LONDON
in the
NINETEENTH CENTURY

First published London 1827-31
Reissued 1968, by Benjamin Blom, Inc.
Reprint Edition 1978 by Arno Press Inc.

LC78-68144
ISBN 0-405-08963-5 (Arno)
ISBN 0-8317-6399-X (Mayflower)

Manufactured in the United States of America

LONDON
in the
NINETEENTH CENTURY

Being a Series of Views
of the New and Most Interesting Objects
in the British Metropolis & its Vicinity
From Original Drawings by *Thomas H. Shepherd*
with Historical, Topographical
& Critical Illustrations by *James Elmes*

MAYFLOWER BOOKS
NEW YORK ● 1978

Engraved by Wm Tombleson.

BANK OF ENGLAND.

TO THE GOVERNOR & DIRECTORS OF THAT NATIONAL ESTABLISHMENT, THIS PLATE IS RESPECTFULLY DEDICATED.

Drawn by Thos H. Shepherd. Engraved by Wm Wallis

LONDON.

RESPECTFULLY INSCRIBED TO THE RIGHT HONB^{LE} THE LORD MAYOR, COURT OF ALDERMEN, & COMMON COUNCIL.

METROPOLITAN IMPROVEMENTS;

OR

LONDON,

IN THE

Nineteenth Century:

BEING A

SERIES OF VIEWS,

OF THE NEW AND MOST INTERESTING OBJECTS,

IN THE

BRITISH METROPOLIS & ITS VICINITY:

From Original Drawings by

THOS. H. SHEPHERD.

WITH

HISTORICAL, TOPOGRAPHICAL & CRITICAL ILLUSTRATIONS,

BY

James Elmes, M.R.I.A.

Author of the Life of Sir Christopher Wren,
Lectures on Architecture, &c

Drawn by Thos. H. Shepherd.   Engraved by J. Allen.

THE KINGS PALACE, PIMLICO.

London,

PUBLISHED APRIL 11, 1829, BY JONES & Cº TEMPLE OF THE MUSES,

FINSBURY SQUARE.

METROPOLITAN IMPROVEMENTS;

OR

LONDON

IN THE

NINETEENTH CENTURY:

DISPLAYED IN A

SERIES OF ENGRAVINGS

OF

THE NEW BUILDINGS, IMPROVEMENTS, &c.

BY THE MOST EMINENT ARTISTS,

FROM

ORIGINAL DRAWINGS, TAKEN FROM THE OBJECTS THEMSELVES EXPRESSLY FOR THIS WORK,

BY MR. THOS. H. SHEPHERD:

COMPRISING THE PALACES, PARKS, NEW CHURCHES, BRIDGES, STREETS, RIVER SCENERY, PUBLIC OFFICES AND INSTITUTIONS, GENTLEMEN'S SEATS
AND MANSIONS, AND EVERY OTHER OBJECT WORTHY OF NOTICE THROUGHOUT THE METROPOLIS AND ITS ENVIRONS,

WITH

HISTORICAL, TOPOGRAPHICAL, AND CRITICAL ILLUSTRATIONS,

By JAMES ELMES, M.R.I.A. ARCHITECT,

Author of the Life of Sir Christopher Wren, Lectures on Architecture, Dictionary of the Fine Arts, &c.

LONDON:

PUBLISHED BY JONES & CO. ACTON PLACE, KINGSLAND ROAD;

AND SOLD BY SIMPKIN AND MARSHALL, STATIONERS' HALL COURT;
AND ALL BOOK AND PRINTSELLERS.

1827.

[ENTERED AT STATIONERS' HALL.]

PRINTED BY J. HADDON, CASTLE STREET, FINSBURY.

TO THE KING.

Sire,

      YOUR MAJESTY, in taking a second
of my works illustrative of ARCHITECTURE,

under your protection, has conferred an honour upon me, as grateful as it is gracious.

The splendid and useful improvements that have been effected in this METROPOLIS, under your MAJESTY's auspices, and which it is the business of this work to describe, will render the name of GEORGE THE FOURTH, as illustrious in the British annals, as that of AUGUSTUS in those of Rome.

The power of *England*, concentrated by peace, and directed by wise counsels, extends its general influence over a greater portion of the habitable globe, than did ever that of *Rome* by the demoralizing influence of the sword. And under the benign reign of your MAJESTY, we derive more advantages from the liberal cultivation of arts of *peace*, than did any other people, from the most triumphant consequences of successful *war*.

In *Rome* the few were prodigiously rich, and the mass of the people as wretchedly poor; in *Britain*, the converse of this unhappy condition prevails : and the majority of your MAJESTY's subjects are in the secure enjoyment of liberty, prosperity and happiness. This state of society arises principally from a due regard for the honours of a noble ancestry; from active commerce, industrious trade, skilful manufactures, agriculture, arts, science, literature, and those magnificent rewards, which are ever the solace of genius and talents, from a patriotic sovereign and an enlightened people.

Industry and a daring spirit of commercial enterprize, have characterized the British nation, from the time of Tacitus to the present day; when the influence of our princely merchants, and the spirit of nautical discovery, which signalize your MAJESTY's reign, have extended the fostering influence of our laws, customs and language, and planted the British standard, from the icy regions of the Polar Seas to the verge of the *terra incognita* of Australasia.

That your MAJESTY's fortunate and happy reign, may be still more fortunate and more happy, by a providential continuance of the blessings of health, and a happy length of days, is the sincere prayer of

Your MAJESTY's

Most obliged and most devoted

Subject and Servant,

JAMES ELMES.

London,
July 1, 1827.

METROPOLITAN IMPROVEMENTS,

OR

London,

in the

NINETEENTH CENTURY:

BEING A

SERIES OF VIEWS,

OF THE NEW AND MOST INTERESTING OBJECTS,

in the

BRITISH METROPOLIS & ITS VICINITY:

from Original Drawings by

Mr THOS. H. SHEPHERD.

WITH

HISTORICAL, TOPOGRAPHICAL & CRITICAL ILLUSTRATIONS,

BY

James Elmes, M.R.I.A.

Drawn by Thos. H.Shepherd.

Engraved by W.Wallis.

SUSSEX PLACE REGENT'S PARK.

LONDON.
Published May 5, 1827, by Jones & Co. 3, Acton Place, Kingsland Road.

METROPOLITAN IMPROVEMENTS.

INTRODUCTORY CHAPTER.

Lo! numerous Domes, a Burlington confess,
For Kings and Senates fit, the *Palace* see!
The *Temple* breathing a religious awe;
E'en fram'd with elegance the plain retreat,
The *Private Dwelling.* Certain in his aim,
Taste never idly working, saves expense.
Lo! *Stately Streets,* lo! *Squares* that court the breeze,
Lo! rayed from cities o'er the brightened land,
Connecting sea to sea, the *solid Road.*
Lo! the *proud Arch,* no vile exactors stand,
With easy sweep, bestrides the chasing flood.

THOMSON.

VAST AND ENCREASING IMPROVEMENTS—CULTIVATION OF ARCHITECTURE OF
NATIONAL IMPORTANCE—ARTS AND ARTISTS PATRONIZED BY THE WISEST
AND GREATEST MONARCHS—EARLIEST IMPROVEMENTS OF LONDON—PARISH
OF MARY-LE-BONE—REGENT'S PARK—ORIGINAL GRANTS, &C.—GEOGRAPHICAL
BOUNDARIES—MR. NASH'S PLAN—VILLAGE OF MARY-LE-BONE—VARIOUS
EMPLOYMENTS—NEW CHURCHES, CHAPELS, &C.—TOUR OF THE NEW PARK—
ENTRANCE LODGES—TERRACES—VILLAS, &C.—CRITICAL AND HISTORICAL
REMARKS.

AUGUSTUS made it one of his proudest boasts, that he found
Rome of brick, and left it of marble. The reign and regency
of GEORGE THE FOURTH have scarcely done less, for the vast
and increasing Metropolis of the British empire: by increasing
its magnificence and its comforts; by forming healthy streets
and elegant buildings, instead of pestilential alleys and
squalid hovels; by substituting rich and varied architecture

and park-like scenery, for paltry cabins and monotonous cow-lairs ; by making solid roads and public ways, scarcely inferior to those of ancient Rome, which have connected the extremest points of the empire, and have brought its provinces and sea-ports, many days journey nearer to the Metropolis, instead of the miry roads through which our respected ancestors ploughed their weary ways, from London to Bath, " by the blessing of God, in four days ;" and, by beginning, and continuing with a truly national perseverance, a series of desirable improve-ments, that bid fair to render LONDON, the ROME of modern history.

So rapidly indeed are these improvements taking place around us, that the absence of a few months from London, produces revolutions in sites, and alterations in appearances, that are almost miraculous, and cause the denizen to feel himself a stranger in his own city.

Could our late revered monarch, the first English sovereign who had the taste to patronize arts and artists, since the days of the elegant minded patrons of Rubens, Vandyck and Inigo Jones, revisit the country of his birth and of his love ; and witness the gigantic alterations and tasteful improvements that have been so rapidly and effectually made, under the auspices of his illustrious son and successor ; he would be lost amid the architectural wonders (the merits of which he was so able to appreciate) of that very Metropolis, in which he lived and reigned for more than half a century.

The business of this work is to record and describe the " wonderful alterations" that have taken place in those com-paratively short periods ; and have rendered the present æra THE AUGUSTAN AGE OF ENGLAND.

Among the glories of this age, the historian will have to record the conversion of dirty alleys, dingy courts and squalid dens of misery and crime, almost under the walls of our royal palaces, into " stately streets," to " squares that court the breeze," to palaces and mansions, to elegant private dwellings, to rich and costly shops, filled with the productions of every clime, to magnificent ware-rooms, stowed with the ingenious and valuable manufactures of our artisans and mechanics, giving activity to commerce with all the enviable results of national prosperity. Fields, that were in our times appropriated to pasturage, are now become the gay and tasteful abodes of splendid opulence, and of the triumphs of the peaceful arts.

The greatest statesmen and philosophers, have ever considered the cultivation of architecture, and the building and adornment of cities, as of primary and political importance. Plato attributes the origin of legislature to the cultivation of the arts. Public buildings are the most lasting and effective ornaments of a country; and at the same time, the cheapest that a people can obtain. By their means nations are established, and obtain "a local habitation and a name;" by them are opulent and ingenious foreigners attracted, and in most cases, more money is brought into a country than all the cost that was originally expended in their construction. It was so at Versailles, as every body knows; and similar causes will always produce similar effects. Such works not only attract great and wealthy foreigners, but at the same time they increase commerce, create wealth, give employment to the labourer, the artisan and the artist; and make a people love their native country; which is a passion that is the parent of all great actions that conduce to the public wealth.

The most learned and philosophic architect, that perhaps ever lived, Sir Christopher Wren, in allusion to such subjects, says,* "The emulation of the cities of Greece was the true cause of their greatness. The obstinate valour of the Jews, occasioned by the love of their temple, was a cement that held together that people, in former ages, through infinite changes. The care of public decency and convenience was a great cause of the establishment of the low countries, and of many cities in the world. Modern Rome subsists still, by the ruins and imitations of the old; as does Jerusalem by the temple of the sepulchre, and other remains of Helena's zeal."

In this opinion of eminent statesmen and philosophers have the greatest princes and monarchs ever coincided. They have invariably distinguished themselves by a just and honourable patronage of the arts, of literature, of philosophy, of science, and of the other heaven-directed workings of the human mind. It has, fortunately, for humanity, almost always happened, that the greatest men of every kind, in art, in literature, in philo-

---

* See ELMES's Life of WREN, Appendix, p. 119

sophy, in science, in politics, and in warfare, have generally been contemporaries, and flourished resplendently in a comparatively short period of time.

When Apelles, Praxiteles, Lysippus and other eminent artists flourished in Greece, her greatest poets, orators, and philosophers were alive; and Socrates, Plato, Aristotle, Demosthenes, Isocrates, Thucydides, Xenophan, Æschylus, Euripides, Sophocles and Menander, flourished almost in the same age. The ages of Pericles, of Augustus, and of Louis the Fourteenth, were similarly celebrated for their several constellations of artists, philosophers, statesmen and warriors; and THE AUGUSTAN AGE OF GEORGE THE FOURTH, emblazoned as it is by a galaxy of talent in poetry, in the sublimest works of imagination, such as no nation has hitherto surpassed, in legislation, in the art of war, and in the more peaceful arts and sciences, will be no less the subject of admiration from the future historian and posterity. It is also no less remarkable, that the duration of these brilliant epochs or times of perfection, have generally been brief in proportion to their splendour. May the duration of our present splendid epoch, contradict the history of past ages, and be no less continuative than brilliant.

The honours conferred by our present enlightened sovereign on literature and the arts, followed up as they are by the legislature of the country, and by our leading nobility and gentry, in the establishment of national libraries, galleries of sculpture and of painting, have given a life and spirit to the genius of our times, that cannot fail of producing an abundant harvest of the richest quality.

The professors of the fine arts, poets, and other cultivators of the human mind, have ever been considered among the benefactors of mankind, and honoured as such by the great. The Greeks rendered as much honour to Polygnotus, as they could have bestowed either upon Lycurgus or Solon. They prepared magnificent public entries for him into cities that he had decorated with his pencil; and appointed, by a decree of the council of Amphictyons, that he should be maintained at the public expense wherever he might choose to go.

Alexander the Great and Demetrius Poliorcetes, are alike celebrated for their attentions to illustrious artists; and paid the greatest homage to the rare talent and superior merit of those extraordinary men, who flourished in their days. Alexander issued a remarkable edict in favour of three of the most eminent artists of his day, whom he honoured with his friendship, by which he granted exclusively to Apelles, the privilege of painting him; to Lysippus, according to Pliny, and to Polycletes, according to Apuleius, that of representing him in bronze statues; and to Pyrgoteles that of engraving his portrait. Rightly judging, says Cicero, that the skill of those two great masters (Apelles and Lysippus), would also immortalize his; for it was not to please them that he published that edict, so much as to enhance his own glory.

One of the greatest emperors of the west, since the days of Charlemagne, conferred the highest honours of Chivalry upon Titian; Francis the first, one of the most enlightened of monarchs, honoured Da Vinci in the highest degree; and our days have witnessed our own sovereigns honouring and delighting in the works of eminent artists, embellishing our metropolis with grand and magnificent edifices, by munificent and splendid presents of books, pictures and statues to our public institutions; by honours conferred upon splendid talent and art, as well as upon eminence in legislation and warfare.

Upon works such as these, alike worthy of a great monarch, and a brave, free and enlightened people, Agrippa, the son-in-law of Augustus, made a magnificent harangue, worthy of the first and greatest citizen of Rome: in which he shews, by several reasons, how useful it would be to the state, to exhibit publicly the finest pieces of antiquity of every kind; for the purpose of exciting a noble emulation in the youth; which, no doubt, he adds, would be much better than to banish them into the country, to the gardens and pleasure grounds of private persons.

Such has been the conduct of the monarch and legislature of these kingdoms, in establishing academies and societies, founding and enlarging libraries, museums, galleries and institutions, enlarging and improving the metropolis; for the magnificence of the buildings, the multitude of good pictures, statues and other monuments of the good taste, munificence and genius of a people, are among the greatest embellishments of a state, and wise princes and enlightened legislators do well in encouraging them.

Persons who remember London as it *was* thirty years ago, may proudly say, regarding it as it *is*,

" Look on this picture and on this."

No city in Europe has undergone such rapid changes and improvements as this metropolis. The first great change was occasioned by that awful conflagration, (calamity it can scarcely be called by us), which consumed the greater part of the ancient city, and purified it from plagues, pestilence and perpetual fear of incendiaries. The magnanimity with which the citizens sustained the calamity which destroyed their houses and estates, the greatness of mind with which they beheld the ashes of their houses, and gates and temples, was a theme of admiration to all their contemporaries. They immediately set about rebuilding their city, while its ruins were still smoking. Wren, Evelyn, Hooke and others presented designs for the new city, and the King, his brother the Duke of York, and the whole court aided the undertaking. The Royal Society forwarded their views. Wren's plan* was adopted by the King and privy council. It possessed such qualities for security, convenience and beauty, that if it had been executed, the city would not have been in that disgraceful, deserted, and dilapidated state, that a comparison with its improved and improving sister of Westminster, has now rendered it. The hurry of rebuilding, and the disputes about property, prevented Wren's beautiful plan from being adopted, and the city became one, whose streets are lanes, and whose lanes are alleys. The sooner the corporation (who have recently appointed a committee of improvements, which it is hoped will not render their important office a sinecure) remove this opprobrium from their city, and emancipate their fine cathedral from its monstrous thraldom, the sooner will their city be enabled to hold its due rank in the splendid metropolis of the empire.

The next alteration or improvement of consequence was the removal of all the signs from the public streets that cut such a grotesque figure in Hogarth's pictures, and the taking away of the projecting water spouts, and dripping eaves, that made " the

* For an engraving and description of this plan, see Elmes's Life of Wren, p. 197. *et seq.* and Appendix No. 13. p. 81.

art of walking London streets," so much more difficult when it was sung by Gay, than in our improved days.

The new thoroughfare called Skinner Street, after an Alderman of that name, whom the city deigned to honour, was the next metropolitan improvement of utility; and certainly the useful was more sought after than the ornamental by the then city Vitruvius. Picket Street near Temple Bar, wherein another Alderman's name is immortalised to puzzle posterity, is another of the useful improvements by the corporation of London.

The parish of St. Mary-le-bone succeeds, though not in strict chronological order, to the improvements within the walls, and the name of " the Mary-bone school of temple builders has damned" its masters and founders " to everlasting fame," by a proverb and bye-word. Clipstone Street, Titchfield Street and their neighbourhood present their venerable ruins to the notice of the artist and antiquary.

The city of Westminster deserves, and shall receive in its proper place, the honour due for its alterations, improvements and restorations, particularly those in and about its venerable minster, and the two houses of parliament. The parish of St. Pancras, and the Duke of Bedford's estate in the neighbourhood of Bloomsbury, and the New Road, present claims to commendation, and shall be noticed in their turns, as shall every other of importance.

But our immediate object is with those of our own days, those which are arising around us from the foot of Primrose Hill, to the banks of Le Notre's canal in the park, which have metamorphosed Mary-le-bone park farm and its cow-sheds, into a rural city of almost eastern magnificence; and changed Swallow Street and its filthy labyrinthine environs, into the most picturesque and splendid street in the metropolis.

Therefore, although it is intended that our work shall comprehend a succinct, but COMPLETE HISTORY of the BRITISH METROPOLIS, *yet,* with a view of gratifying that interest which is universally excited, we shall begin with the Regent's Park, and proceed onwards through the most splendid and magnificent architectural undertakings now in progress.

THE REGENT'S PARK.

This compages of splendid architecture, and tasteful garden-ing, was named after our present king, during his sovereignty as regent of these kingdoms. It is a part of the ancient manor of Mary-le-bone, still more anciently called Tybourn, from its situation near a small bourn, or rivulet, formerly called Aye-brook, or Eye-brook. The Rev. Mr. Lysons, the indefatigable author of the historical account of the environs of London, imagines with great reason, that when the site of the church was altered to another spot* near the same brook, it was called St. Mary at the bourn, and became corrupted to its present ap-pellation of St. Mary-le-bone, or Mary-bone.

This immense parish which is larger, more opulent, more populous, and possessed of more public and private buildings of good taste and real beauty, than many METROPOLISES of the continent, is situated in the hundred of Ossulston, which gives a baronial title to the heir apparent of the noble family of Tan-kerville. Its extent may be gathered, when it is known that it is bounded on the *east* by the parishes of St. Giles's in the fields, and St. Pancras; on the *west* by that of Paddington, to the Kilburn Road; on the *north* by Hampstead to the foot of Prim-rose Hill; and on the *south* by those of St. Anne Soho, St. James Westminster and St. George Hanover Square. It is eight miles and a quarter in circumference, and computed to contain above two thousand five hundred acres of land.

The brook, or bourn, whence the parish derives its name, runs on the south side of Hampstead, and passes near Bellesize park to Barrow Hill farm. Thence through the Regent's Park, to Marybone lane, it crosses Oxford Street near Stratford Place and Piccadilly under a bridge, near Hay Hill, which is supposed by some antiquaries to derive its name from this Aye† brook. It then passes through St. James's Park, near Buckingham House, through Tothill fields, and falls into the Thames at a place called King's Scholars' Pond, a little below Chelsea.

---

* This event occurred in the year 1400, in consequence of the church at the de-serted village of Tybourn having fallen into decay, and being robbed of its books, vestments, bells, images, and other decorations.

† This derivation to be complete, must borrow the cockney aspiration of the H.

The manor of Tybourn is described in Doomsday book, as appertaining to the crown, and was held under it by various noble families, whose names and titles are all recorded in the third volume of Lyson's " Environs of London." The manor was granted by several successive kings to various persons, but the park was often reserved or reclaimed by the crown. The manor became afterwards the property of the Duke of Portland; whose grandfather married Lady Margaret Cavendish Harley, (whose names are given to several streets), heiress of the two noble families of Newcastle and Oxford.

The manor house, which during the time that it was vested in the crown, was occasionally used as a temporary royal residence, particularly by queen Elizabeth, who appears by many accounts to have used her various palaces in rapid succession, was pulled down in the year 1791. From a drawing by Rooker, in the possession of Mr. White the architect, it appears to have retained, in spite of many alterations, some traces of the style of architecture used in that queen's reign; at which period, the park of Mary-le-bone was abundantly stocked with game. In the history of the royal progresses of that queen it is recorded, that " on the 3rd February, 1600, the ambassadors from the Emperor of Russia, and other Muscovites rode through the city of London to Marybone park, and there hunted at their pleasure, and shortly after returned homeward."

When the manor of Mary-le-bone was granted to the before mentioned Edward Forsett, King James reserved the park in his own hands. It continued to be the property of the crown till the year 1646, when Charles I. by letters patent dated at Oxford May 6, granted it to Sir George Strode, and John Wandesforde, Esq. as security for a debt of £2318. 11s. 9d. due to them, for supplying arms and ammunition during the civil wars. After the death of the king, when all the crown lands were disposed of by Cromwell, this park, without any regard to the claim of the before-mentioned grantees, was sold for £13,215 6s. 8d., including £130 for 124 head of deer, and £1774. 8s. for the timber, exclusive of 2976 trees marked for the navy, to John Spencer who is described " of London, gentleman," in behalf of Colonel Thomas Harrison's regiment of dragoons, on whom Mary-le-bone park was settled for their pay. Sir John Ipsley being appointed by the protector to the office of Ranger.

On the restoration of Charles II. Sir George Strode and Mr. Wandesforde were reinstated in their possession of the park, which they held till their debt was discharged, except the great lodge or palace as it was sometimes called, and sixty acres of land, which had been granted to Sir William Clarke, secretary to the Lord General (Monk) the Duke of Albemarle. A compensation was also made to John Carey, Esq. for the loss of his situation of ranger, which he had held before the protectorate.

When Cromwell disposed of the park, for the support of a regiment of dragoons, it was disparked and never afterwards stocked. It was let on lease in the year 1668 to Henry Earl of Arlington; in 1696 to Charles Bertie and others in trust for the Duke of Leeds; in 1724 to Samuel Grey, Esq. whose interest in the lease was purchased by Thomas Gibson, John Jacob and Robert Jacomb, Esqrs. who renewed their lease successively in the years 1730, 1735, and 1742. In 1754 a lease was granted to Lucy Jacomb, widow and Peter Hinde, Esq. In 1765 William Jacomb, Esq. had a fresh lease for an undivided share of fifteen twenty-fourths. The term of this share was prolonged in 1772, and again in 1780 for eight years which commenced on the 24th January, 1803, and expired at the beginning of the year 1811. In 1784 Mr. Jacomb sold his interest to the Duke of Portland. In the years 1765 and 1772 Jacob Hinde, Esq. had a new lease of the remaining nine twenty-fourths; which lease not being renewed, expired in 1803, eight years before the Duke of Portland's.

So passed away the destinies of Mary-le-bone park, till it attained its present state of richly adorned beauty. These curious and authentic details were originally communicated to the Rev. Mr. Lysons by William Harrison, Esq. of the land revenue office in Scotland yard, by permission of the late John Fordyce, Esq. the then surveyor general of his Majesty's woods and forests; and continued to the present day from similar authentic sources of information.

This estate, the late Mary-le-bone park, now the Regent's park, contains 543 acres, 17 perches, according to an actual survey made in the year 1794 by the late Thomas Leverton, Esq. under the direction of John Fordyce, Esq. the late surveyor general of the crown lands, and by order of the Lords of the treasury.

About two thirds of this magnificent property lies in the parish of St. Mary-le-bone, and the rest in that of St. Pancras. It extends along the New Road, from Portland Street, on the east, to the end of Harley Street, Portland Place, on the west.

Shortly after the before-mentioned survey, the Lords of the treasury empowered the surveyor-general to offer premiums for the best plans for building on this new estate; and selected two (we believe) as the best, one by John Nash, Esq. which embraced all those beauties of landscape gardening, which his friend, the late Humphrey Repton, so successfully introduced, with the splendour of architectural decorations, in detached villas; and the other by Messrs. Leverton and Chawner, which was more *urban* and builder like, than the enchanting *rural* plan which their lordships adopted.

The park no sooner became once more the property of the crown, than the commissioners of his Majesty's woods and forests commenced operations to carry Mr. Nash's plan into effect. Following the sound advice of Cato the elder, in his book upon rural life,* that when we intend to *build*, we ought to deliberate; when our intentions are to *plant*, we should not *deliberate*, but *act*; they began by planting the whole demesne according to the plan; and it has therefore had the advantage of so many years growth while the buildings are in progress.

There is another advantage in this process, much in favour of the divine art of landscape gardening, which is, that from the moment of finishing either building or planting, the former begins to decay, and the latter to flourish.

Thus has the public spirit of the king and his government secured to the inhabitants of London a magnificent park, whose beauties and splendour cannot be surpassed by any metropolis in Europe.

What the melodious poet Waller sung of St. James's Park, as improved by Charles the Second, may truly be applied to this noble appropriation of the royal demesne, whose beauties are the subject of the following pages.

---

* Ædificare diu cogitare oportet, conserere cogitare non oportet, sed facere. CATO *de re Rust*

" For future shades, young trees upon the banks
Of the new stream appear in even ranks,
The voice of *Orpheus*, or *Amphion's* hand,
In better order could not make them stand;
May they increase as fast, and spread their boughs,
As the high fame of their great owner grows!
May he live long enough to see them all
Dark shadows cast, and as his palace tall!"

The extension and improvement of the metropolis in this princely parish and district, within the memories of not very aged people, have been more rapid and surprising than those of any other country in Europe. They present to the astonished spectator, so magnificent are the buildings, and so tasteful is the scenery, more the appearance of the newly founded capital of a wealthy state, than one of the suburbs of an ancient city.

The progress of the metamorphoses of this farm-like appendage to our metropolis, into its present superb state, is a curious subject of investigation, as a series of historical facts in the history of our Metropolitan Architecture. We again refer to the circumstantial authority of Mr. White, as furnished by him to Mr. Lysons.

At the beginning of the last century, Mary-le-bone was a small village, nearly a mile distant from any part of the metropolis. In the year 1715 the plan for building Cavendish Square, and several new streets on the north side of Oxford Street, then called indiscriminately by that name and Tybourn Road, was first suggested. About two years afterwards the ground was laid out, and the circular plantation in the centre inclosed, planted and surrounded by a parapet wall and iron railings.

The whole of the north side was taken by the celebrated James Bridges, Duke of Chandos, who acquired a princely fortune as pay-master to the army in Queen Anne's reign, and whose magnificent buildings, particularly his unrivalled mansion at Canons, and stately style of living, which fell little short of that of a sovereign prince, were celebrated by Pope in his satires under the name of Timon. Of his magnificent conceptions in building the satirist says, that

" Greatness with Timon dwells in such a draught
As brings all Brobdignag before your thought;
To compass this, his building is a town,
His pond an ocean, his parterre a down.

The Duke (then Earl of Carnarvon) it is said, took this large portion of the ground, which reached an immense way back towards the north, for the purpose of building a town residence, correspondent with that of Canons. Of this he built no more than the wings, which were sufficiently spacious to become mansions. One, was that large mansion at the corner of Harley Street, formerly occupied by the late Princess Amelia, mother to King George the Third; subsequently by H. P. Hope, Esq.; and recently, with its spacious court yards and stable offices, built upon by George Watson Taylor, Esq.; and the other the corresponding mansion at the corner of Chandos Street. The centre part is occupied by two splendid mansions of the Corinthian order, which stand on the sides of an opening leading to a place still known by the name of Chandos' Folly. They were designed, I believe, by James of Greenwich, who was architect to the Duke at Canons.

At this period, Harcourt House, the large mansion on the east side, and Bingley House, now Harcourt House, on the west side, a noble mansion designed by Inigo Jones were the only houses in Cavendish Square. The prison-like walls which close up the latter on every side like a fortress, were then necessary from its solitary and dangerous situation. It is now the residence of the Duke of Portland, who has recently added a handsome range of stable offices at the back of the house, in Wimpole Street, in the style of the mansion, from the design, and under the superintendance of Samuel Ware, Esq. his grace's architect.

Portions of ground on the east and west sides were taken by Lord Harcourt and Lord Bingley; and the rest was let to builders and other speculators. The failure of the celebrated South Sea adventure in 1720, caused a temporary cessation to these improvements, and it was several years before the square was entirely finished. In the year 1770, an equestrian statue, was erected in the centre of the enclosure to the memory of William Duke of Cumberland the hero of Culloden; who is represented in the full military costume of his day. It is of lead gilt, cast by Chew, a statuary of some eminence in his day; and was placed there, as the inscription on the pedestal informs us, by Lieutenant General William Strode, in gratitude for private kindness, and in honour of public worth.

During the stoppage of the buildings in Cavendish Square, a new chapel and market-place were projected, not only as an inducement for the builders to proceed, but also for the inhabitants of the square and new street. The designs were made by James Gibbs, the architect of the beautiful church of St. Martin in the fields. They were both completed in 1724, but the market-place was not opened for business till 1732, in consequence of the opposition of Lord Craven, who feared that it would abridge the value of Carnaby Market.

This chapel named after the Earl of Oxford, on whose estate it was built, was the first of the established church that was erected in the parish of Mary-le-bone, and is situated at the corner of Vere Street and Henrietta Street, both named after the noble family of Vere Earl of Oxford. The market is called Oxford Market from the same cause.

The houses on the north side of Tybourn road, were completed in 1729, and it was then first called by its present name Oxford Street. About the same time, most of the streets, which lead from Oxford Street to Cavendish Square and Oxford Market, namely, Henrietta Street, Vere Street, Holles Street, Margaret Street, Cavendish Street, Wimpole Street, Princes Street, Bolsover Street, Castle Street, John Street, Market Street and a few others, were built; and the sites marked out for Lower Harley Street, Wigmore Street, Mortimer Street &c.

This magnificent parish has five splendid churches : one, the parish or mother church, and four district churches, which it is probable will hereafter become parochial, by a division of the parish; like that of St. George Hanover Square, from its parent St. Martin in the fields. The old parish church, which was built in 1741, has been converted, by act of parliament, into a parochial chapel of ease, and a large chapel that was begun in July, 1813, was enlarged, altered from the Ionic to the Corinthian order, and by other requisite improvements converted into the parish church. It was finished in February, 1817, from the designs of Thomas Hardwick, Esq. and will be fully noticed in its proper place.

Since that time, the other four churches have been erected under the authority of an act of parliament passed during the regency of our present king, at an expence of about £20,000 each.

The church of ST. MARY in Wyndham Place, Bryanstone Square, was designed by Robert Smirke, Esq. and consecrated in January, 1824; that of ALL SOULS, in Langham Place, by John Nash, Esq. was commenced in 1822, and finished in 1825; that of CHRIST CHURCH, in Stafford Street, Lisson Green, by Philip Hardwick, Esq. was began in July, 1822, and opened for divine service in May, 1825; and TRINITY CHURCH, now building opposite the north end of Portland Street, by John Soane, Esq. the professor of architecture in the Royal Academy. Full descriptions of these new churches will be found in their proper places.

The several episcopal chapels, or chapels of ease, were built about the following years. Oxford Chapel, in Vere Street, designed by Gibbs, in 1724; Bentinck Chapel, in 1772; Portman Chapel, in 1779; Margaret Street Chapel, first used as a place of worship for the Church of England, about 1779; Baker Street Chapel, and Brunswick Chapel, in Upper Berkeley Street, about three years afterwards.

In the beginning of the reign of George the Third, there was nothing but a dreary, monotonous waste of dank pasturage, between the new region of Cavendish Square and the village of Mary-le-bone. The first improvement, westward of this site, was the erection of Portman Square; which was laid out and the north side begun about 1764, but it was nearly twenty years before the whole was completed. Even in 1772 the now densely populated site between Duke Street and Mary-le-bone Lane, was entirely unbuilt upon. Portman Square consists principally of large and splendid mansions, without any pretensions to external display in architectural embellishments. At the north-west angle is Montague House, formerly the residence of that amiable philanthropist Mrs. Montague, who was celebrated for her literary talents, and for her custom of entertaining and regaling all the little chimney sweepers of the metropolis in her house and gardens on the first of May in every year; in gratitude, it is said, for having recovered a lost child from among that pitiable class of infant sufferers.

In 1770, the continuation of Harley Street was begun, as well as Mansfield Street, on a site of ground that had formerly been a basin or reservoir of water. Soon afterwards Portland Place, formerly reckoned the most magnificent street in the

metropolis, was built; and also most of the streets that intersect it. It was originally terminated by Foley House on the
south, and by the fields of Mary-le-bone Park farm on the
north. In the year 1772, according to a plan and description
given in Northouck's History of London, a new square was then
building on the site of Portland Place, called Queen Square,
bounded by Foley house and gardens on the south by houses;
abutting on Portland Street on the east; by Harley Street on
the west; and by an island of mansions on the north; with two
grand streets, one on the east, called Highgate Place; and the
other on the west, Hampstead Place. Westward, towards the
south, is Great Queen Anne Street, and opposite to it, on the
east, Little Queen Anne Street.

This design was abandoned, and Portland Place built, as before described; but recently, Foley House has been taken down
and this spacious avenue of mansions, being 125 feet in
breadth, is continued, by an elongation called Langham Place,
by a handsome sweep round Sir James Langham's elegant
mansion and grounds to Regent Street and St. James's Park on
the south: and by Park Crescent, New Road, and its plantation, with a bronze statue of heroic size of the late Duke of
Kent, by Gahagan, and the splendid creations of picturesque
art of the Regent's Park, on the north. Portland Place is
principally erected from the designs of Robert Adam, one of
the architects of the Adelphi Buildings, and Park Crescent,
Langham Place, and the continuation into Regent Street, from
those of Mr. Nash.

Stratford Place was built about the year 1774, on ground
belonging to the Corporation of London, then called Conduit
Mead, where the Lord Mayor's banquetting house formerly
stood. Old Stowe informs us that it was customary, in those
days, for the Lord Mayor, accompanied by the Aldermen and
other citizens on horseback, on the 18th of September of every
year, to visit the fountain heads whence the conduits in the
city were supplied, hunting a hare before dinner and a fox
after dinner, in the fields beyond St. Giles's. The dinner was
served in the banquetting house. The site was granted on
lease renewable for ever on certain covenants, from the corporation to Edward Stratford, after whom the place was named, and
others. It consists of two handsome wings, which form an

entrance, two rows of large dwelling houses, and a mansion on the north, which faces the entrance. It was formerly decorated with a column supporting a statue of the king, commemorative of the naval victories of Great Britain. It was erected by the late General Strode, and taken down in 1805, in consequence of the foundation giving way.

Cumberland Place, now a Crescent, but originally intended to have been a Circus, was began about 1775, in a "plain brown-brick" style of architecture. Every war and every peace created fresh revolutions and improvements in the architecture of the metropolis.

From 1786 to 1792 the additions and improvements increased with rapidity. All the Duke of Portland's property in Mary-le-bone, except one farm, was let at that period on building leases; and the new buildings in the north-west part of the parish increased with equal rapidity. Manchester Square,* which had been began in 1776 by the building of Manchester House, one of the finest mansions in London, was finished in a neat manner in 1788.

The large estates at Lisson Green have all been largely, and in many instances, tastefully built upon. Their principal beauties will also be dilated upon hereafter, as well as those in the Regent's Park, Regent Street, &c.

The causes of the extension of the metropolis in the style of the Mary-le-bone school of temple builders, whose motto was, that their buildings should only be strong enough to last till they were sold, has been so well depicted by Mr. Nash, to whom the public are beholden for the most picturesque improvements that ever were bestowed upon their metropolis, in each of his reports to the commissioners of His Majesty's woods and forests, that we cannot do better than to extract a few of the more important passages. This eminent architect says, that "the artificial causes of the extension of the town, are the speculations of builders, encouraged and promoted by merchants dealing in the materials of building, and attorneys with monied clients facilitating, and indeed, putting in motion, the whole system,

---

* Mr Britton, in his last edition of "*the Original Picture of London,*" says, this square " originally was intended to have been called Queen Anne's Square." A reference to page 16, will prove this assertion of that generally correct antiquary, to be incorrect in this instance.

by disposing of their client's money in premature mortgages, the sale of improved ground rents, and by numerous other devices, by which their clients make an advantageous use of their money, and the attorneys create to themselves a lucrative business from the agreements, leases, mortgages, bonds and other instruments of law, which become necessary throughout such complicated and intricate transactions. It is not necessary for the present purpose to enumerate the bad consequences and pernicious effects which arise from such an unnatural and forced enlargement of the town, further than to observe, that it is the interest of those concerned in such buildings that they should be of as little cost as possible, preserving an attractive exterior, which Parker's stucco, coloured bricks and balconies, accomplish; and a fashionble arrangement of rooms on the principal floors, embellished by the paper hanger, and a few flimsey marble chimney pieces, are the attractions of the interior. These are sufficient allurements to the public, and ensure the sale of the houses, which is the ultimate object of the builders; and to this finery every thing out of sight is sacrificed, or, is no further an object of attention, than, *that no defects in the constructive and substantial parts shall make their appearance while the houses are on sale;* and, it is to be feared that for want of these essentials which constitute the strength and permanency of houses, a very few years will exhibit cracked walls, swagged floors, bulged fronts, crooked roofs, leaky gutters, inadequate drains and other ills of an originally bad constitution; and, it is quite certain, without a renovation equal to rebuilding, that all those houses, long, very long, before the expiration of the leases, will cease to exist, and the reversionary estate that the proprietors look for, will never be realized, as it is not till the end of the builder's term that the proprietor of the fee will be entitled to the additional ground rents laid on by the builder. It is evidently, therefore, not the interest of the crown, that Mary-le-bone Park should be covered with houses of this description."

The commissioners wisely and tastefully adopted Mr. Nash's plan, and their bosoms must glow with satisfaction at the results which are now so splendidly budding, and promising of future fruit, before their eyes.

The noble appropriation of this royal domain, is in every respect worthy of the nation and of the metropolis. It is the

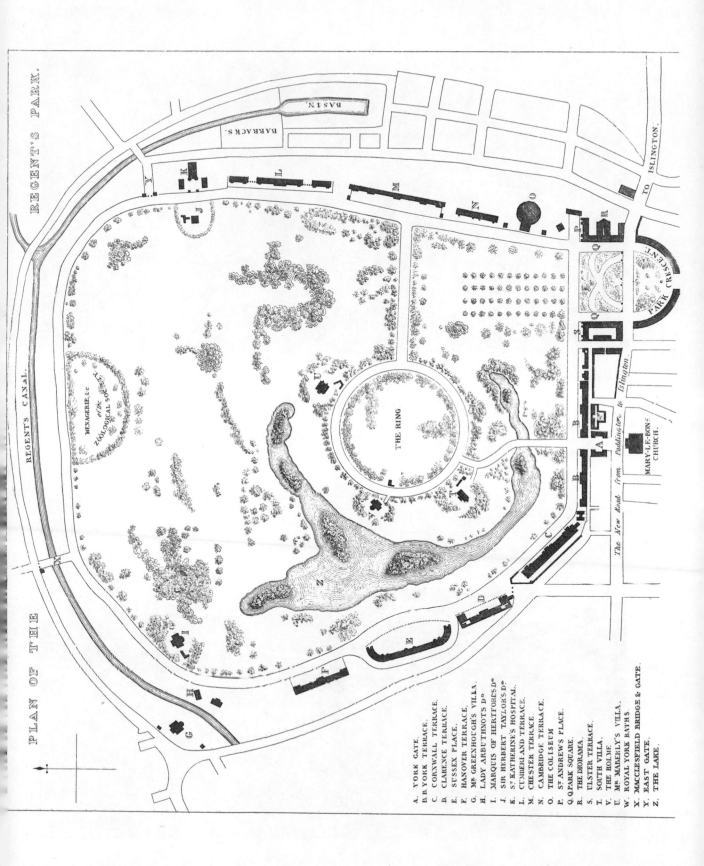

PLAN OF THE REGENT'S PARK.

REGENT'S CANAL.

BARRACKS.

BASIN.

TO ISLINGTON.

PARK CRESCENT.

MENAGERIE, &c of the ZOOLOGICAL SOCIETY.

THE RING

MARY-LE-BON: CHURCH.

The New Road from Paddington to Islington.

A. YORK GATE.
B.B. YORK TERRACE.
C. CORNWALL TERRACE.
D. CLARENCE TERRACE.
E. SUSSEX PLACE.
F. HANOVER TERRACE.
G. Mr GREENHOUGH'S VILLA.
H. LADY ARBUTHNOT'S Dº
I. MARQUIS OF HERTFORD'S Dº
J. SIR HERBERT TAYLOR'S Dº
K. Sⁱ KATHERINE'S HOSPITAL.
L. CUMBERLAND TERRACE.
M. CHESTER TERRACE.
N. CAMBRIDGE TERRACE.
O. THE COLISEUM.
P. Sⁱ ANDREW'S PLACE.
Q. PARK SQUARE.
R. THE DIORAMA.
S. ULSTER TERRACE.
T. SOUTH VILLA.
V. THE HOLME.
U. Mʳˢ MABERLY'S VILLA.
W. ROYAL YORK BATHS.
X. MACCLESFIELD BRIDGE & GATE.
Y. EAST GATE.
Z. THE LAKE.

Drawn by Thos. H. Shepherd.

Engraved by W. Tombleson.

AN ISLAND ON THE LAKE & PART OF CORNWALL & CLARENCE TERRACE,
REGENT'S PARK.

Drawn by Thos. H. Shepherd.

Engraved by W. Tombleson.

THE COLISEUM AND PART OF THE LAKE REGENT'S PARK.

largest of the parks, and the trees and shrubs are becoming umbrageous and park-like.

In performing a tour of the Regent's Park on a fine day, the enquirer into its beauties and merits should perform it leisurely and on foot. This will take some hours, or a long morning; but two distinct visits, one *generally* to become acquainted with its geography, and the other *specifically* to examine its details, will be preferable. An engraved plan, which accompanies the present work, will be found greatly to facilitate this object. Its best approach is to go up Portland Place, turn to the left, under the beautiful Ionic colonnade of Park Crescent, survey the tasteful plantation of Park Square, and proceed along the New Road as far as the new parish church. Then cross over, and enter the park by the entrance called YORK GATE. Turn round, and take what is perhaps the best view of the church from the road, to which the gate makes a picturesque accessary. As we are now performing the office of *Cicerone* in the *general* visit, we shall leave detail and criticism till the *specific* inspection.

On entering the park, it may be as well to proceed for a few minutes to the elegant little bridge which faces you, and admire the fascinating beauties of the artificial lake which it crosses, adorned as it is with rare and beautiful water fowl, aquatic plants, and other appropriate embellishments.

Return then to the main road, survey the architectural beauties of York Terrace, which extends to both sides of the entrance road. We shall not stop farther than to call your attention to the palatial splendour of these two grand rows of buildings, which, instead of resembling a series of dwelling houses, carry upon their faces the semblance of the residence of a sovereign prince.

Proceed then by Cornwall Terrace, the richness and correctness of style of whose architecture is aptly embellished by the sylvan scene before it. Pass then by the entrance from Baker Street, in a northerly direction, by the elegant arcade of Clarence Place, and by the fanciful cupolas of Sussex Place. Continue your pedestrian treat, forgetting the driver's maxim of never looking to the right or left, and keeping your eye continually between your horse's ears; which, as you have no horse to be troubled with, may rove delighted " from earth to heaven, from heaven to earth," in perpetual transport at this scene of ever varying delight.

Those who can remember with us, padding over the poached soil, about ten years since, when the roads were forming, the canal digging, the plantations trenching, and the infant trees, looking like bundles of useless sprigs, being dropped into their places where now they have taken root and are flourishing; may remember, at least we do, the aërial castles that we formed in our minds, which we were fearful would fail as such fragile architecture generally does. If they do so, they may perhaps agree with us, that the prophetic vision is more than realized.

We next arrive at Hanover Terrace, still on the left hand, with all the sylvan beauties of the Park before it; and a few detached villas of tasteful beauty. Behind their plantations that beneficial stream, the Regent's Canal, enters the northern circuit of the park, and conveys the produce of the inland part of our island, in a beautiful dell, to the bosom of old father Thames.

In order then we pass by Albany Cottage, the residence of Mr. Raikes; Hanover Lodge, Sir Robert Arbuthnot's; Grove House, Mr. Greenough's; and being arrived at nearly the northern extremity of the park, we incline to the eastward. We next pass by (the as yet unbuilt) Munster Terrace, named after one of the Hibernian royal titles, and by the beautiful site marked out for Carrick Terrace.

Now we arrive at the north-eastern boundary of the park; let us sit down for a few minutes in one of the recesses, and survey the delightful prospect before us. Surely the gardens which Dioclesian preferred to his throne, could scarcely have surpassed what these will be, when the present gigantic undertaking is accomplished. Cowley exclaimed, when excited by associations, such as might well be raised by the present enchanting scene,—

> " Methinks I see great Dioclesian walk
> In the Salonian garden's shade,
> Which by his own imperial hands were made:
> I see him smile, methinks, as he does talk
> With the ambassadors, who come in vain
> T' entice him to a throne again.
> ' If I my friend,' said he, ' should to you show
> All the delights which in these gardens grow,
> 'Tis likelier far that you with me should stay,
> Than 'tis that you should carry me away;
> And trust me not, my friends, if every day

PARK VILLAGE EAST, REGENT'S PARK.

PARK VILLAGE EAST, REGENT'S PARK.

Drawn by Tho? H.Shepherd. Engraved by S.Lacey.

JUNCTION OF THE REGENT'S CANAL, AT PADDINGTON.

Drawn by Tho? H.Shepherd. Engraved by S.Lacey.

VIEW IN THE REGENT'S PARK;

EAST GATE, A VILLA AND ST. KATHERINE'S HOSPITAL.

Published May 24. 1828. by Jones & C? 3. Acton Place. Kingsland Road. London.

I walk not here with more delight,
Than ever after the most happy fight,
In triumph to the capitol I rode,
To thank the gods, and to be thought myself a god.' "

What a prospect lies before us? splendour, health, dressed rurality and comforts such as nothing but a metropolis can afford are spread around us. " Trim gardens," lawns and shrubs; towering spires, ample domes, banks clothed with flowers, all the elegancies of the town, and all the beauties of the country are co-mingled with happy art and blissful union. They surely must all be the abodes of nobles and princes! No, the majority are the retreats of the happy free-born sons of commerce, of the wealthy commonalty of Britain, who thus enrich and bedeck the heart of their great empire. Well might the poet ask with honest pride and patriotic exultation,

" Where has commerce such a mart,
So rich, so throng'd, so drain'd and so supplied,
As LONDON—opulent, *enlarg'd* and still
Increasing LONDON? Babylon of old
Nor more the glory of the earth than she,
A more accomplish'd world's chief glory now."

COWPER.

Before we proceed further, let us return a short distance and walk out of the north gate of the park, called Macclesfield Gate. This outlet is over a flat topped bridge, the road or viaduct of which is supported on arches sprung from the capital of iron columns of the Doric order. Under us winds the canal in a lovely dell. The grounds of the park descend to a precipitous bank which protects them from the incursions of the bargemen and other persons whose occupations lead them to frequent the canal and the towing path. The gate on the northern end of the bridge, which with others is closed at ten o'clock every night to all but those who are going to the houses within the park, is in three divisions, a carriage way and two posterns for foot passengers divided by stone piers, and a plain lodge on the western side for the attendant porter. See the Plate of Macclesfield Bridge.

Now return we, and proceed onward, bearing a little to the eastward till we come to the eastern entrance of the park. See the Plate of the East Gate. This is north of the noble pile of buildings of the Corinthian order, flanked by two lofty arches decorated with columns of the same graceful order of architecture, which is called Chester Terrace.

This gateway or entrance, which we believe is to be called Chester Gate, leads to the great north road by Camden Town, Hampstead and Highgate. It has more pretensions to architectural character than either of the other gates, being flanked by the well proportioned stone lodges, and its entrance divided by Doric columns. The entablature, which, with the whole of the composition is Palladian, runs through, and connects the lodges over which it finishes in two pediments. The columns are of cast iron, and fluted after the manner of the Italian architects, and the whole order is selected from their best works. The columns have bases and plinths, with cubical sub-plinths of granite beneath them, as if they were too short for their places, and required the aids of such appendages to raise them to their architraves. This is a fault never found in the pure and sublime architecture of Greece, and rarely in that of ancient Rome, except where they stand as divisions or piers between steps, the column standing on the uppermost, as in Wren's beautiful colonnade at Greenwich hospital.

Each lodge has a well proportioned semi-circular headed window towards the park, and the face of the building is broken and diversified by rustics. The composition is pretty and Italian like, it harmonizes well with the scenery, but the tasteful connoisseur must forget every recollection of a Propyleïum, when viewing this architectural entrance of the Regent's Park, for it must be allowed, that from the time of the Romans to the present day, all deviations from Grecian art, have in the same proportion been deviations from beauty.

Over the two central columns is a projecting and raised blocking course, which, contrary to the rules of good architecture, does not rise so high as the side pavillions, and is moreover weakened in character by a row of projecting reeds in a panel, which give it the appearance of wood scored by a carpenter's reeding plane. Nor does it accord with the sides, which gives the centre an appearance of depression. Sir Christopher Wren* says that " fronts ought to be elevated in

---

* ELMES's Life of Wren, Appendix, page 121.

T.H.Shepherd. del.

T. Barber. sculp.

EAST GATE, REGENT'S PARK.

Pl. 5.

TO THE Rt HON: C. ARBUTHNOT, M.P. &c. &c, THIS PLATE IS MOST RESPECTFULLY INSCRIBED.

BY THE EDITOR.

T.H.Shepherd. del.

T. Barber. sculp.

CLARENCE TERRACE, REGENT'S PARK.

Pl. 6.

TO HIS ROYAL HIGHNESS THE DUKE OF CLARENCE, &c. &c. &c. THIS PLATE IS HUMBLY DEDICATED.

BY THE PUBLISHERS.

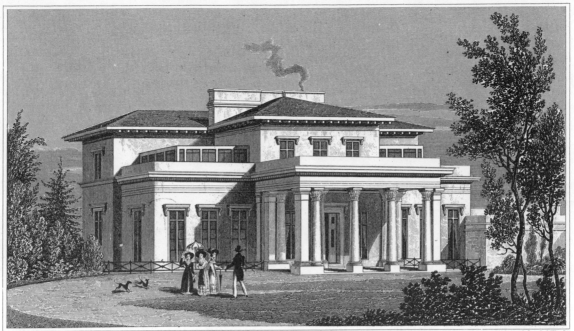

VILLA IN THE REGENT'S PARK.

THE RESIDENCE OF THE MARQUIS OF HERTFORD, TO WHOM THIS PLATE IS RESPECTFULLY INSCRIBED.

CUMBERLAND TERRACE REGENT'S PARK.

TO JOHN NASH, ESQ: ARCHITECT TO THE KING &c. THIS PLATE IS RESPECTFULLY DEDICATED.

the middle, not the corners; because the middle is the place of the greatest dignity, and first arrests the eye; and rather projecting forward in the middle, than hollow. For these reasons, pavillions at the corners are naught; because they make both faults—a hollow and depressed front. The ancients elevated the middle with a tympan and statues, or a dome. The triumphal arches, which now seem flat, were elevated by the magnificent figure of the victor in his chariot with four horses a breast, and other statues accompanying it." A trophy or other pyramidal composition placed on this centre acroterium would remove this objection.

As a composition in the Italian or Palladian style of architecture, as adapted to garden scenery, the East Gate of the Regent's Park is harmonious in design, and graceful in proportion. As the chimneys could not very well be hidden, they are very properly ornamented. The iron carriage way and the postern gates accord in style with the rest of the composition. The view selected by the artist, Mr. T. H. Shepherd, gives a favourable display of this handsome gateway.

We now proceed to the south, having the new hospital and chapel of St. Catherine on the left, and its old English looking house for the master (Sir Herbert Taylor), on our right. We pass by the row of mansions called Cumberland Terrace, and approach Chester Terrace, its lofty arches and spacious plantation; till Cambridge Terrace, the last on the east, connects itself with the towering majesty of the Cupola, and well proportioned Doric portico of Mr. Hornor's prodigious undertaking, the Coliseum, intended as a panorama of the metropolis and its environs, from an elevation loftier than the summit of the cross of St. Paul's Cathedral. This terminates the circuit, and leads us into Park Square, on the east side by the Diorama, where the powerful pictorial illusions of Messrs. Bouton and Daguere, have so often delighted the amatuers and cognoscenti of the metropolis.

We now return by Park Square, leaving its fine gardens and splendid circus, opening its defiles to the vista of Portland Place, on our left. At the north-west angle of Ulster Street begins Ulster Terrace, which passed, leads to Ulster Street, opening into the new road, opposite Harley Street. Then we continue by Brunswick Place, a less ostentatious row of buildings, and to the eastern division of the before mentioned magnificent terrace, which bears the name of the lamented Duke of York, whose illustrious memory is about to be justly commemorated by a national monument.

The entrance between the two divisions of this splendid terrace is called York Gate, and is the subject of a Plate, which gives a view of the architecture on each side, terminated with a view of Mary-le-bone church in the distance. The gate itself consists of ornamental iron work of no prevailing style of architecture. The houses themselves and the church will be described in our future pages, where they will furnish subjects for distinct plates.

Having now made a circuit of the park, we shall conduct you to the interior, and point out the sites of the various villas that are built, and proposed to be built in this terrestrial paradise.

It is proposed by the commissioners of his Majesty's woods and forests, under whose tasteful directions, not only Mary-le-bone Park, but also the splendid improvements of Regent Street, Carlton Palace, and those which are about to commence in the Strand, are being carried on; to erect no more than twenty-six villas within the park. The sites of these villas are all marked on the plan which accompanies this work. Several are already built, the plantations for the rest are completed and growing, and preparations are making, as you may perceive on the northern side, for the erection of others, and for the grounds and menageries of the Zoological Society.

Those which are built, belong to the Marquess of Hertford; to James Burton, Esq. an architect of eminence, (to whom the metropolis is indebted for many fine improvements about Russell and Tavistock Squares, Regent Street, and other places); John Maberly, Esq. M. P. called St. John's Lodge; Grove House, to George Bellas Greenough, Esq.; Hanover Lodge to Colonel Sir Robert Arbuthnot, K. C. B.; Albany Cottage to Thomas Raikes, Esq.; and South Villa, the first in passing the bridge opposite York Gate, to William Henry Cooper, Esq. Mr. Burton's villa called the Holme, designed by his son Decimus Burton, Esq. is the subject of one of our plates, and will be described when we come to it.

Drawn by Tho. H. Shepherd.

Engraved by W. Wallis.

WEST GATE, REGENT'S PARK.

Drawn by Tho. H. Shepherd.

Engraved by W. Wallis.

THE CENTRE OF CUMBERLAND TERRACE, REGENT'S PARK.

ST. MARY LE-BONE CHAPEL, ST. JOHN'S WOOD ROAD.

DORIC VILLA, REGENT'S PARK.

As our round has rather fatigued you, let us sit down on one of these seats that the commissioners have liberally scattered about the park, and before paying a visit to Mr. Burton's tasteful villa, we will chat a little about our opinions as to what a villa is and should be.

With the Greeks we can have little to do. We know but little of their domestic architecture, save and except, about their palaces and hovels; and these indeed more from their writers than from their ruins.

Of the Romans we know more, but I am not going to dis tract you with long discussions about their architecture in general, but only to discuss with you a little concerning their villas, which with those of their bastard successors the Italians, has had much influence upon the domestic architecture of England. Nay, do not start, madam, at my epithet about your favourite Italians, I mean the word as of their architecture only, as the noble author of Childe Harold does of their language, when he calls it

> " that soft bastard Latin,
> Which melts like kisses from a female mouth,
> And sounds as if it should be writ on satin,
> With syllables which breathe of the sweet south."

So of their architecture I adapt another quotation from the same illustrious bard, and you may see it illustrated around you. They, the Italian architects I mean, (and I reckon Messrs. Nash, Joseph Gwilt and Ware to be as much Italian architects, as I do Messrs. Soane and Smirke, to be Grecian), attempted too much variety in compositions which are to be seen at once, and in such cases, too much variety creates confusion. Hence their architecture like their language possesses all the vices of beauty, and is too rich, too redolent of charms, too redundant in variety, has too many parts " joined " as the noble poet says.

> " By no quite lawful marriage of the arts,
> Might shock a connoisseur; but when combin'd
> Form'd a whole which, irregular in parts,
> Yet left a grand impression on the mind."

A *villa*, as generally understood at the present day, is a rural mansion or retreat, for wealthy men. The *palace* with us, belongs to the sovereign and is sometimes applied to the episcopal residence of a bishop. The *mansion* implies the residence of state of a nobleman or gentleman, and sometimes the house of the lord of a manor.

The *villa*, on the contrary is the mere personal property and residence of the owner, where he retires to enjoy himself without state. It is superior to the ornamented cottage, standing as it were between the cottage cornée of the French, and the mansion or hall of the English. The term is never more properly applied than when given to such suburban structures as those which are rising around us, serving as they may well do from *situation* as to the town, and from *position* as to rural beauty.

Quite unlike those merchant's and sugar-baker's boxes which croud the sides of Clapham Road and Kennington Common,

> Suburban *villas* highway-side retreats,
> That dread th' encroachment of our growing streets,
> Tight boxes, neatly sash'd, and in a blaze
> With all a July's suns collected rays,
> Delight the citizen, who, gasping there,
> Breathes clouds of dust, and calls it country air.
>
> COWPER.

With the Romans the villa was quite a different affair. Pliny's villas at Laurentinum, Tuscum, Tusculum, Tybur and Preneste, of which he has left such ample and entertaining descriptions in his epistles, were complete mansions, with residences for retinues of servants, families of his friends, whole regiments of slaves, and other auxiliaries.

Hadrian's villa was a city of palaces, temples and theatres, with an hippodrome, a naumachia, a palestra, a nymphëum, a stadium, a pretorium, splendid galleries of pictures and statues, libraries, porticoes, residences for his ministers, officers, &c. barracks for his soldiers, and an immensity of apartments fitted up in a style of magnificence and splendour, worthy of a Roman emperor.

The villas of Cicero, of Lucullus, and of many other eminent Romans, which are so numerous and so thickly set at Tusculum, and to which they retired from the fatigues of their professions, are more in accordance with our ideas of such a structure. So was that which the infamous Agrippina, according to

THE HOLME, REGENT'S PARK.

THE RESIDENCE OF JAMES BURTON ESQ^R ARCHITECT, TO WHOM THIS PLATE IS RESPECTFULLY INSCRIBED.

Published Sep. 15, 1827, by Jones & Co 3, Acton Place, Kingsland Road, London.

ULSTER TERRACE, REGENT'S PARK.

TO THE RESIDENTS OF WHICH, THIS PLATE IS RESPECTFULLY INSCRIBED.

Drawn by Thos H.Shepherd. Engraved by W.Wallis.

HANOVER TERRACE, REGENT'S PARK.

INSCRIBED TO JOHN NASH, ESQ.^R THE ARCHITECT OF THIS & OTHER SPLENDID WORKS IN ITS NEIGHBOURHOOD.

Drawn by Thos H.Shepherd. Engraved by W.Wallis.

VILLA IN THE REGENT'S PARK.

THE RESIDENCE OF G. B. GREENHOUGH ESQ: TO WHOM THIS PLATE IS MOST RESPECTFULLY INSCRIBED.

Tacitus, so often made the scene of her dissolute pleasures in the same vicinity.

The villas of the modern Romans are nothing better than large city palaces removed into the country. They consist of rooms of state, not of domestic convenience, such as we associate with the word *villa*. They seem more for show than use, and if properly named, would be called *palaces*, instead of villas. Such is the villa Ludovisi, such is the villa Aldobrandini, and such is the villa Albani, whose magnificent galleries and spacious porticoes are filled with the most precious collection of ancient sculpture that any private cabinet ever contained, and which is as appropriately called a villa as if we were to name the spacious mansions of Chatsworth or Blenheim by the name of the villa Devonshire, or villa Marlborough. The villa Mondragone has more windows than there are days in the year, and the villa Borghese bears as much resemblance to a villa as any of those just cited.

Palladio's villas more approach the utility and comfort of such a structure. They are admirably adapted to the country and climate for which he designed them, and are models of beauty and arrangement.

Inigo Jones introduced the Palladian villa into England with more taste than propriety. Lord Burlington continued its practice, and accomplished its greatest beauties in his beautiful gem at Chiswick; but it is too cold, too dreary, and above all, too comfortless, for our climate and our habits of society.

Campbell, Ware and Brettingham built mansions both large and small, but scarcely any thing to be remembered as a villa. Wren built town houses, and Vanburgh palaces, but neither of them accomplished a villa. The houses of the former, many of which are to be seen in London, and are commemorated in his memoirs, cannot be considered, according to his own canons, as *architectural;* for he conformed to the French taste and Parisian fashion of the day, and satirised them by avowing that "architecture aims at eternity, and is therefore the only thing incapable of modes and fashions."

The various villas in the park, the consideration of which have occasioned this digression, shall now be visited, if you are sufficiently rested to proceed. The first that we arrive at, is that of Mr. Burton, which he has named the Holme, a Saxon word, meaning a river island. Good views of it are obtained over the lake and island whence it derives its name, from Hanover Terrace, along Sussex Place, and from Clarence Terrace. From the gardens opposite these buildings our view is taken. Its charming plantations and lovely evergreens, on a fine autumnal day, when we viewed it from the opposite grounds last year, and surveyed the glassy surface of the silver lake,

> " Sloped downwards to its brinks and stood,
> With their green faces fixed upon the flood."
>
> LORD BYRON.

This villa, appears from the grounds, to consist of but two stories, the principal and the chamber story; but in reality it consists of three, the offices being contained in a basement, which is concealed by a lawned terrace, and protected from damps by concealed area walls. This story is lighted and approached from the outside by areas on its flanks, which are hidden by the plantations.

The entrance is on the opposite front to that shown in the view, under an Ionic tetrastyle portico. It consists of a door and two windows, one of which lights the study and the other the eating room. This portico corresponds in width with the bow, or rotunda in the garden front, and is covered with a well proportioned pediment; and the windows agree with those seen in the view: except those under the portico which are smaller, and light the stair-case on one side, and a closet or small dressing room on the other. The door is in the centre, and opens to a hall 16·0 by 10·0, with only one door besides that by which you enter. This door leads to a corridor that communicates with all the apartments of the principal story and the stairs to the chamber story, which are on the left side (on entering) of the hall. The apartments consist of a handsome drawing room which occupies the bow, a library on the side next the conservatory and a billiard room on the other side. These three rooms, occupy the garden front, and can be easily thrown together into one or two apartments, by means of large folding doors. At the back of the library is a spacious dining room, entered under a circular recess; and behind the billiard room, which is as large as the eating room, is a study or gentleman's room, in a retired situation suited to its purposes. The chambers and dormitories are above stairs. The bow is decorated by attached columns of the same order as those in the entrance front, and the entablature is continued on every face of the building except the wings, where the architrave is omitted to make room for the dressings of the windows. The bow is surmounted by an attic, and covered with a well proportioned cupola. Each end of the flanks are finished with a pediment formed by the roof itself, not as in some modern instances, by an appliqué of a different shape. The length of the building on the ground story is sixty-six feet, and the depth on its flanks forty-four feet.

The style of the building is villa-like and characteristic, and the appearance from the grounds rural and pleasing. It is the work of a young architect, and is creditable to his rising abilities.

There is time yet to inspect another of these suburban villas, if you are not too tired :—therefore in our way to our friend's house in St. John's Wood, where we are to dine, we will pass again along the terraces that adorn the outer circle. Look ! what a fine effect the portico of the new church has, now the setting sun illuminates its northern aspect. It is singular, that most of our best porticoes and façades have this dull and sunless aspect. From the India House to Somerset House, and thence to Carlton Palace, which by the way is now being removed, and again, this before us, all face the dreary north.

Look ! I say, at the effect, (the detail and proportions we will defer till to-morrow), see how the long gray shadows contrast with the mellow sunny hue of the lights ; and how playfully they break, and cross each other. What a beautiful carved frame, in appearance, the houses on both sides of York Gate form to the church, (see the print,) and how well the Ionic orders of the houses carries on the eye to the richer Corinthian of the church.

Well, let us proceed dinnerward, and cast another look as we proceed at the terraces on the left, and at the beautiful plantations and lovely lake on our right. See ! the sparkling undulating line of beauty, formed by the curved neck of that swan, sailing majestically by the dark green shrubs of the Holme. The united powers of the magic pencils of Ruysdael and Claude would hardly do justice to that bit of brilliant nature. See again at that charming groupe of (angels, I was going to say,) children, who are sporting between the shrubs. By heaven, I could stay here all day feasting my eyes, till my more corporeal nature would command me to attend to other senses.

Before we cross the bridge at Macclesfield Gate, I will call your attention to the picturesque groupe before us, formed by Albany Cottage in the fore-ground, Hanover Lodge a little behind it, and Grove House, that which has the Ionic portico and niches, in the distance.

GROVE HOUSE, the residence of *George Bellas Greenough*, Esq. is another of Mr. Decimus Burton's elegant designs, and is completely in the villa style of architecture. It is larger and has more pretensions to architectural character, than that of his father. The garden front, which forms the principal feature in the print, is divided into three portions, a centre and two wings. The wings are backed with the flanks of the side elevations, which give a value to their outlines.

The centre of the garden front, is composed of a tetrastyle portico of the Ionic order, raised on a terrace. Three windows fill the apertures between the columns, and a long panel over them, gives an apparent height to the apartment thus decorated. The wings have recesses, the soffites of which are supported by three quarter columns of the Doric order. Between these columns are well proportioned niches, each of which contains a statue. No other window or door appears on the front, which gives a remarkable and pleasing *casino* or *pleasure-house* character to the house.

The portico, which is composed of one of the purest of the Grecian orders, is surmounted by a well proportioned pediment and acroteria; and the cornice of the wings, by a blocking course, the beauty of which is injured, by its integrity being broken and its character weakened, through raising the angles and depressing the centre, contrary to all the sound rules of the art, and of the elements of beauty. The curvilinear dipping lines of these finials to the wings are discordant to the eye, and should have been avoided. Sir Christopher Wren * says, that "an artist ought to be jealous of novelties, in which fancy binds the judgment; and to think his judges, as well as those

---

* ELMES's Life of WREN, Appendix, p. 120.

that are to live five centuries after him, as those of his own time. That which is commendable now for novelty will not be a new invention to posterity, when his works are often imitated, and when it is not known which is the original; but *the glory of that which is good is eternal.*"

The entrance front, also consists of three parts, or divisions, a centre and two wings. The centre, however, is kept subordinate to the garden or principal front, by having no pediment, but is finished with a simple straight blocking course over the level Ionic cornice, which is continued through both fronts and flanks, as the *theme* or subject of the composition. This variety of uniformity gives perfect beauty and an *Ionic* character to the house; although the lower portico and decorations of the niches have a *Doric* accompaniment. These uniformities carried alternately in the fronts, affect the eye, as the key notes in music, or the alternate rhymes in poetry, do the ear. The blocking course is finished by a panelled acroterium, surmounted by a sub-cornice and lesser blocking course; shorter by about a fourth than its plinth, and carried into a pyramidal form by well proportioned trusses, which have the merit of appearing really as supporters to their centre.

Under the architrave of the leading entablature are the windows of the chamber story. Three in the centre and one in the flanks. The entrance door is protected by a spacious semi-circular portico of the true Doric order, which harmonizes with the livelier Ionic, as Linley's inimitable violoncello does with Spagnoletti's brilliant fiddle :—or to take a higher character, like one of Mozart's majestic accompaniments, to his brilliant and inventive *arias*.

The blocking course of this order is carried horizontally in a straight line, and vertically in a beautiful curve, censuring by its harmony the discord of its weak and inefficient neighbour. I cannot help again quoting Wren while we are here, although our friend may be getting warm, and his dinner cold, by our delay. It is from the same unfinished sketch that I before quoted from, and is germain to our subject.

" Beauty, firmness and convenience," says our great master, " are the principles of architecture: the first two depend upon geometrical reasons of optics and statics; the third only makes the variety. There are natural causes of beauty. Beauty," observes he, making a fine definition, " is a harmony of objects, begetting pleasure by the eye." Then he proceeds to say that there are two causes of beauty, " natural and customary. Natural is from geometry, consisting in uniformity, that is, equality and proportion. Customary beauty is begotten by the use of our own senses to those objects which are usually pleasing to us for other causes; as familiarity, or particular inclination, breeds a love to things not in themselves lovely. Here lies the great occasion of errors; here is tried the architect's judgment; but always the true test is natural or geometrical beauty."

Put your tasteless watch into your hungry fob, I will not detain you from your dinner many minutes, and the subject is so apt, that I must finish it. We will take gallant's law, and lay the blame on the enticing beauties that have surrounded and accompanied us. " Geometrical figures," continues my master, " are naturally more beautiful than other irregular figures; in this, all consent as to a law of nature. Of geometrical figures, the square and the circle, are most beautiful. Next, the parallelogram and the oval. Straight lines are more beautiful than curved : next to straight lines, equal and geometrical flexures. An object *elevated* in the middle" (mind that friend Decimus, and violate no more the purity of thy blocking courses) " is more beautiful than *depressed*."

The general composition of Grove House, accords (excepting only the inharmonious discord of the aforesaid blocking course, which affects the eye like a badly resolved chord in music does the ear), with the definition of beauty, that I have just quoted. The principal, or garden front, is harmonious, both in its principal features and in its accessories; the entrance front is equally harmonious in itself, and secondary to the leading ideas, forming an admirable tenor to the soprano façade of the garden, and the whole forms a pretty architectural *sinfonia* of a few parts; the composer wisely leaving the more magnificent and grander features of the art for fuller compositions :—to such as where

" The pillar'd dome magnific heaves
Its ample roof; and luxury within,
Pours out her glittering stores."

THOMSON.

The interior of this modest mansion is commodiously arranged, both for convenience and utility. The study of this department of our art, *convenience*, particularly in domestic architecture, is one of the most useful, and at the same time, one of the most difficult parts of an architect's profession. Sir Henry Wotton, in discussing this subject, says, that "every man's proper *mansion-house* and *home*, being the theatre of his hospitality, the seat of self-fruition, the comfortable part of his own life, the noblest of his son's inheritance, a kind of private princedom; nay, to the possessors thereof, an epitome of the whole world, may well deserve, by these attributes, according to the degree of the masters, to be decently and delightfully adorned. For which end there are two arts attending on architecture, like two of her principal gentlewomen, to dress and trim their mistress—picture and sculpture." I know not what our old friend Fuseli would have said to this doctrine of making painting a dressing maid to architecture. Flaxman would have shaken his venerable head at any one who would have promulgated such an heresy concerning his art. Courage! I see land, our friend's house is in view, the chimneys are delightfully telegraphing us with their smoak, and I have just time to finish the diplomatic-architecto-critic's opinion of the three arts; " between whom," continues he, " before I proceed any farther, I will venture to determine an ancient quarrel about their precedency, with this distinction; that in *the garnishing of fabrics*, sculpture no doubt must have the pre-eminence, as being indeed of nearer affinity to architecture itself, and consequently, the more natural and suitable ornament. But, on the other side, to consider these two arts, as I shall do, philosophically, and not mechanically, an excellent piece of painting is to my judgment the more admirable object, because it comes near an artificial miracle to make divers distinct eminences appear upon a flat by force of shadows, and yet the shadows themselves not to appear, which I conceive the uttermost value, and virtue of a painter, and to which very few have arrived."

As we have yet a few minutes, I must say something of the horticultural decorations, which " garnish " this villa.

They are at present young and incomplete, but looking with a pictorial eye, at their present capabilities and prospects of future growth, they are beautifully diversified, and give a characteristic back-ground and accompaniment to the principal feature—the house.

CHAP. II.

"Fountains and Trees, our wearied pride do please,
E'en in the midst of gilded palaces;
And in our towns, that prospect gives delight,
Which opens round the country to our sight.

SPRAT

TOUR OF THE REGENT'S PARK, BEGINNING AT YORK GATE—YORK GATE AND THE NEW CHURCH OF ST. MARY-LE-BONE, THE WORK OF TWO ARCHITECTS, CONSIDERED AS ONE COMPOSITION—CONVERSION BY ACT OF PARLIAMENT OF AN IONIC CHAPEL INTO A CORINTHIAN CHURCH—OBSTINACY OF THE BASES, CONTRASTED WITH THE SUBSERVIENCY OF THE CAPITALS—YORK TERRACE—CORNWALL TERRACE—ARCHITECTURE COMPARED WITH MUSIC—CLARENCE TERRACE—OBSERVATIONS—SUSSEX PLACE—HANOVER TERRACE—DESCRIPTIONS OF AND REMARKS ON ALBANY COTTAGE—HANOVER LODGE—GROVE HOUSE, THE VILLA OF MR. GREENOUGH—THE MARQUESS OF HERTFORD'S VILLA—MACCLESFIELD BRIDGE—THE GROUNDS OF THE ZOOLOGICAL SOCIETY—THE COLLEGIATE CHURCH AND HOSPITAL OF ST. CATHERINE—THE MASTER'S RESIDENCE—CHESTER TERRACE—CAMBRIDGE TERRACE—MR. HORNOR'S COLISEUM—THE DIORAMA—MR. SOANE'S NEW CHURCH.

GOOD morning to you gentlemen, we are betimes and punctual, and it is well we are so, for we have much to do. The morning, however, is auspicious, and we go to our task with affection. Let us, as the French say, begin with the beginning, and by walking gently along the New Road, enter upon our undertaking at

YORK GATE.

To see this place (for York Gate is not only the entrance gateway to the park, but also comprises the two rows of mansions that flank it, forming an architectural avenue to the park on entering it, and a brilliant border to the church on leaving it) we should go upon the bridge.

The entrance is formed by the porches of the eastern and western ends of York Terrace, which is thus divided into two halves. These porches give the effect of lodges to the gates which cross the avenue, and break the perpendicularity of the line of houses. Of the terrace itself, I will say a word or two as we pass round the park, after examining the two rows of mansions that flank this handsome entrance to it.

One side is similar to the other, and consists of a centre and two wings. The wings project from the main body of the building, and are plain in their elevation, except where their perpendicular lines are broken by the string course, which forms the plinth to the stylobate of the Ionic order of the centre, and by the cornices of the principal and attic orders.

The centres recede, and are decorated by semi-circular headed windows in the ground story; by a colonnade of the Ionic order, to the principal and two pair stories, and by an attic surmounting the cornice of the principal order. The inter-columniations, are appropriated to the windows; those of the principal story having balconies formed by a balustrade, between the pedestals of the order. Both the buildings are insulated, their northern extremities being bounded by the mews and entrances to the houses of York Terrace, and their southern ends by the buildings and gardens of Nottingham Terrace, which reach to the New Road.

Before we proceed to a brief examination of the church, let me call your attention to the rich and varied effect of the three architectural façades of which this stereotomous scene, like that of Palladio's sculptured scenery at the Olympic theatre of Vicenza, is composed. The western front is in positive shadow, relieved only by the atmospheric reflection, that faintly delineates the details, and gives a massive effect approaching to that of moon-light; while its opposite brother sparkles with all the radiance of the morning sun, having shadows and lights, reflexes and demitints in varied harmony. The church connects this light and shade, this treble and base, as it were, of the composition, by a middle tint of half shadow, a sort of tenor to the others, and is illuminated into complete detail by the reflected lights from the eastern front of the buildings, from the surface of the road in its front, and from the atmosphere. These lights produce almost the effect of perfect day-light without sun-shine, upon the portico and aisles of the church; and give softened instead of cast shadows, like those in sun-shine, and the west front is comparatively dark, from the excessive light of the eastern building.

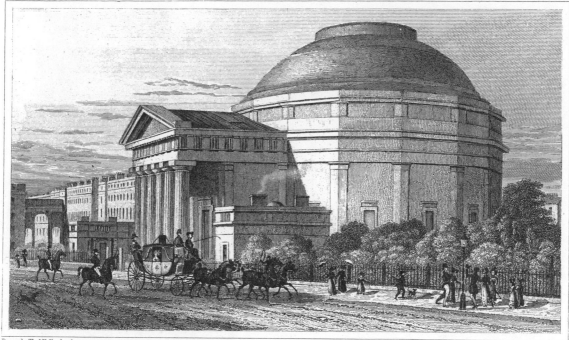

Drawn by Thos H Shepherd.

Engraved by H.Wallis.

THE COLISEUM, REGENT'S PARK.

Published April 21, 1827, by Jones & Co 3 Acton Place, Kingsland Road, London.

Drawn by Thos H.Shepherd.

Engraved by H.Wallis.

YORK GATE, REGENT'S PARK, & MARY-LE-BONE CHURCH.

Drawn by Thos. H. Shepherd.

Engraved by Thos. Dale.

ST PETER'S CHURCH.

EATON SQUARE, PIMLICO.

Drawn by Thos. H. Shepherd.

Engraved by Thos. Dale.

CHAPEL OF EASE.

TO MARYLEBONE, STAFFORD ST. NEW ROAD.

They form a complete architectural pictorial symphony of three parts, in perfect harmony as a composition, although the work of two masters. True it is, there are some defects in the detail, the attic cornice is too trifling and petite, and the upper blocking course too insignificant, and not exactly in good keeping with the rest, or in good taste :—but, when the adapter of the accompaniments (Mr. Nash), has succeeded so well in completing the whole subject, of which the church, the theme as it may be called of the composition, is the work of another artist (the late Mr. Hardwick), and rendered it so picturesque and harmonious as a whole ; we must not seek too rigidly for the accidental carelessness of an appogiatura note or two, that may offend against the strict rules of the art, the entire composition being so pleasing and satisfactory.

One more look, as that passing cloud is beautifully varying the bright lines of the columns with a dioramic effect, and then we will cross the road, and take a closer view of the new church.

The New Church of St. Mary-le-bone.

The first church of this parish was dedicated, say the antiquaries, to St. John, and the second one, of which I have before spoken, to the Virgin Mary. Of this idol of the Catholic church, in those days England possessed many, even as there are still a plurality of Madonnas in those countries where the Roman Catholic faith prevails. This saint in particular, was called *St. Mary of, or at, the bourn,* and now by corruption and acceptation, *St. Mary-le-bone,* which, with your leave I shall call it, with the *vulgar* million, leaving its etymology and correct orthography to the *wise* few, who patronize word-catching and antiquarianism.

The original church stood on or near the present court-house of the parish, at the end of Mary-le-bone Lane, near Oxford Street. The second church was built on the site of a chapel near the upper end of High Street; which becoming dilapidated, was taken down in the year 1741, and a new one, now called *the parish chapel,* erected in its place. It is, as Cobbett says, in The Rejected Addresses, " a plain brown brick edifice."

This church becoming inadequate to the population and respectability of the parish, in spite of the many chapels of ease which had been built within its circuit, the parishioners for many years past had been endeavouring to procure the erection of a new parish church, commensurate with their wants. In 1770 they procured an act of parliament for building one, for making a new cemetery, and other purposes connected therewith; and a design for its construction by Sir William Chambers was approved by the proper authorities. In 1772 or 1773 the vestrymen procured a new and enlarged act, empowering them to provide an additional public cemetery, and to erect a new parish chapel of ease. The plot of ground before us, was therefore purchased and enclosed, but no farther steps were taken till after the passing of a fourth act in 1811, which repealed all the former acts, and gave new powers to the vestrymen and their successors.

These gentlemen, therefore, determined in the beginning of the year 1813 to build a new chapel of ease on this spot, and adopted a design for such purpose, made by Thomas Hardwick, Esq. The works were accordingly commenced in the July of that year, and the edifice was proceeding rapidly to completion, when the building was suddenly stopped; and various alterations effected. It was then much smaller and of a different order, the Ionic. Some of the capitals, I well remember, were carved, and I believe one or two were erected upon their proper shafts. When this smaller building was at this stage of its operations, the select vestry came to the resolution of converting their incipient *chapel of ease*, into a complete *parish church :* and as parliament is proverbially said to be omnipotent, they procured another act to empower them to make that metamorphosis, and to convert, by its magic influence, good Ionic columns into substantial Corinthians. This occasioned a perfect chaos among the materials and elements of the building; which, when order was restored, all the shafts of the Ionic columns became elongated to Corinthian proportions, and were surmounted by capitals of that splendid order. But the humble attic bases of the original design, not having the fear of being called to the bar of the house before their eyes, would not give way to the parliamentary enactment, and remain to this day vouching for their Ionian origin.

The more modest maidenly tower, was also compelled to resign her claims, in order to make way for the riper and more matured beauties of a sedate matronly campanile steeple. The aisle-like additions of the stair-ways to the galleries, received the embroidered decorations of a pair of orthodox columns, the tetrastyle Ionic porch of the chapel was extended to the hexastyle Corinthian portico of the church, and various other alterations were made, to give the *daughter chapel*, now married by authority of parliament, the character of a *mother church*.

When completed and consecrated, the new edifice was named, with all due solemnity, *the parish church of St. Mary-le-bone;* and was invested with all the rights and privileges of its decrepit and divorced predecessor, which was obliged to retire into the humble rank of *parish chapel*, and to act as a handmaid to its more favoured, and more youthful successor.

The Duke of Portland, as rector of the parish, nominates the curate, who is to be licensed by the Bishop of London. This ecclesiastical officer is now paid a stipend suitable to the rank and wealth of his flock. But, as a contrast to the present day, Mr. Lysons informs us in his valuable researches into the history of the environs of London, that in 1511 the curate's stipend was only thirteen shillings a year, which was paid by Thomas Hobson, then lessee under the priory of Blakemore. In 1650 the impropriation was valued at £80 a year, and the curate was paid £15 a year, his other emoluments averaging generally about the same sum. From the prodigious increase of first-rate buildings, and of population in the parish, particularly in the Regent's Park, the contingencies of the minister's stipend are now such as to make it divisible into several valuable benefices.

The plan of this church, like most of those in the metropolis, is a parallelogram, with its longest sides distributed to the north and south, instead of to the east and west, as is usual with Christian churches. This method of construction, which throws the principal or entrance front to the north, and the altar to the south, is an arrangement that doubtlessly was thought of but little importance when its original destination was for a Chapel; but is objectionable in many points of view, as I will presently shew you, in a Church.

The north front is elongated by lateral projections to the east and west, which are both faced by detached columns. These wings contain the staircases which lead to the galleries. The south ends of the east and west fronts are also elongated by similar projections, which, lying diagonally in relation to the main building, form internally a semi-hexagonal recess for the altar ; and externally, that to the eastward a direct portico or façade of entrance from High Street, and that to the westward a corresponding form, which, however, faces only the church-yard. The eastern diagonal wing, contains a vestibule and staircase to the gallery, and to the private family pews above, which have the heterodox and profane appearance of the private boxes of a dramatic theatre. The western corresponding appendage, contains a similar staircase upon a smaller scale, and a vestry room below, and family pews corresponding with those opposite to them, above.

Before entering the church, the doors of which fortunately for us are open, we will take a view of the principal elevation now before us. The portico, which is raised upon six steps, is Corinthian, of the proportions and after the chaste example of the Pantheon at Rome, and is hexastyle in front. It is crowned by a proper entablature, and a well proportioned pediment. Behind the principal range of columns, which have a return column and an anta on each flank of the portico, are three doorways, with well proportioned architraves and dressings. The centre entrance leads to the nave, and the sides to the aisles and galleries. The elevation is divided into two stories by a string course, on which, in front, are two semi-circular headed windows over the side doors, and between the four central columns, is a long blank sunk panel, which was in the architect's original design, filled with a basso-rilievo representing the entry of Jesus Christ into Jerusalem. Few subjects of sacred history, could be either more appropriate to a Christian edifice than this narrative, the selection of which is highly creditable to the taste and judgment of this able pupil of Sir William Chambers, or compose better for a sculptural embellishment to a Christian temple. The select vestry could not do better than to order Mr. Westmacott, whom the Royal Academy have with great judgment elected professor of sculpture, to fill up the void by a sculptural representation of this very appropriate and analogous subject from his able hand ; and thus complete the principal elevation of their handsome church.

The ceiling of the portico is divided into panels by the architraves from the columns to the wall or cell of the building, which are crossed by the epistylium of the columns in flank. These panels are filled with flowers of a broad, bold and appropriate character, peculiarly suitable for their situation.

" Honour to whom honour is due," says a high authority, therefore I should have been sorry had we left the portico without noticing the inscription over the centre doorway ; which, like that of the portico of Agrippa from which this is copied, records the honoured names of its pious founders.

" This Church was erected at the expense of the PARISHIONERS, AND CONSECRATED VI. FEBRUARY,
A.D. MDCCCXVIII.

The Duke of Portland, } CHURCHWARDENS.
Sir James Graham, Bart. }

George Allen, } SIDESMEN.
John Russell, }

I had almost forgotten my promise of animadverting upon the practice of reversing, or neglecting, the ancient custom of building churches east and west, which makes the entrance or portico face the west, and the altar or posticum face the east or rising sun. To say nothing of religious principle in this mode of construction, which however, like most principles founded on such grounds, will always be found consistent with good sense, the custom of placing churches east and west is of very ancient practice, and independently of the Christian feeling of the early ages, is founded on good taste, and is the most beautiful in practice ; not only for the sentiments that it inspires from its antiquity, and from the feeling of adoring the Creator of all things, looking towards the east, where his bounteous source of light and heat rises to beautify and benefit our mundane globe ; but from the circumstance, that such a mode of distribution gives more beauty and variety of light and shade, than any other. In a northern aspect, such as this of Mary-le-bone new church, the portico, which is always the most distinguishing feature of a church, is turned towards that part of the heavens, from whence the sun never shines ; and it rarely catches its enlivening rays, but receives on the contrary the gloomy sepulchral reflected light of a northern aspect, and bears more the character of a pagan sepulchre, than of the enlivening features of a Christian temple.

The steeple partakes of the same gloomy character *in front*, but being circular in its upper part, and having every face alike, the same objection does not entirely hold good. Therefore to catch the best character of this feature of the church, which by the way is the most difficult thing to design in modern architecture, and may be called both the touch-stone and opprobium of modern art, let us walk a little way down the New Road towards Portland Place, and observe the charming effect of the light and shade upon its varied forms.

To compare this steeple with the best of Gibbs' or any of Wren's, that are executed in stone, would be trying its architect by too severe a standard, for who of modern days has surpassed that of St. Martin's in the Fields, or has equalled those of St. Bride's, Row, or many others that may occur to an observing spectator? But it has its beauties, which are principally those of detail, and its defects, which are entirely those of outline and of appropriateness. In outline it is bulky and inelegant, and in appropriateness, either the pediment should have been omitted, or the campanile should not have been placed a straddle upon its back. It has no precedent in any work of Wren's, who always brings up his spire from a sufficient tower, and base from the ground; nor do I remember at this moment any in the great Italian masters. Gibbs furnishes an example in St. Martin's, and so does the elder Dance in St. Leonard, Shoreditch, two specimens of great beauty, elegance and solidity, but deficient in this first requisite of a bell tower, a sufficiently apparent foundation.

The steeple, as you may perceive, commences on the summit of the pediment and roof, by a square rusticated tower of twenty-one feet on each side. In the centre is a clock, which breaks the monotony of the masonry. On the upper part of this is a circular peristyle of columns of the Corinthian order. A blocking course and two lofty steps surmount the cornice and form a base to eight caryatic figures of the winds, which support an entablature, a blocking course, and a series of eight trusses, bearing up as many ribs, upon a cupola, which finish upon its vertex, and support a pedestal and weathercock.

The setting off of the square tower to the circular temple is too abrupt for symmetry, and consequently fails in producing a beautiful effect. The composition is not sufficiently pyramidal, nor lofty, but the female figures, and the semicircular headed apertures between them, are novel in design, and elegant in effect. Its height is about seventy-five feet from the roof, or 120 feet from the ground.

As we are on this side, let us go down High Street, take a look at the Eastern front, which has an original and striking appearance on this side, from the effect of the almost meridian sun which is now shining upon it ; and enter the church, by the south eastern entrance. Over the corresponding door, is a similar niche to that before us, and the wing is ornamented in every respect in a similar manner.

The floor of the church is raised five or six steps above the level of the cemetery, which is a method that should always be adopted, as the ground of the church-yard is always increasing in height. Witness the number of churches in the country whose floors are become by such means much below the level of the surrounding soil, to the great injury of the healths of the congregation.

The interior, which we are now entering, is, as you perceive, spacious, airy and commodious ; and, having a second gallery, will accommodate an immense congregation, the members of which can all hear and see as well as in any church in the metropolis. The arrangement of the galleries and pews, and the distribution of the seats, are all excellent as far as hearing and seeing are concerned, but are too theatrical in appearance, for an edifice of so sacred a character as a church. This appearance is still farther increased by the private pews, which standing in the diagonal sides in tiors bear also too great a resemblance to the private boxes, and the altar and its decorations, with the organ in its centre, and the flimsy linen transparency in its front, to the proscenium of a theatre. With these exceptions, the interior is rich and splendid, and bears evidence of a sound and pure taste in its architect. The lower part of the altar-piece is also in excellent style, and the altar picture of a holy family, by West, is one of the best productions of that facile painter.

The pulpit and desks are beautifully carved in mahogany,

and are very appropriate to their destined purposes. The ceiling, as you may perceive, is broad and bold in style, and effective in execution. The splendid effect of this church on Sundays, when filled by a congregation of the first wealth and information in the British metropolis, cannot be surpassed.

Our morning is wasting fast, we have much to see and to talk about, and the pew-opener is waiting to lock the doors after us; therefore, if you please, we will leave this singularly original design, return into the Park by York Gate, and pursue our peregrinations. I almost had forgotten to say, that the expense of building the church, including the charge incurred by the alterations from the original design of a chapel into a church, was about £60,000.

See the rich embroidered prospect now before us! Look on our right how the huge cupola of the Coliseum spreads its ample rotunda among the groves of mansions, pleasure grounds and squares. See the bizarre minarets of Sussex Place on our left, in direct opposition to it; and the tasteful pilasters of Cornwall Terrace, how they play in the sunny corruscations of this brilliant morning. With how much more justice might the poet exclaim, had he lived to see our metropolis in this our day,—

> " this splendid city
> How wanton sits she, amidst nature's smiles ;
> Nor from her highest turret has to view,
> But golden landscapes, and luxuriant scenes,
> A waste of wealth, the store-house of the world."
>
> Young.

York Terrace.

Now we are again in the confines of the park. The buildings on our right and left are York Terrace, designed by Mr. Nash. That which is eastward of York Gate, we will leave till we return to it after our circuit, and inspect that on our left. This splendid row of princely mansions, has the appearance of one single building, of a complete palatial character; owing to all the entrances being in the rear, where large and characteristic porches protect the vestibules, and serve for the reception of dressed company from carriages in bad weather. All the doors and windows in this lawn or principal front, are uniform, and have the appearance of a suit of princely apartments rather

Drawn by Thos. H. Shepherd.   Engraved by T. Barber.

VILLA IN THE REGENT'S PARK,

THE RESIDENCE OF JOHN MABERLY ESQ: M.P. TO WHOM THIS PLATE IS RESPECTFULLY INSCRIBED.

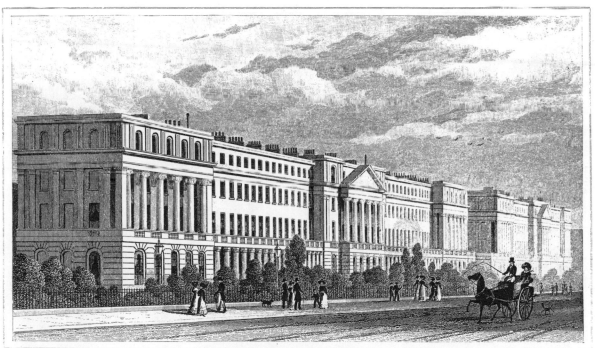

Drawn by Thos. H. Shepherd.   Engraved by T. Barber.

YORK TERRACE, REGENT'S PARK.

Drawn by Thos. H. Shepherd.

Engraved by W. Tombleson.

HANOVER LODGE, REGENT'S PARK.

THE RESIDENCE OF LADY ARBUTHNOT: TO WHOM THIS PLATE IS RESPECTFULLY INSCRIBED.

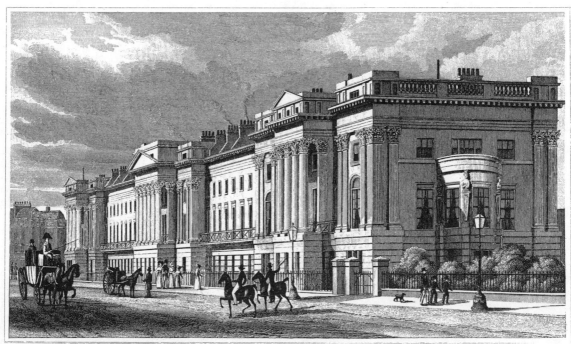

Drawn by Thos. H. Shepherd.

Engraved by W. Deeble.

CORNWALL TERRACE, REGENT'S PARK,

TO THE RESIDENTS OF WHICH, THIS PLATE IS RESPECTFULLY DEDICATED.

than a row of private dwellings. This idea is kept up by the pleasing and judicious arrangement of the gardens, which have no divisions, but are laid out in the style of grounds belonging to the palace. The elevation is in a good Italian style of architecture in composition, with Grecian detail; and consists of an entrance or ground story, with semicircular headed windows, and rusticated piers. A stylobate, or continued pedestal above the rusticated arches of these windows, runs through the whole composition, divided between the columns into balustrades in front of the windows of the one pair or principal story, to which they form balconies of a handsome architectural character, much superior to the trivial thread-like iron balconies of its predecessors. Lofty, well-proportioned windows, that give light to the elegant drawing-rooms of the principal story, are perforated immediately on the cornice of the stylobate, and in accordance with the majestic simplicity of the order to which they belong (the Ionic of the Ilyssus), they are left without decoration. A similar range of windows, of the same width but less in height, are constructed for the use of the principal chamber story, and like those of the drawing-room story are also without dressings. These two stories form the principal architectural features of the terrace, and are decorated with a colonnade of the Ilyssus Ionic order. The angles are finished in antis, and the order is completed by a well proportioned entablature, adapted with great propriety from the same beautiful specimen of the order. On the summit of the cornice is constructed an attic story, which by prescription is allowed to wander a little into the bizarre, but this strays rather too much into the irregular, to accompany so chaste a composition as the Ionic, to which it forms a crown. The cornice and blocking course are both also too small in proportion for the majesty of the lower order. A contrast there should be certainly, but not in style. It is in a different key, and is a false concord, when only an harmonious discord was required. The windows between the piers or pilasters of this story, are of the same width as those below, and finished with semicircular heads and sash windows in correspondence with those of the lower story.

Now we will proceed in our excursion, but hark! at that delightful harp. The very circumstance of not seeing the charming player enhances the romance of the scene. How the swelling chords wander about the ear. It comes from the open window, with the tamboured muslin curtains, and it accords so completely with the harmony of the scene, that I cannot tear myself away. The lovely musician is revelling in all the brilliancy of Arpeggio variations upon the beautiful Venetian air *sul margine del rio*. Mark the rapidity with which she executes that *brillante* passage, swelling from the minutest *piano* to the most powerful *forte*, stopping as if by magic in an instant and then reverting to the original air. It ceases! Well! the highest enjoyments are often the most brief. Therefore now let us proceed.

Cornwall Terrace.

This next row of buildings is one of the first, and at the same time one of the prettiest, that have been erected in the Park. It is called Cornwall Terrace, after our present King's ducal title, when Regent of these kingdoms. The houses are not on so large a scale as those in York Terrace, but possess a character for regular beauty that some of their more colossal neighbours want. This terrace is erected from the designs of Mr. Decimus Burton, and possesses a character of beauty and scholastic regularity, that is highly creditable to the talents of this young architect. It consists of a rusticated ground story, which forms a well proportioned basement to the Corinthian order of the principal stories. The doors and windows correspond in character, and preserve an appearance of unity highly agreeable to the eye. This rusticated story projects beyond the face of the upper, which is of the Corinthian order, with fluted shafts, well proportioned capitals, and an equally well proportioned entablature. The windows, dressings, accessories and other architectural and sculptured embellishments of this very elegant row of houses, are in good taste, and present to our view an architectural façade of singular beauty.

Clarence Terrace.

Let us now continue our ramble. This picturesque row of houses is named after his Royal Highness the Lord High Admiral of England, and is also from the drawing board of Mr. Burton, junior. It is in three portions, a centre and two wings, of the Corinthian order, connected by two colonnades of the Ilyssus Ionic order. This terrace is the smallest in the park; and from the circumstance of its projecting wings, and its Ionic colonnade, it presents a greater variety in its composition, and a more imposing effect, than if it were straight upon its face, and had not such bold features. The elevation is divided into three stories; namely, a rusticated entrance, which serves as a basement to the others, a Corinthian order embellishing the drawing-room and chamber stories, and a well proportioned entablature : these form the principal features of this pleasing composition.

If we cross over to the pavement of the terrace, and turn our backs upon the houses, we shall enjoy one of the most pleasing views in the park. Look at the beautiful expanse of the lake before us ! See the exquisite diversity of scene, occasioned by the islets or holmes that lay upon its tranquil bosom, in all the variety of nature, when at the same time they are the effects of art. Such power has the artist of pure taste, who looks to nature as his guide, in the formation of living pictures like the scene that we are now enjoying.

A house, situate like one of these, possesses the double advantage of town and country. By its contiguity to the fashionable and business parts of the metropolis, it forms a complete town residence; and by the romantic beauty of the decorated landscape scenery by which it is surrounded, it is equal to any part of the country for health and domestic retirement, for men of business,

> " When weary they retreat
> T' enjoy cool nature in a country seat,
> T' exchange the centre of a thousand trades
> For clumps and lawns, and temples and cascades."
>
> Cowper.

How charming is the appearance of those two beautiful villas, the Holme and South-villa, from this spot; surrounded as they are by such luxuriant vegetation of shrubs and trees, and flowers, redolent of beauty and of the sweetest perfume.

Now let us proceed. The whimsical row of houses, that we are now approaching is,

SUSSEX PLACE,

designed, I believe, by Mr. Nash. In elevation it presents a singular contrast to the chaster beauties of the other terraces and places, by which it is surrounded ; and was perhaps introduced purposely by its able architect for the sake of picturesque variety. For architectural beauty or good taste, if we separate the pagoda-like cupolas of this pile, and the bizarre style of decoration which it displays, from its adjacent scenery and accessories, it is entitled to no commendation on the score of pure style : but, when considered with the eye of a landscape painter, it presents a variety of form, and an assemblage of picturesque outlines, which diversify the scene, and prevent a monotony of effect that might otherwise have been tedious. The horticultural accessories, are pleasingly adapted to the houses, and the situation, which commands some of the most charming prospects in the park, is one of the most delightful suburban sites in this region of beauty. The lake spreads its tranquil bosom before the façade, and reflects its eastern-like cupolas with pleasing effect. The varied plantations of the park, group with singular felicity, and the delightful season, that we are now enjoying, gives a double relish to the natural beauties of the place.

Now let us proceed, as the morning is wearing away apace, and we have much to occupy our attention.

Our next object is the handsome row of mansions on our left, named after his Majesty's continental kingdom and hereditary dominions,

HANOVER TERRACE ;

which is also a design of Mr. Nash's, and in a more grammatical style of architecture than that which we have now left. It has a centre and two wing buildings, of the Doric order, the acroteria of which are surmounted by statues and other sculptural ornaments in terra cotta. The centre building is crowned by a well proportioned pediment, the tympanum of which is embellished with statues and figures in a wretched style of art, which the architect would do well to remove. The style of

ROYAL YORK BATHS, REGENT'S PARK.

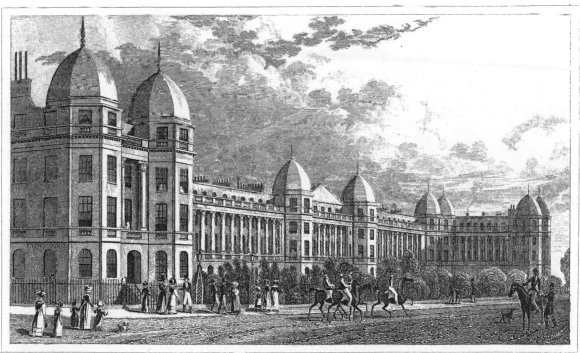

SUSSEX PLACE, REGENT'S PARK.

ALBANY COTTAGE, REGENT'S PARK.

THE RESIDENCE OF THOS RAIKES ESQ

APSLEY HOUSE, HYDE PARK CORNER.

THE RESIDENCE OF HIS GRACE THE DUKE OF WELLINGTON TO WHOM THIS PLATE IS RESPECTFULLY INSCRIBED

architecture employed by the artist is Italian or Palladian, and remarkably well adapted for the description of dwelling houses, of which the structure is composed. The capitals are well proportioned in design, and well executed, but the entablature is weak in profile and inefficient in character, for the height of the building to which it is appropriated.

The stories of the mansions are lofty, and elegantly finished, and the domestic arrangement of the various rooms convenient, and laid out in a masterly style. The situation of this very pretty terrace is near the north western extremity of the western branch of the lake which embellishes and refreshes the park. The islet which faces its northernmost wing sweetly diversifies the scene, and gives a charming sylvan character to the prospect from the houses.

The knoll of Primrose hill which appears above the tops of the young plantations, looks charmingly, as that passing cloud is diversifying its emerald bosom, and removing a somewhat too great monotony. A large reservoir of water is being formed upon its summit for the supply of the houses in the park, as high as their upper stories. This undertaking will add to the character which our countrymen have ever enjoyed of adding the useful to the ornamental.

Now let us rest a while, and enjoy the passing by of this bevy of fair demoiselles on their prancing jennets, who appear proud of their lovely burthens; accompanied by the gentle cavaliers who are escorting them, with beaming eyes and rejoicing hearts.

How beautiful that group of detached buildings, north of Hanover Terrace, composes from the situation in which we now are. The first on our left is Albany Cottage, the picturesque residence of Thomas Raikes, Esq. As a specimen of the English cottage ornée, it is scarcely to be surpassed, even in this region of architectural and picturesque beauty. The plantations accord with the architecture in a singularly happy manner, and at this youthful season of the year, give out delicious and health-inspiring perfumes.

" Welcome thou mother of the year, the spring,"

sings old Kit Marlow in his masque of the Sun's darling,

" That mother, on whose back Age ne'er can sit,
For Age still waits upon her ; that Spring, the nurse
Whose milk the Summer sucks, and is made wanton,
Physician to the sick, strength to the sound;
By whom all things above and under ground
Are quicken'd with new heat, fresh blood, brave vigour,
That spring that on fair cheeks in kisses lays
Ten thousand welcomes."

What can surpass the health-inspiring odour that now surrounds us ; the gaiety of our lightened spirits, the suavity of
that cloudless sky, or the mirthful carols of the little birds,
which in this " violet-breathing May," are exulting in the very
joyousness of their being ?

" Hark ! the cuckows sing
Cuckow to welcome in the spring.
Brave prick-song ! who is't now we hear?
'Tis the lark's silver leer-a-leer.
Chirrup the sparrow flies away :
For he fell to't ere break of day.
Ha, ha, hark, hark ! the cuckows sing,
Cuckow, to welcome in the Spring.

MARLOW.

Shall we rise ? The next pretty house on the left beyond
Albany Cottage, is Hanover Lodge, the tasteful dwelling of the
gallant Colonel Sir Robert Arbuthnot K. C. B. This modest
mansion has greater pretensions to architectural character, than
its rural neighbour, and its accessaries of course, are in a more
sculptural style.

The house is entered under a handsome portico, which opens
into a spacious hall ; the cieling of which is supported by marble
columns, and its floor decorated with a handsome tessellated
pavement. A well-proportioned dining room nineteen feet six
inches in length, by sixteen feet in width adjoins the hall on
one side, and on another is a splendid suit of three elegant
drawing rooms, extending above sixty feet in length when the
doors are opened, by eighteen feet in breadth. A stone staircase of good proportions leads to the upper story, which comprises nine handsome bed-chambers, a bathing room with every
accommodation for that healthful luxury, dressing rooms, and
other requisites for a respectable family. The basement story
contains an extensive range of culinary, and serviceable domes-

tic offices, and the out buildings of a neat lodge on each side of the entrance, a gardener's lodge, dormitories for men servants, a double coach house, four stall stable, coachman's room and and other conveniences.

The grounds, for a town residence are spacious, and laid out with considerable taste and elegance. The variety of form, and apparent natural effect of the meandering walks, and irregular shaped beds, and baskets cut out in the emerald-velvet turf, give greater delight to the tasteful eye, and more pleasure to the cultivated mind, than the banished formalities of the mathematical school of gardening, of Kent and his contemporaries.

Had that artist been entrusted with the laying out of these grounds he would have sought jokes and conceits in every walk, and have dug practical puns in every bed : even as he sent ladies to court, (for he was as often employed in designing garments for the gaudy nymphs of his day, as he was mansions and pleasure grounds), with bodices and flounces decorated with the five orders of architecture. Entablatures on their lovely backs, columns wreathed round their wavy limbs, and bases and pedestals on their capacious petticoats.

Had Kent I say, laid out these grounds, he would have displayed in cut box, or more formal yew, the star and insignia of the commander of the military order of the Bath, with which the gallant proprietor is ennobled. The white horse of Hanover would have shone in chalk in commemoration of the name which graces the mansion, and the crest, family arms and honorary additions would have been emblazoned in all the honours of London pride, and Virginia stock, in proper colours ; with multangular and polygonal beds ; in which all the geometrical figures in the first book of Euclid would have been practically demonstrated.

Now to pursue our journey. The Italian villa before us on the right hand side of the road, is the suburban retreat of the Marquess of Hertford, designed by Mr. Decimus Burton. Its buildings and offices are on a larger scale than any other in the park, and are accordant in style with the wealth of its noble owner. Simplicity and chastity of style, characterize its exterior, and its interior is in the same style of beautiful simplicity. The entrance hall is protected by a hexastyle portico of that singular Athenian order, which embellishes the door of the octagonal tower of Andronicus Cyrrhestes, known to Grecian antiquaries, as the tower of the winds. The roof is Venetian with projecting eaves, supported by cantalivers, and concealed gutters to prevent the dripping of the rain water from the eaves. The wings are surmounted by spacious glass lanterns, which light the upper rooms. The offices are abundantly spacious, being spread out like the villas of the ancients upon the ground floor, and are designed in the same style of chaste simplicity as the mansion.

The entrance lodge is particularly chaste, and the gates solid and park-like; the plantations eminently beautiful, and the *tout ensemble* of the whole demesne in good taste.

This is decorated simplicity, such as the hand of taste, aided by the purse of wealth can alone execute. Yet less expense, aided by a pure taste, may accomplish beauty. Even in the recesses of a distant country village, taste may improve the most rigid economy. Such as a poet, whose name I do not at present remember, describes as

" Close in the dingle of a wood
Obscur'd with boughs a cottage stood :
Sweet-briar deck'd its lowly door,
And vines spread all the summit o'er.
An old barn's gable end was seen,
Sprinkled with nature's mossy green,
Hard on the right, from whence the flail
Of thrasher sounded down the vale :
A vale where many a flow'ret gay
Sipp'd a clear stream—let on its way :
A vale, above whose leafy shade
The village steeple shows its head."

Here is a beautiful spot, between the north eastern boundary of Lord Hertford's villa, and the portion in preparation for the use of the menageries and gardens of the Zoölogical Society, for such a Cottage-ornée as my friend Dashwood wishes to have for his London residence, since he has been returned by his independent neighbours as their representative in parliament.

In such a place as this, nothing like a town house should be allowed to insinuate its brazen face. No Grosvenor Square mansion, nor Grecianized sugar-house, should be skirted by emerald lawns, like those about us. Nor, as the animated author of " Sayings and Doings" says, should " an upright villa, with a flight of steps leading up to the door, with a round weedy pond on a lawn, looking like a basin of green pease soup on a card table," be allowed to contaminate the hallowed place.

A rural style of architecture, should alone preponderate in a spot of such polished rurality as this before us. A house in full puff, or a mansion in a court-cut coat and bag wig, would be as preposterous, among the green fields and gay plantations of the Regent's Park, as my friend Dashwood himself would be in his full bottomed wig and silk gown, following the Leicestershire fox hounds, breast high among the sportsmen. In this paradise of rural charms, the architect who would compose his design in accordance with the natural beauties of the surrounding scenery, should say with the poet, before he commences his sketch.

> " To me more dear, congenial to my heart
> One nature charm, than all the gloss of art."

Were comfort my aim, in composing a fit dwelling for my friend, in the very best part of the park, it should be a cottage, an English cottage, not, as Dr. Johnson defines it, " a low mean house in the country," but a genuine English cottage in the vicinity of the metropolis. Such, as my friend could unbend in, amidst his beloved domestic circle, and renovate his mental and bodily powers, in true and friendly hospitality and enjoyment.

My friend's cottage, therefore, shall not be the abode of either poverty or penuriousness. It shall not be, as a witty writer in Blackwood's Magazine asserts all cottages are, infested with colonies of rats, or communities of sparrows. It shall have neither damp walls, nor smoky chimneys; nor will I allow a scolding wife ever to enter its love-inspiring doors, without being metamorphosed into a resemblance of its handsome mistress, who is an example of perpetual smiling good humour, and amiable cheerfulness.

The plantations are almost to my mind, therefore a very few additions will accomplish that necessary appendage to the grounds of my friend's proposed cottage residence. It should be built on that rising knoll, with its entrance front towards the north-west, and, as a good name is every thing, I would call it Belle-grove.

The front I would place at a moderate distance from the road, inasmuch as the canal, and the opposite plantations, vouch for the impossibility of having opposite neighbours too near. The elevation should be simple, with a plain portico, of a size sufficiently ample to admit a carriage under its roof, to set down their fair cargoes in rainy weather without danger to their delicate habiliments.

The first hall, or vestibule should be sufficiently large, to contain the cloaks, garden-bonnets, hats, coats, parasols, and other exuviæ of the drawing-room guests ; for all strangers, servants, tradesmen, &c., should have a distinct entrance near to the servants' hall, so that robbery need not be apprehended. In this general apartment, I would provide room for the bows and arrows of Dashwood's boys, who are famous archers, and their father encourages this exercise as tending to expand the chest, and strengthen the muscles of the arms and back. In it should also be a good sized billiard table, around which my friend may walk from six to eight miles of a rainy day, by way of exercise, and afford active amusement to his visiters.

Of guns, I say nothing, for although our park abounds with game, my friend is a man of too studious habits to be much of a shot, and even if he equalled Colonel Hawker himself, he would carry his fowling propensities farther a field than the cockney counties of Middlesex or Surry.

The gentleman's own room should adjoin this general apartment, and have also a communication with the common hall of entrance, and have the accommodations of a bath, a dressing table, and other suitable apparatus, besides that of a small writing table.

The dining room, should be placed on the right, or westward side of the hall, and should be so situated, for I like to assign a reason for my dispositions, because the view from this corner of the building, being the least interesting, suits in my mind the occupation of the dinner hour, when all eyes being engaged upon the banquet, they require less external attraction. In fact, the finest prospects fade before that of the table ; for who, I would ask, at the hour of six, the eye is satiated by the highly dressed scenery about this charming neighbourhood, and the body fatigued by exercise or business, would not rather survey the gratifying display of the hospitable and well arranged family dinner table, than even the magnificent expanse of *Table* bay itself?

Then, when the banquet is removed, and the snow white damask is carried off, leaving the fine green baize cover, as a preservative of the richly polished table; does it not, at such an interesting moment, when the produce of the Madeiras, of Oporto, of the east and of the west are about to be arranged for our gratification, more than rival the smiling beauties of the first fine day at the close of winter, such

> " As the young Spring gives,"

> SPENSER.

when the balmy air, warmed by the increasing power of the sun, dissolves the wintry snow upon the verdant lawns, and as Horace says,

> " Fled are the snows, the verdant turf appears."

On the opposite, or left hand side of the hall, I would place the morning room, or room of general occupancy; which should have a private door opening to a passage leading to the stable yard, the offices of which, should be at a sufficient distance from the house, not to be offensive. The door of the coach house, should face the south, which is a rule never to be deviated from, for the benefit of the sun to dry the carriages when wet. Adjoining the stable yard, I would arrange the melon and cucumber grounds, for the conveniency of the dung-pit, and to keep the kitchen garden free from litter.

The summer breakfast room, the withdrawing room, the ladies' room, for a professed boudoir would not be strictly in character with a cottage, should be in the rear, opening to the south-east, and all on the ground floor. It is matter of faith with me, and orthodoxy in my creed, that it is the character of the genuine cottage to have all the before-mentioned rooms on the ground floor. Indeed, for myself, I should prefer even my bed chamber to be on the ground floor, and adjoining to my own dressing room.

These apartments, I would shelter from the meridian sun, by a broad verandah, the supporters of which should be overgrown with woodbine, jessamine, honey-suckles, the white fragrant clematis, called from the circumstance of its pouring forth its greatest profusion of odours in the evening, " the labourer's welcome home," monthly roses, which in such a situation would bloom even in merry Christmas tide, the twice flowering amber-coloured corcorus japonicus, the sweetly scented pea, the darling mignonette, which, by a new mode of culture, can be had in bloom, nearly all the year.

Then in front of this verandah, the windows under which, should all open as French sashes down to the floor, and which facing

> " the sweet south,
> That breathes upon a bank of violets,
> Stealing and giving odour,"

should be a wide gravel walk, as yellow and as smooth as a Limerick glove ; then a lawn, as level and as shorn as the cloth of a billiard table, interspersed with a few irregularly shaped patches, like a slashed doublet, filled with nature's embroidery, hardy annuals, geraniums sunk in pots, so as to be removed into the conservatory in hard weather ; Lady Holland's botanical pride, the splendid and hardy Dahlia and other beautiful

> " flowers, as many
> As the young spring gives, and choice as any."
>   SPENSER.

On the south treillage raised against the back of the kitchen chimney, for the sake of the warmth, I would have a splendid plant of the Magnolia grandiflora, to scent the apartments and grounds with its almond-like fragrance. I would have an abundance of sweet-briers, and many of the best varieties of the scented cabbage rose, some of which I would have grafted on lofty stocks, that they might be smelt or gathered without stooping.

Of the dormitories, I shall say but little, except that as my friend's cottage is to be only one story high above the principal floor ; those for the servants should be approached by a different staircase, and separate from those of his family. The men servants' rooms should be in the stable offices.

As the cottage would be detached, I would have it thatched, not that rough sort of thatch like an Irishman's wig, which, one might suppose, covered Miss Hamilton's celebrated cottage at Glenburnie, or many of the cabins in Ireland,

" That keep every thing else but the weather clean out ;"

DIBDIN.

where a hurdle or an old cart wheel is thrown upon the roof to keep the thatch from being blown away. The thatch that I would have, should be formed of combed wheat straw, laid thick and smooth, and trimmed at the eaves, with compact ornamented ridges and verges. This sort of roof is not only very handsome and appropriate to the gentleman's cottage, but is the warmest covering in winter, and the coolest in summer, while slating is directly the reverse.

But to return to the garden, which I have not quite finished. I would have a small fountain, the jet of which should be supplied from an elevated cistern in the stable yard. This would be a source of admiration and amusement to my friend's children, and at the same time give an agreeable undulation to the air in sultry weather, while a basin at its base would afford protection to a few brace of gold and silver fish, and without the pretence of a regular aquarium, would accommodate a few water lilies and other fragrant and curious aquatic plants.

I would also have a small rosarium which would provide rosebuds for the pot-pourri, and leaves for scent-bags, and the use of the still worm. Near to the rosarium I would have a hedge of the gray and spikey lavender, and beds of other fragrant flowers, and herbs for the same domestic purpose. A small orchard should also be provided, if the size of the grounds permitted, to furnish the dessert with choice specimens of fruit; while beneath the trees, for due economy, I would sow lucerne, sainfoin and clover for green meat for the horses.

Such should be the sort of cottage that I would build for my friend Dashwood in the Regent's Park, and I think you must give me some credit for my talents of building castles in the air, in this instance.

Let us now cross Macclesfield Bridge, and mount the easy summit of Primrose Hill. The construction of this bridge, designed by Mr. Morgan, is very picturesque, appropriate and architectural. Its piers are composed of a series of cast iron columns of the Grecian Doric order; from the summits of which spring the arches which support a flat viaduct or road-way, and cover with their lofty heads, the road-way of the towing-path, the canal itself, and the shrubberies on its southern bank. The abacus, echinus and hypotrachelion of the order, are in beautiful proportion, and the shafts of ample size.

The archivolts that form the support of the road-way, are also in accordance with the order; although fastidious critics may object to the dignity of the pure ancient Doric being violated by degrading it into supporters of modern arches. *See the plate of Macclesfield Bridge.*

If any excuse can be found for this error in taste, it is in the necessity of the case, or rather in the advantages that result from it. The centre arch is appropriated to the canal and the towing-path, and the two external arches to the accommodation of foot passengers beneath them, and as viaducts for the road above them. Solid piers, therefore, would have rendered the two external arches, dark vaults; and perforations in them, would only have furnished dingy apertures with awkward angles. By carrying the springings of the arches on columns, these diffi-culties were removed, and by springing minor arches transversely to the road, cutting the main arches with bonnet groins, the whole is rendered light, airy, and convenient. The only objection is in the choice of columns of the *Grecian order*, the first born of archi-tecture, for this degrading office, and in depriving them of their natural and effective epistyles, which might have been agree-ably and tastefully connected with the archivolts of the vous-soirs, by the substitution of common place bonnet groinings of the coal cellar; whilst the less pure architecture of Rome would have furnished abundance of precedents for the support of arches by columns—and the architecture of Greece does not afford even a solitary example of the practice. It has, however, a beautiful and light appearance, and is an improvement in exe-cution upon a design of Perronet's for an *architectural* bridge, that is, a bridge of *orders*. The columns are well proportioned, and suitably robust, carrying solidity, grace and beauty in every part; from the massy grandeur of the abacus, to the graceful revolving of the beautiful echinus, and to the majestic simplicity of the slightly indented flutings. Had indeed the archivolt, formed after the architrave of the order, been surmounted by a proper entablature and blocking course, with *scamilli* set back

REGENT'S QUADRANT.

Published June 16.1827 by Jones & Co 3. Acton Place, Kingsland Road. London.

MACCLESFIELD BRIDGE, REGENT'S PARK.

TO JAMES MORGAN ESQ: ARCHITECT, THIS PLATE IS MOST RESPECTFULLY DEDICATED BY
T. H. SHEPHERD

Drawn by Thos H.Shepherd.   Engraved by W. Tombleson.

THE ROYAL HOSPITAL OF St KATHERINE, REGENT'S PARK.

TO THE REVD G.F. NICOLAY, SENR BROTHER OF THE HOSPITAL, &c. THIS PLATE IS REPECTFULLY INSCRIBED.

Drawn by Thos H.Shepherd.   Engraved by W. Tombleson.

RESIDENCE OF GENL SIR HERBERT TAYLOR, BARt REGENT'S PARK.

MASTER OF THE ROYAL HOSPITAL OF St KATHERINE, &c. TO WHOM THIS PLATE IS MOST RESPECTFULLY DEDICATED.

Published Dec. 8, 1827, by Jones & Co. 3, Acton Place, Kingsland Road, London.

as the rise, or perforated with panels, the bridge would have been unexceptionably the most novel, and the most tasteful in the metropolis.   Even as it is, it is scarcely surpassed for lightness, elegance, and originality by any in Europe.   It is of the same family, with the beautiful little bridge in Hyde Park, between the new entrance and the barracks.

Let us now re-enter the park, and proceed with our journey. The grounds in preparation on our right, are for that very useful and praiseworthy institution the Zoölogical Society, and are intended for the reception of their living animals, after the mode of the establishment called the garden of plants at Paris.   This new establishment will consist of a spacious menagerie, an aviary for choice birds, a museum for stuffed and preserved specimens ; and fish ponds, with other necessary appendages for the cultivation of Zoölogical studies.

The east gate, or, as I believe it is to be called, Chester Gate, is now before us.   We examined it yesterday in our general perambulation, (*see page* 22), therefore shall pass it by, and keep within the delightful verge of the park.

The pile of buildings that we are now approaching is the new

Collegiate Church, and Hospital of St. Katherine,

and is building in lieu of the ancient foundation of that name, which has lately been pulled down to make way for the great commercial establishment, the dock of St. Katherine, near the Tower, now in progress.

As the sun is passing hot, and this seat opportunely vacant, we may rest ourselves before we approach the building, and view its grouping at a distance.   Being very little of an antiquary, I must refer you to Dr. Ducurel's elaborate history of St. Katherine's, for historical accounts of its founders, and other particulars.   But it is a singular instance of the mutability of human affairs, that a portion of our vast metropolis, which one of our most splendid monarchs, Edward III., the magnificent founder of Windsor Castle, intended as a metropolitan court, under the name of *East Minster*, or the Abbey of St. Mary of the Graces, and as a rival to *West Minster*, should become in after times, as " *St. Katherine's*," the most disgraceful and abominable of all the low precincts of the metropolis.

The memory of this foundation is recalled to my mind, as having been for years past under the spiritual guidance of the mild, amiable and truly Rev. G. F. Nicolay, who was presented to the honourable office of senior brother, together with the parish of my ancestors, St. Michael Royal in the city, by the late Queen Charlotte, to whom his father, the celebrated composer, was music master.

This small ecclesiastical establishment, whose proper title is " the peculiar and exempt jurisdiction of the collegiate church or free chapel of St. Katherine, the Virgin and Martyr," was founded by the bold and ambitious Matilda, queen consort of king Stephen, in the year 1148, and dedicated to St. Katherine. It was dissolved in 1272, and the present hospital founded in the following year by queen Eleanor, and dedicated to the same saint.   It has continued unaltered till its present removal.

The establishment of this college, or hospital, consists at present, as it did on its second foundation by queen Eleanor, of a master, three brothers, who must be in priest's orders, three sisters, single women, ten bedes-women usually nominated by the master, a registrar, a high-bailiff, and some other officers.

The buildings of this Royal college, as I before mentioned, were all swept away, by the spirit of commercial enterprize, to make way for the new docks, and are rebuilding, as we now see them, in the more royal situation of the Regent's Park. The old church, as I well remember, was a handsome structure, though much concealed from sight by the confined nature of its situation ; and had a more modern appearance, from the neat state of repair, in which it had been kept, than its real antiquity warranted.   The interior was well deserving of notice, but all that remains of it now, are descriptions in the works of our archaiologists, and fragments collected and preserved by some curious admirers of our ancient architecture, at the sale of its old materials.   Among these, Mr. Cottingham the architect, who is known to the public by many excellent prints of the ancient architecture of England, has completed a Gothic museum adjoining his office in Waterloo Road, from its interesting fragments.

The ancient structure consisted of the church, cloisters, a

burial ground, the sister's close and dwellings, the brother's houses, the master's house, bedes-women's houses, a court-room, chapter-room, &c.

The church was divided into a body and a choir by a handsome carved screen. The choir consisted of a nave, and two aisles. The windows were handsome and light, particularly the east window, which was deservedly admired for its magnificent size and elegant proportions, by every connoisseur and admirer of our ancient ecclesiastical architecture. This splendid window was the largest in and about the metropolis, being thirty feet in height, by twenty-four in width, and contained 561 feet of glass, exclusive of the stone mullions and tracery. It poured a majestic and almost overpowering flood of light, over the antique pillars and venerable monuments that were in the church, and set forth their beauties in the highest perfection. The altar-piece that was under this emblematical eastern source of light, was of pure design, and in the richest style of the florid Gothic. The beautiful stalls, which I am happy to learn, are, with other parts of this venerable fabric, carefully preserved for re-erection in the new chapel, were began by William de Erldesby, master of the hospital, in 1340, and were finished by John de Hermesthorp, who was master in 1369.

Among the valuable antiquities that are to be thus reinstated in the new chapel, is the singular and curiously carved historical pulpit that was given in 1621, by Sir Julius Cæsar, the then master; who repaired the entire edifice, and was otherwise a great benefactor. It is hexagonal in plan, each angle has an Ionic pilaster, with a fanciful entablature that forms the upper rim or desk of the pulpit. Each pilaster is panelled, and has a scroll of foliage within it. Between each pilaster, that is on every face, is an arch springing from an impost; under the archivolt of which is carved in relief a view of some part of the then buildings.

As the pulpit is under repair in the carpenter's shop, and I have permission to view it, we will examine its unique carvings, before we go. No. 1, Ducarel informs us is the north, 2, the east, 3, the west, and 4, the south views of the ancient hospital; 5, is the outer gate, and 6, the inner gate. By these sculptures, the artist has conveyed to our time, four views of the hospital, and also two of its gates, as they were in his days.

This is one of the most ancient wooden pulpits now remaining to us, as before the Reformation, pulpits of stone of great size were more usual. To commemorate this, the donor has caused to be carved round the base, the following inscription in large and bold characters, "EZRA THE SCRIBE STOOD UPON A PULPIT OF WOOD, WHICH HE HAD MADE FOR THE PREACHEN." NEH. viii. 4.

The splendid tomb, consisting of a canopy of curious fret-work, under which lie the marble figures of John Holland, duke of Exeter, his first wife, and his sister, is also to be reinstated in the new chapel; as are also the other monuments, and the valuable organ that was erected in the old church, in 1778, by the celebrated Mr. Green, which is reckoned to be one of the finest, particularly in its swell, of any in England.

This duke of Exeter, whose tomb will occupy a conspicuous place in the new chapel, was a great benefactor to the hospital. He was lord high Admiral of England, in the reign of Henry VI., and also constable of the tower, and master of the hospital. He died August 5th, 1447; when this monument, with statues of himself, his first wife Constance and his sister, was erected by his second wife, who survived him.

On the death of this lady, she by will desired her executor, Dr. Pinchbeke, to bury her in the same vault, and to avoid all unnecessary pomp and expense, which he strictly complied with. This is probably the reason why her figure was not placed with that of her husband and the other two ladies, as there is sufficient room.

THE QUEEN CONSORTS OF ENGLAND, are by *law* the perpetual patronesses of St. Katherine's; this hospital being considered as part of their dower. They nominate, as the lawyers say, *pleno jure*, the masters, brothers and sisters; and may increase or lessen their number, remove them, alter any statutes, or make new ones at pleasure; for their power in these instances is unlimited.

When there is no *queen consort*, the king nominates the master, brothers &c. (to borrow another law phrase) *pro hac vice*. But the *Queen Dowager* has no power or jurisdiction, when there is a queen consort. All the attempts that have been made in ancient and modern times for this purpose, have proved ineffectual; and the sentences of the courts of law have unanimously confirmed the great and unlimited powers of the QUEEN CONSORTS of England, over this small ecclesiastical jurisdiction.

The business of this house is transacted in chapter, by the master, brothers and sisters; and it is singularly remarkable that by the statutes, the sisters have therein a vote equally with the brothers; and that no business can be done there, without the votes of four of the members, one at least of which must be a sister. The other officers of this house are elected by a majority of votes, and their patents confirmed under the chapter seal.

The principal officers so elected, are the commissary or officer principal, who in his licenses is styled, " Commissary or official of the peculiar and exempt jurisdiction of the collegiate church, or free chapel of St. Katherine, the Virgin and Martyr;" the registrar, the steward, the surveyor, receiver, and chapter-clerk, besides a clerk, sexton, &c.

The architect of the new building, which, if you are sufficiently rested, we will now approach, had therefore a splendid original to compete with; and it is but doing justice to well cultivated talent, to admit that he has eminently succeeded.

The quadrangle on our left is the hospital, composed of the collegiate church or free chapel in the centre, with dwelling houses on both sides for the brothers and sisters, the chaplain and other officers; and the building on our right directly opposite and overlooking it, is for the residence of the master. *See the plate of St. Katherine's Hospital.*

The present master is Sir Herbert Taylor, the senior brother the Rev. George Frederick Nicolay; and the architect, whose talents in designing and executing the buildings which I have just recommended to your notice, is Ambrose Poynter, Esq. a pupil of Mr. Nash.

The church is a handsome building in the Gothic or old English style of architecture, and bears a truly collegiate character in its composition. The west window is well proportioned and in good taste, the doorways judicious and appropriate to their purpose. The turretted buttresses at the angles are also in good proportion, but fail in effect as they rise, by being too plain in their crockets and finials, whereas a greater richness in these upper parts, increasing as they rise from the ground, in con-

formity with all our best examples, would have been productive
of a much better effect; whilst on the contrary, their present
meagre finishing is too much in the French style, and resembles
the modern Gothic of Strawberry Hill and Arlington Street
too much, to be pleasing to the genuine admirer of the old
English style of architecture. The wings which improve the
effect of the composition, are for the purpose of a school-house
on one side, and the chapter-room on the other.

The dwellings are extremely commodious, and exhibit both
externally as a part of the composition, and internally as intended for convenience and utility, a skilful and artist-like
arrangement.

As soon as this group of horsemen are passed, and the dust
which they have raised has a little subsided, we will pass over
to the master's house, and take a general view of the quadrangle.
But stay, one of the workmen has just opened the door of the
church. Let us therefore walk in and take a peep at Mr.
Poynter's interior arrangement.

Well gentlemen! what think ye? Indeed this much surpasses the outside, of which, however, I make no complaint,
except as to the want of a little more richness in the turrets.
This ceiling is really masterly, and characteristic, and the whole
in plain good taste, and in excellent keeping. That east window
is very fine, and the smaller windows in the north and south
walls harmonize well with the master key that governs them.
The joinery is in equally good taste with the rest of the design,
and is admirably executed. A little more richness of colour
from the employment of more costly materials might be wished
for; but penuriousness towards our architects, is one among the
vices of our patrons, that it would be well for them to amend. A
charming air of chaste simplicity pervades the whole, which is
in strict accordance with the appropriation of the sacred edifice.
Its proportions are ninety feet in length, thirty in width, and
forty-five in height. The shields under the windows are to be
emblazoned with the arms of the Queen consorts, patronesses
of the hospital.

Now gentlemen, if you have satisfied yourselves with this
inspection of the re-edifying of the proud empress Maud's
liberality and piety, we will cross the road, and see what modern
liberality and science is doing for the protestant lay master of

the once Catholic hospital of St. Katherine. Whether there
are any pretty blue-eyed nuns of St. Katherine's now among
the sisters, is a question, I fear, we must not ask of the brave
and gallant master of the sisterhood.

Stay! before crossing let me call your attention to the ends
of the houses, that form the north and south sides of the quadrangle. They are admirably characteristic of the intention of
the founder, whilst the sculptures of the Royal and other arms,
and inscriptions indicative of the nature of the buildings, are
in happy accordance with the architecture and style of sculpture, and the mode of inscriptions of the day.

Now for the master's mansion. Truly were it finished, and
some of the tawny tints of time deposited upon its surface, we
might really take it for the habitation of the prior to some rich
and mitred abbot. Its separated angle chimney flues, their
ornamented tops, the fastigated gables, and narrow cell-like
windows in the attics, the mullioned windows of the upper
story, the bow, and bay windows, and porches to the doors of
the principal story, give the whole a conventual or rather a
collegiate look. *See the plate of the dwelling-house of the master
of St. Katherine's Hospital.* The handsome well-laid out plea
sure grounds, the store of kitchen gardens, and the stable offices,
reminding one of the tithe-barn, keep up the illusion: and nothing but a father Paul or two at the windows, rubifying the
scene like the coloured bottles in a chemist's window, and a
living skeleton or two in the shape of lay brothers, labouring in
the gardens, are wanting to complete the picture.

But in reality we shall see, instead of the high and mighty
empress's original intention of cloistered monks, and earth-
bereaved nuns, supporting a few bigotted paupers; a set of
high spirited gentlemen, worthy brethren, and amiable sisters of
the protestant order of St. Katherine; at least we may so con-
jecture from the domestic arrangements of the house, living a
life of equal jollity, and of much less hypocrisy.

Truly, these rooms are very handsome and well proportioned;
the cornices and other mouldings are also in due character with
the leading features of the design, and the whole arrangement
of the plan is judicious, convenient and appropriate. Much as
I love the Greek style for real beauty, and apt as I am to exclaim with Dr. Johnson " so much Greek, so much gold," I

must admit on viewing this beautiful specimen of English domestic architecture, that a villa of the Grecian style, for the master of St. Katherine's Hospital, in the sight of and overlooking as it does, the church and dwellings of the hospitallers, would have been as inappropriate, as it would be to raise the beautiful spire of Salisbury cathedral upon the apex of the pediment of the temple of Minerva Parthenon, and finishing its acroteria with gothic pinnacles, crockets, and florid finials.

The materials with which this assemblage of buildings are constructed, are similar to those of our ancient architects, *brick* and *stone*. But modern art, in giving a fine and pure stone colour, and more than the hardness of stone to brick, has improved upon the heterogeneous mixture of red and black bricks, and white stone of our ancestors, by a happy union of stone-coloured bricks, and free stone. Some critics have decried bricks, as inimical to architecture, grounding their objections upon the marble edifices of Greece. Let these critics, before they decry the use of bricks, or attribute the want of grandeur in modern architecture to the use of that comparatively homely material, reflect, that the Romans, to whose works no want of grandeur can be imputed, used them in their structures with prodigious effect, and that we may almost attribute the invention of the arch, the vault, and the cupola, with which they so gloriously displayed their architectural powers, to the practice of brick-making. Palladio constructed some of his finest works of brick, as did Wren and other eminent modern architects. The judicious mixture of the white brick and stone by Mr. Poynter in these buildings, is infinitely better than the common grey brick, either coloured, or its native poverty concealed by a deceitful covering of cement.

Wishing the gallant lay-master of the collegiate church and hospital of St. Katherine, a long life to enjoy his new and commodious abode, and thanking him for this last half hour's shelter of his roof, we will with your leave, gentlemen, proceed on our perambulation.

That palatial-looking pile of buildings before us on our left, with the majestic cupola of Mr. Hornor's Colosseum rearing itself over its corniced head, is

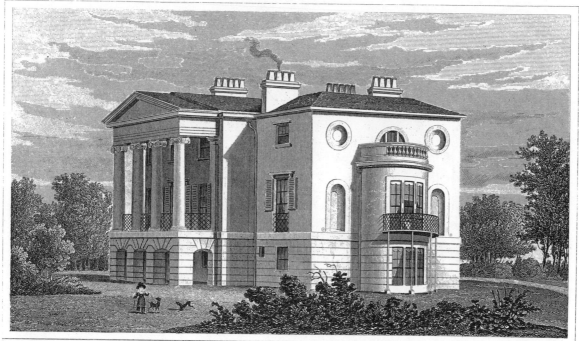

Drawn by Thos. H.Shepherd.

Engraved by J.Tingle.

SOUTH VILLA, REGENT'S PARK.

THE RESIDENCE OF Wm. H.COOPER, ESQr.

Drawn by Thos. H.Shepherd.

Engraved by H. Melville.

CHESTER TERRACE, REGENT'S PARK.

Drawn by Thos H.Shepherd.

Engraved by R.Acon.

BUILDINGS ON THE EAST SIDE OF REGENT STREET.

Drawn by Thos H.Shepherd.

Engraved by R.Acon.

CAMBRIDGE TERRACE AND THE COLLISEUM REGENT'S PARK.

Chester Terrace,

named from the royal earldom of Chester. It is designed by Mr. Nash, and like most of that gentleman's works, combines genius and carelessness. Genius, and powerful conception, in the composition, and a grasp of mind equalled by no artist of the day in the design: and carelessness, sometimes degenerating to littleness, with a deficiency of elegance in the details.

It is of the Corinthian order of architecture, of a feeble and effeminate character in its details, surmounted by a balustrade of lanky proportions and tasteless forms. The capitals do not spread sufficiently for the graceful beauty of the gay Corinthian, and the volutes are too small, and are pinched up, as if the acanthus, whence the Callimachus of Chester Terrace gathered them to decorate his order, had been withered by a frost. *See plate of Chester Terrace.*

Passing by these defects of detail, and of material of which the composition is constructed, Chester Terrace is a grand, bold and commanding row of mansions; and forms a noble composition, and a charming series of residences for such whose good fortune may enable them to take up their abode in this new city of palaces.

The Corinthian arches at each end are novel in idea, grand in conception, imposing in effect, and have the appearance of some of the lesser triumphal arches of Rome. Inscriptions in memory of some of our minor but splendid victories, such as that of Maida, or the defence of St. Jean d' Acre against Napoleon Buonaparte, would make them pleasing records of British prowess.

Before we part from Chester Terrace, let me call your attention to the pavilion-like houses which project at each end, and are connected with the main body of the terrace by the Corinthian arches, as productive of a fine and novel effect.

The next row of houses past the Corinthian arch of Chester Terrace, is named

Cambridge Terrace,

after his Majesty's royal brother the duke of Cambridge, the popular viceroy of Hanover. It is smaller in every respect than its neighbour of Chester, and has less architectural pretensions. The centre, and the two wings are distinguished by porticoes of the Roman or pseudo-Doric order, with rusticated columns, which, although in bad taste, are productive of variety, in a situation where variety is much wanted, and form a good contrast with the delicate Corinthian of Chester Terrace on the one hand, and the majestic Doric of the Colosseum on the other. The superstructure, above the porticoes, which are of the height only of the ground story, is plain and sufficient for the purpose to which it is applied. The plantations which fill up the interval, between Cambridge Terrace and the Colosseum are judiciously executed, and when more grown will prevent too great a contrast between the isolated Colossus and the group of dwelling houses.

Now we will sit ourselves down, before one of the greatest individual enterprises, of which modern art can boast. That magnificent polygonal structure, covered with the vast cupola, and embellished with that beautiful hexastyle portico of the Doric order, is named, (why and wherefore is yet to be discussed),

The Colosseum;

and is intended for the reception and exhibition of a general panoramic view of London and its surrounding country as far as the eye can see, taken by Mr. Hornor from an observatory that was raised above the cross of St. Paul's Cathedral, during the recent construction of the new ball and cross. In taking the views, Mr. Hornor was aided by his topographical knowledge of the country as a skilful land-surveyor, by powerful telescopes, and by curious machinery, for executing his sketches. The distant buildings, villas and features of the country, were also taken on the spots, and the artist-like atmospherical distances, are detailed from them with a fidelity, rarely found in pictures of this nature. The view from this elevated spot which I enjoyed during the progress of the works, furnishes a fine illustration of the poet's view of the vast metropolis of the United Kingdoms, from an elevated spot in Surry,

" Th' impatient muse ascends the Turret's height
Where ample prospects charm the roving sight:
A richer landscape ne'er the sun survey'd,
With lovelier verdure crown'd, or nobler shade;
The whole horizon, to its utmost bound,
One bright and beauteous picture glowing round!
Here freighted with the gems of India's clime,
On Thames' broad wave rich navies ride sublime:
There, proudly crowning her imperial stream,
The lofty turrets of AUGUSTA gleam.
New objects on the dazzled vision break,
And in th' admiring soul new transports wake.
Here, many a league along th' admiring tide,
A thousand villas stretch in rural pride;
There glittering spires and swelling domes ascend,
And art and nature all their beauties blend."

MAURICE.

During the progress of the work, I was often a witness to the indefatigable perseverance and intrepidity of the artist in making his sketches, which he has executed with a correctness that cannot be surpassed. Circumstances have since separated us, and I can now only bear witness to his progress as any other of the public. The painting of the panorama is in a very forward state, and ere long the public will be gratified with its exhibition.

The building is a polygon of sixteen sides, 130 feet in diameter. Each angle is strengthened by a double anta of the Doric order, which supports a continuous entablature without triglyphs, that circumscribes the edifice. The cornice is crowned by a blocking course, and surmounted by an attic, with a suitable cornice and sub-blocking, to give height to the building. On the summit of this upper order, the majestic cupola, supported by three receding *scamilli* or steps, is constructed. The lower part is covered with sheet copper, and the upper part with a curvilinear sky-light, and finished with an immense open circle or eye to the cupola.

The grandest feature of this handsome building is its portico, which is one of the finest and best proportioned of the Greco-

Doric in the metropolis, and gives a majestic feature to this part of the park, that cannot be surpassed. The lodges are in equal good taste, and do great credit to their architect, Mr. Decimus Burton.

Looking at the Colosseum, either in front, on the opposite side of the road, from the north in coming from Chester Terrace, or, from the south, (*see the plate of the Colosseum*) it forms a grand and majestic composition; imposing from its size, and varied from its connection with the beautiful (little I was going to say, from their contiguity to their colossal chief) lodges that support the pyramidal principle of the group, and add to its beauty by the creation of an agreeable variety. The plantations, laid out by Mr. Hornor, add their share of embellishments to the majestic scene, and the whole picture is a fine specimen of architectural grandeur and sublimity, alike creditable to Mr. Burton, jun. the architect, and his talented employer Mr. Hornor.

Now, as to its name, which I have just hinted, deserved some discussion. True it is, that Shakspeare says, a rose under any other name, will smell as sweet, and no doubt this building under any name would look as grand. But naming it after the largest edifice in the world, and to which it bears no affinity either in shape or destination, is doing it a manifest injustice, if not a serious injury.

What associations of ideas, does this name "THE COLOSSEUM" give rise to? "As long as the Colosseum stands," runs the proverb, "Rome shall stand, when the Colosseum falls, Rome shall fall, and when Rome falls, the world will perish." "Quamdiu stabit Colosseus, stabat Roma, quando cadet Colosseus, cadet et Roma; quando cadet Roma, cadet et mundus," runs the original, which is attributed to the Anglo-saxon pilgrims who visited Rome in the early part of the eighth century, and is thus versified by a modern poet in quoting the historian of the decline and fall of the Roman empire,

" While stands the Colosseum, Rome shall stand."

There can be but one Colosseum, any more than there can be but one sun. The building more resembles, and might with more justice be placed in contact and cognomen with the Pantheon, but when by a mere name, it is brought to the mind's eye, in competition with that mountain of architecture,

> " Which in its public shows, unpeopled Rome,
> And held, uncrowded, nations in its womb;"

it makes one wish such an inappropriate symbol had never been adopted. Why! the huge blocks of Travertine marble, heaped on high by command of Vespasian, outnumber even the nine inch bricks of the modern Colosseum.

Fie upon it, give it some other name, a name *per se*, and then it will stand *second* to no other edifice in Europe of its sort. In some of the newspapers, and in Mr. Britton's Illustrations of the public buildings of London, it is called *" The Coliseum,"* deriving it, I presume, from the French *Colisee;* a language that also emasculates the manly Titus Livius into *Tite Live*, and other lingual abominations.

Now I presume, that the sponsor of Mr. Hornor's panorama, named it " COLOSSEUM" in allusion to its colossal dimensions, either from the Latin Colossus, a statue of enormous magnitude, or from the Greek *Kolossaion* (whence Colosseium or Colosseum) an edifice dedicated to, or containing, a colossal statue, as THE-SEIUM, the temple dedicated to *Theseus;* PANDROSEIUM, that of the nymph *Pandrosus;* ERECTHEIUM, the temple of *Erectheus,* and so on; and careless writers indiscriminately named it *the* Colosseum or Coliseum.

The interior, as I mentioned before, is being fitted up for *a panoramic view of London, as seen from the summit of the cross of St. Paul's Cathedral.* It has already employed Mr. Hornor, the projector, and a host of artists upon the painting, more than four years; it is now rapidly advancing towards completion, and will, I understand, be opened to the public in the course of the next spring. The costliness with which every part of it has been executed, is commensurate with the scale of the majestic building that contains it, and the importance of the subject to be delineated.

The object of the artist in this gigantic undertaking is to present, through the medium of a panoramic painting of unparalleled size, and mode of exhibition, a full and accurate representation of the metropolis and all the surrounding country that is visible from the summit of our magnificent cathedral.

The preparatory sketches, the most of which I have seen, had for several years engaged a considerable portion of Mr. Hornor's attention. They were completed during the summer of 1821, from an observatory purposely constructed on the top of the scaffolding that was then erected for the construction of the new ball and cross, and other repairs of the lantern over the cupola of the cathedral, under the direction of Mr. C. R. Cockerill, the tasteful architect of St. George's Chapel, in Regent Street; whose veneration for the great architect of the building that he was intrusted to renovate, was a sure warranty of his success.

Dividing the panorama, into four quadrants corresponding with the four cardinal points of the mariner's compass, the first or western view commences with the banks of the Thames towards the south, and the picturesque arches of Blackfriars bridge.

The leading features of this portion of the panorama, are the beautiful meanderings of the silver Thames, the four great bridges that bestride the flood, (that of Waterloo being particularly fine and effective,) the venerable abbey of Westminster, the antique hall of Rufus, the distant palaces of Westminster and the Parks, which are now undergoing such extensive and manifest improvements. The sites and plantations of the spacious squares, and the mansions of the leading streets of the western end of the town are predominant beauties. The foreground is finely marked by the two campanile towers of the west front of the metropolitan cathedral; and those double triumphs of the architective skill and taste of their author, are productive of an effect almost approaching to reality, by the value that they give to the distance, and the scale which they form to the lineal perspective of the streets and houses, between and on each side of them. The rear of the pediment, and backs of the colossal apostles that decorate the acroteria of the upper order, are also productive of singular effect.

Beyond these, Ludgate Hill traversed by Bridge Street, showing the gap by the side of the Norwich Fire Office, the western end of the proposed New Street, that I have suggested among other improvements to the corporation of London, and leading on by Chatham Square over Blackfriars bridge along the wide expanse of the Surry Road to the Obelisk, where it is lost in the labyrinth of roads and houses of that mazy neighbourhood.

The centre part of this quarter of the panorama is occupied by a multitudinous mass of buildings, in which are principally distinguished the gardens and antique turrets of the temple; the spacious squares and plantations of Lincoln's-inn, Gray's-inn, the Foundling Hospital, and the adjacent pretty modern squares in that vicinity. The British Museum, and its substantial new additions for the library of George the Third, which has been most munificently presented to the nation by the patriotism of his son GEORGE THE FOURTH, stand also predominant in this grand national picture; with a great portion of the new streets of Somers Town, St. Pancras, the site of the New London University, and Camden Town, with the palace-like workhouse of St. Pancras.

In the northern portion of this quarter of the view, Newgate Street, the three great prisons of the metropolis, the late College of Physicians, the churches of St. Sepulchre and of St. Andrew, Holborn, and the adjacent neighbourhood, are conspicuous.

In the southern portion, the principal part of the canvas is occupied by a considerable part of Lambeth, extending to Vauxhall Gardens. The windings of the river, which here forms so fine a feature in any elevated view of our metropolis, has additional interest from the distinct view, which is obtained from the elevated spot whence Mr. Hornor traced his sketches of the fine bridges of Blackfriars, Waterloo, Westminster, and Vauxhall.

The handsome buildings of Somerset Place, and the Adelphi, with their lofty terraces, and the succession of noble residences between the latter place and Westminster Bridge are next in consequence. In this portion of the picture, Westminster Hall, the pinnacles, and the east end of St. Stephen's Chapel, the Abbey, Whitehall, the Horse-guards, the Admiralty, and numerous other public and private edifices in this opulent quarter of the metropolis, form conspicuous and picturesque features.

Further westward, we see the polygonal Penitentiary at Milbank, with its curious towers, a considerable portion of Chelsea, with its noble college, the ranges of new buildings, between that low point, and the new palace of Buckingham House, the park—and onwards to the great expanse of the west end of the town, to the Regent's Park, where the colossal cupola of the building which contains the picture itself shines conspicuous, with its glossy glazed cupola. Primrose Hill, with the new reservoir of water for the supply of the park overtops this part of the picture; and ranging northward, are the lovely hills, crowned with the beautiful villages of Hampstead and Highgate, in which almost every house, that can be seen, will be found faithfully delineated. In the distant parts of this quarter of the picture will be seen many of the prominent features of Hertfordshire, Middlesex, and Surry, with the numerous beautiful villas and hamlets that bespangle that range of country.

Turning, directly opposite to the eastern portion of the panorama, the view commences, with the east end of the choir of the cathedral, and the eastern side of the churchyard, where the portico and cupola of the new St. Paul's school forms a fine architectural fore-ground. It embraces portions of the north and south sides of the church-yard, to which the fine balustrades of the church, and the colossal statues on the pediments of the transepts afford both a fine contrast and a picturesque relief. The New Post Office comes particularly grand, and when I tell you that it occupies nearly 300 superficial feet of the canvas, you may form some opinion of the colossal dimensions of the whole picture.

The view is then extended down Cheapside, to the centre of the commercial part of the city. In this the Mansion House, the new fronts of the Bank of England, and the majestic stone cupola over the Broker's Rotunda are eminently conspicuous. The Royal Exchange, the numerous spires of the churches that embellish this portion of the city, and other public buildings, lift up their architectural heads in proud grandeur amidst thousands of chimneys and roofs, upon which they seem to look down with supreme contempt.

From these the eye is carried onward to the East India House, where a dozen or two of English merchants rule an eastern empire, and communicate wealth to two extremities of the globe. The ancient turrets of the Tower of London, the space now excavating for the intended docks of St. Katherine, the Mile End and Commercial Roads, the forests of masts in the river, the populous suburbs that surround the great commercial docks, the spacious expanse of the Isle of Dogs, Plaistow Marshes, and the high grounds of Essex, to near Gravesend, fill up a lively portion of the colossal picture. From thence the windings of the Thames appear in occasional glimpses, progressively to the magnificent and truly Royal Hospital of Greenwich, which, with its spacious range of buildings and beautiful twin towers, complete the fascinating picture in this point of view.

Tracing the course of the river upwards from Greenwich towards the Pool, the view embraces its different reaches, its multitudinous masses of shipping and countless masts, and the costly establishments that line both banks of the river. On the southern side, the elevation of nearly every edifice is distinctly visible as it presents its front in almost a right angle to the eye.

Toward the south, the view takes in a portion of the Borough, nearly the whole of the hamlet of Bermondsey, the high grounds and numerous villas of that portion of East Kent, terminating with the beautiful distance of Shooter's Hill, and the well known reminiscent tower of Severndroog Castle on its summit.

Toward the north-east, are seen the ranges of streets that lead to Finsbury Square and the City Road ; embellished by the new City Circus, with the London Institution in its centre, St. Luke's Hospital and Church, the handsome spire of Shoreditch, with the extensive village of Hackney, the hamlets of Lower and Upper Clapton and the surrounding neighbourhood, on both sides of the extensive and beautiful vale of the river Lea, and the fine wooded uplands of Epping Forest, to Havering Bower.

The nearer and more conspicuous portions of this quarter of the circle, relates to the great city itself, and give a very faithful representation of the architecture of many of its public buildings, with portions of thousands of its well-known houses, the lines of its principal streets, and the towers and spires of its numerous churches.

The direct north view, includes the north side of St. Paul's Church-yard, the colossal saints of the north transept, the Blue Coat School or Christ's Hospital, with its magnificent new gothic dining hall now building, the spacious hospital of

St. Bartholomew, and the misapplied area of Smithfield, with its numerous diverging avenues. In the mid-distance are delineated the Charter House and its gardens, the Artillery-ground, part of Finsbury Square, Old Street, the City Road, the numerous mercantile establishments on the banks of the Regent's Canal and its basins, the greater portion of Clerken-well, Cold-bath Fields, a considerable portion of Pentonville, Islington, Britannia Fields, the London Field, Hoxton, the two mills by the Rosemary-branch, Kingsland Road, Crescent, and adjoining fields, Highbury and its commanding terrace, Stoke Newington, Stamford Hill, Muswell Hill and Hornsey. The extreme distance embraces a part of Epping Forest, with the high grounds eastward towards Enfield, and the neighbouring parts of Hertfordshire.

The south quarter of the circle, commences with the south side of St. Paul's Church-yard, including part of Thames Street, St. Andrew's Hill, Blackfriars', St. Bennet's Hill, with the college of Doctor's Commons, and the building formerly occupied by the heralds:—all the adjacent churches, among which are many of the best of Sir Christopher Wren's, and other public buildings, the Southwark Bridge, the New London Bridge and Bankside, from St. Saviour's Church, along the line of warehouses and manufactories to the southern foot of Blackfriars' Bridge.

The mid-distance of this view includes a considerable part of the Borough of Southwark, with the line of Blackfriars' Road, the Greenwich Road, and particularly displays the situation of its numerous public buildings from Bethle'm Hospital to the Kent Road. The more distant part comprises Kennington, South Lambeth, Newington, Camberwell, Peckham, Denmark Hill, Hearn Hill, the fine woods of Dulwich, Norwood and a great extent of the surrounding country, with its numerous villas, parks, paddocks and champaign scenery of the delightful county of Surry.

Thus, this gigantic and unparalleled undertaking will give a perfect representation of a continuous scene, from a lofty central situation, of a prospect unequalled in extent, variety and grandeur, whether considered in regard to those interesting objects which characterize the great metropolis with its extensive port, to the accumulated memorials of architectural splendour of various ages, or to the diversified beauty of the environs, and rural residences by which they are surrounded.

The sketches that Mr. Hornor took, with an apparatus of his own construction, by which the most distant and intricate scenery may be delineated with mathematical accuracy, comprised nearly 300 sheets of large drawing paper, and extended over a surface of 1680 superficial feet: a space which will not appear surprising, when it is considered that they include a portion of almost every public building and dwelling-house in the metropolis, with all the villages, fields, roads, rivers, canals &c. that are visible from the summit of the Cathedral.

It is not exactly correct to describe the operations of an artist during his progress, because of the probability of his altering his intentions before their completion. But this great undertaking is so nearly advanced to that desirable stage, that there is now but little fear of such an event taking place in its arrangements.

The mode in which Mr. Hornor proposes to exhibit his panorama, when completed, is novel and ingenious. As the building is of great height, more than 150 feet, and different views at different heights are to be given, it would be a work of some labour to ascend a staircase from the bottom to the top. To avoid the necessity for this exertion, the room in which the spectators are placed to see the picture, is raised by one effort, visiters and all, from the level of the floor of the structure, to the first platform or gallery, a height exceeding that of lofty four storied houses, such as those of Portland Place. The machinery by which this elevation is accomplished, is both simple and effective. The power employed is that of water, so contrived as to proportion its strength to the number of persons it has to raise; as each individual who enters, adds to the power by such entrance in passing the door, a force equal to his own weight. At a given signal the apartment then rises: the panorama being all the while invisible to the spectator; until at length, arriving at the first platform, he stands on what appears to be that portion of the cathedral that is called the iron gallery; with the enormous cupola, the turrets, and all those parts of the cathedral which are visible from that position immediately below him; and the whole of the metropolis of London, with its various great features, the rivers, the bridges, the suburbs &c. spreading on all sides, and in every direction, around him. This is a scene that, looking to the accuracy with which all its details are painted, will not merely be highly interesting both to Englishmen and foreigners; but it is also a view, which there are few opportunities of witnessing. For the prospect from the iron gallery of the cathedral, is so often dimmed and obscured by the smoke and vapour which hangs over the city, that it is very uncertain when to obtain a clear prospect, except at those very early hours in the morning when access cannot be had.

The great size of the picture, added to the number of objects contained in it, gives it indeed the appearance of a model on a gigantic scale, rather than that of a painted panorama; and the first impression that strikes the general spectator is, how little he was acquainted with the great outline of the city, in which, perhaps, he habitually resides.

From this first stage, the visiters then proceed by a spiral staircase to a second gallery, about thirty feet above the first, the ascent to which is so managed that they appear to be mounting by a scaffolding erected round the lantern of the cathedral, and they actually pass round the ancient ball and cross, that was originally erected by Sir Christopher Wren, and removed at the recent repairs; two relics of that period which Mr. Hornor has preserved. From this gallery a second view of the picture is given; and still higher up I think there is a third; and from thence winding still higher, the spectator suddenly emerges into an extensive gallery, built round the exterior of the building, where it is no longer a picture that is before him, but a living panorama of the whole circle around him, with the Regent's Park, and the whole of its magnificent improvements; with the hills of Highgate and Hampstead one way, and St. Paul's and Westminster Abbey the other. This part only forms an exhibition which thousands of persons in the metropolis alone, would willingly pay a consideration to view.

The improvements in the park proceed so rapidly, that, I purpose, in the spring, taking another tour with you to inspect their progress, and as I trust Mr. Hornor's panorama will then be finished, we will make a day for the whole.

As our long rest before the panorama, has given vigour and

excitement to our spirits, let us take a finishing turn along the front of Ulster Terrace, up the road opposite to York Gate, by Mr. Burton's villa, make a circuit of the ring, come out opposite Chester Terrace, and conclude our perambulations by an inspection of Mr. Soane's new church at the south-eastern extremity of the park.

Park Square, as I have before mentioned, is the improved alteration of the originally intended circus, which is not, as the celebrated Irish orator, Sir Boyle Roche, observed, "*an amendment for the worse.*" The row of houses that adjoins it at the north-western angle, with four bow-windowed houses, is

Ulster Terrace.

It has nothing particularly architecturally striking in its composition. The entrance story is of the Ionic order, with semicircular headed windows between the columns. The entablature is imperfect, being without a frieze, the upper stories are composed of windows with handsome architraves and entablatures by way of dressings, and the whole surmounted by a well proportioned balustrade. *See plate of Ulster Terrace.*

York Terrace looks well with this oblique western sun upon its bold projections; and the panoramic turns of the terraces beyond, have a splendid variety of gilded lights and broad shades, as they alternately present their faces or rears to the glorious luminary that is now enlightening our hemisphere.

Let us hasten over the bridge, or time will press upon us. South Villa, the seat of Mr. Cooper, does not present its best aspect towards us in this road. It is best seen from the lake, as is Mr. Burton's, which we before examined in every view. This on our left, on the northern periphery of " the ring," is the villa that was designed by Mr. Raffield, for C. A. Tulk, Esq. the late member for Sudbury, and now the residence of John Maberly, Esq. the member for Abingdon. *See plate of Mr. Maberly's villa.*

The house is in the Grecian style of decoration, partaking somewhat of the Etruscan. The centre is ornamented by two piers, which supports a pediment with acroteria; and include between them two pilasters of the Corinthian order. Between these, is a large and lofty Palladian window. The wings project a little from the centre, and these are likewise embellished by two large piers, with neat panels, and Grecian honeysuckles in the caps.   Below the large window is a spacious porch of two well-proportioned piers, each supporting a lion.   The centre is marked by two columns and an entablature of the Pœstum Doric, with a string-course substituted for the cornice, and a blocking course in unison with those which support the lions. A belfry of rather a pretty form, disfigures the design, which, otherwise, has animation and variety in every part, and a happy accordance between the flanks and the principal front.   The house, which I have several times been over, previous to Mr. Maberly's occupation, is remarkably well built, by the Messrs. Baileys, whose beautiful indurated cement, resembling the finest Portland stone, shows off the architect's tasteful design to the greatest advantage.

Let us now proceed, once more by THE PORTICO of the Colosseum, pass by the Diorama, through Park Square, and finish our morning's walk by an investigation of Mr. Soane's new church, at the south-eastern angle of the park, on the verge of the New Road.   The exterior of the Diorama has nothing more than the adjoining houses on either side, and its interior has nothing in common with any thing else in the metropolis ; nor has St. Andrew's Terrace much more to recommend it, except the pretty pavillion-looking building of the Corinthian order at the further end, which forms two houses, so contrived as to appear like one.   Therefore, as the unruly sun has been looking upon us with his warmest regards for some hours, suppose we enter the cool rotunda of the Diorama, and rest our wearied bodies, and refresh our tired eyes, with the artificial beauties of Messrs. Bouton and Daguere.

This delightful exhibition (let us sit down in the hall, while the theatre and its audience, like that of Scribonius Curio at Rome, is turning from one subject to another, during which operation we cannot enter), is a display of architectural and landscape scenery, painted in solid, and in transparency, arranged and lighted in a peculiar mode, so as to exhibit changes of light and shade, and a variety of natural pheno-mena in a really wonderful manner.   The body of the picture is painted, on what scene-painters technically term a flat, and this main or perpendicular subject is aided by wings or side

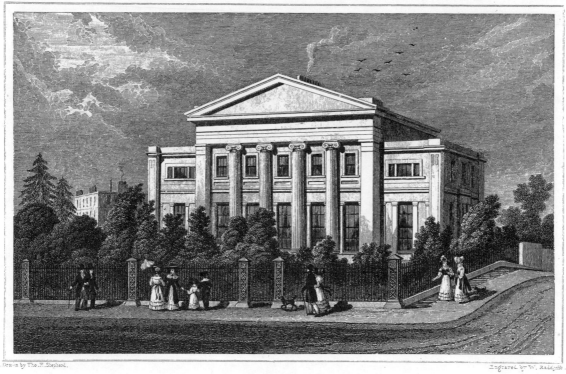

VILLA IN THE REGENT'S PARK.

ST. ANDREWS PLACE, REGENT'S PARK.

Drawn by Thos H Shepherd.   Engraved by Archer

ST MARY'S CHURCH, WYNDHAM PLACE, & DISTRICT

RECTORY TO ST MARY-LE-BONE.

Drawn by Thos H Shepherd   Engraved by H. W. Bond

TRINITY CHURCH, NEW ROAD.

scenes, by painting on the floor, by raised bodies and by other optical and pictorial effects, till the delusion is perfect and almost incredible. These paintings are lighted from behind by large windows as big as the pictures, and by sky-lights over and in front of them; and by the aid of opaque and transparent screens and curtains of various colours and degrees of transparency, the various effects of light, shade and gradations of colour are produced.

These pictures, or scenes, are viewed from a very elegant circular theatre, with pit, boxes and passages, through an opening, decorated by a proscenium. While the opening in the theatre is before one picture, the whole body of the audience part is slowly moved round by some admirable machinery below, and the spectators, seats, attendants and all, are moved imperceptibly round, from the Mary Chapel of Canterbury Cathedral to the lake of Lausanne, or from the city of Rouen in France, to the interior of Rosslyn Chapel in Scotland. The elevation next Park Square is from the designs of Mr. Nash, and the interior of the theatre from those of Mr. Morgan and M. Pugin.

The theatre has now revolved upon its axis, and one of the openings removed to the door in the hall, therefore we may enter, and be mystified by the delusions of these eminent pictorial enchanters.

I hope you will admit, that I have not misapplied the epithet of enchanters to these artists, and if you are sufficiently rested and gratified by your inspection of the Diorama, we will walk gently onward towards the new church, which is just completed on the eastern extremity of the immense parish of St. Mary-le-bone. This new church is called the church of the Holy Trinity, or for brevity sake,

TRINITY CHURCH.

This very handsome and well built church is erected by the commissioners for building new churches, from the designs and under the superintendance of Mr. Soane, the most original and painter-like in conception, of modern English architects.

We have in this building the satisfaction of seeing, almost for the first time since the days of Sir Christopher Wren, a steeple not sitting a straddle upon the back of the pediment, like the giant Gog, in the Rabbinical fables, riding astride upon Noah's ark during the flood. Mr. Soane has cut this Gordian knot of church architecture, rather than unravelled it; for to accomplish his object he has omitted the pediment altogether, instead of giving his tower a base from the earth, like the campaniles of Wren and the best Italian architects. However it is a tasteful reformation of a contemptible practice, to which Gibbs in his beautiful blunder of St. Martin's in the fields, and the elder Dance, in his Wren-like imitation of Bow church steeple, in the parish of Shoreditch, have given currency.

This church, like its opposite neighbour St. Mary-le-bone near York Gate, stands in the unorthodox position of north and south, instead of the more general posture of east and west; but has its portico in the pleasing and more evidently necessary situation of its face to the south, and its altar, or principal end, at the north.

The portico is tetrastyle and Ionic, after one of the chastest of the Greek specimens, that of the Temple on the banks of the Ilyssus at Athens, and is raised upon a plinth, which is level with the floor of the church. The floor of the portico is approached by a flight of steps, guarded by a projecting block of the same height as the plinth. Under this portico is the door which leads to the nave, and on each side of the portico is a lofty semicircular headed window, lighting the ailes, and divided into two heights by a panelled transom between the jambs; the upper portion lights the galleries and the lower portion the pews beneath them. The cornice is continued on every side of the building, but the architrave and frieze of the entablature, only over the columns of the portico and of the flanks. The frieze is sculptured with the formal Greek fret, which is by no means so graceful or so elegant as the foliated scroll and intervening honeysuckle of the same school. The flanks have projecting sub-porticoes of six half-columns in antis, corresponding in height and proportion with the portico-in-chief; and windows of a similar height and width, and similarly divided into two heights, fill up the intercolumniations. The whole is surmounted by a parapet composed of a balustrade with piers raised upon a well-proportioned blocking-course, breaking with the entablature over each portico. These side sub-porticoes are both original and pleasing, and the long windows, divided between the frames instead of two stories of windows, or the galleries seen through the glass, are equally novel and effective. The lower story of the tower, or rather belfry story, has two projecting columns on each face, with entablatures breaking every way over them, of the Tivoli-Corinthian order, which at this height has a remarkably bold and pleasing effect. The blocking-course over each column, is finished by a very beautiful cinerary urn, or pyramidal sarcophagus, which form pleasing finials, and carry the eye with good effect, to the circular story which surmounts it and fill up the angles of the square.

This upper story is a peristyle of six columns of the composed order used in the portico to the octagon temple of Andronicus Cyrrhestes, commonly called the temple of the eight winds at Athens. The capitals of this order are too minute and ineffective for the height in which they are placed in this steeple, and are very inferior to those of one row of very bold leaves, and large volutes, which are used by Wren, in the tambour of the cupola of St. Paul's. These upper columns are supported on a circular stylobate, which gives elevation to the edifice, and are surmounted by a semi-elliptical cupola of rather lofty proportions, that carries the vane.

Since the days of Gibbs and Wren, I consider this steeple, belfry, or whatever it may be called, as the fashion of the day, or the will of the commissioners, insist on the perpetration of such horrors on the roofs of modern churches, to be the best, always excepting that of Shoreditch. The omission of the pediment gives some approach to the solid tower, emanating from the ground, and surmounted by the steeple, that was the invariable practice of Wren and the best Italian architects.

If the worthy professor of architecture in the Royal Academy were now with us, I would ask him, considering that he was not bound to an east and west longitude, whether he might not have made his Ionic portico, being either tetrastyle to the nave as at present, or hexastyle, embracing at once the nave and the aisles, complete with a pediment; and instead of placing his beautiful belfry a cock-horse on its apex, have erected it on a square unornamented tower, the lower part of which would have served for a sacristy or vestry room, at the north end ; giving it, that is the plain square tower, a greater height to allow for the distance?

A student should not dictate to his professor, but he may ask respectful questions.

Now, my good sirs, we have finished our perambulation of the Regent's Park, but hope that more villas may yet recall our steps, as there is certainly no place in the whole metropolis so completely fitted for the *rus in urbe* as this beautiful spot.

Before finishing our walk, I cannot conclude without reading to you a sketch of this delightful place, written by Mr. Charles Ollier, one of the proprietors and editors of the Literary Pocket Book for 1823, which is often my pocket companion in literary excursions.

" When we first saw," he begins, and I well remember having a similar feeling, although my professional propensities lead me to think lightly of the destruction of fair fields for formal buildings, " that the Mary-le-bone fields were enclosed, and that the hedge-row walks which twined through them were gradually being obliterated, and the whole district artificially laid out, (there is nothing more wretched than the first process of planting and making roads), we underwent a painful feeling or two, and heartily deplored the destructive advances of what generally goes by the name of improvement. Old recollections —recollections of youth, upon which we love to dwell as we advance into the shadowed part of our life's road, are remorselessly stricken aside by this change in pleasant localities ; we almost mourn over the loss of the old trees and paths which stood as quiet mementos of the cheerful rambles of our boyish days, or, it may be, of love-hallowed walks and looks, and tender words first ventured under the influence of the fields and the comparative retirement. Nothing makes the lover bold and the mistress tender, so well as the fresh and fragrant air, the green herbage, the quiet and the privacy of country spots, which, when near towns, are more exciting by the contrast.

"A few years, however, have elapsed, and we are not only reconciled to the change alluded to, but rejoice in it. A noble park is rapidly *rising up*, if we may use such an expression, and a vast space, close by the metropolis, not only preserved from the encroachment of mean buildings, but laid out with groves, lakes, and villas, with their separate pleasure grounds, while through the whole place there is a winding road," *(see the engraved plan of the Regent's Park)* " which commands at every turn some fresh features of an extensive country prospect.

" This is indeed a desirable appendage to so vast a town as London, more especially as the rage for building fills every pleasant outlet with bricks, mortar, rubbish and eternal scaffold-poles, which, whether you walk east, west, north, or south, seem to be running after you. We heard a gentleman say, the other day, that he was sure a resident in the suburbs could scarcely lie down after dinner, and take a nap, without finding, when he awoke, that a new row of buildings had started up since he closed his eyes. It is certainly astonishing: one would think that builders used magic, or steam at least, and it would be curious to ask those gentlemen in what part of the neighbouring counties they intended London should end. Not content with separate streets, squares, and rows, they are actually the founders of new towns, which in the space of a few months, become finished and inhabited. The precincts of London have more the appearance of a newly discovered colony, than the suburbs of an ancient city. For instance ; in what a very short time back were the Bayswater fields, there is now a populous district, called by the inhabitants, ' Moscow ;' and at the foot of Primrose Hill, we are amazed by coming upon a large complication of streets, &c. under the name of ' Portland Town.' The rustic and primeval meadows of Kilburn are also filling with new buildings and incipient roads ; to say nothing of the charming neighbourhood of St. John's Wood Farm, and other spots nearer town.

" The noble appropriation of the district of which we are now speaking, is not so much a change as a restoration. It was formerly a park, and had a royal palace in it, where, we believe, Queen Elizabeth occasionally resided. It was disparked by Oliver Cromwell, who settled it on Colonel Thomas Harrison's regiment of dragoons for their pay ; but, at the restoration of Charles II. it passed into the hands of other possessors, till, at length, it has reverted to the crown, by whose public spirit a magnificent park is secured to the inhabitants of London. The expense of its planting, &c. must have been enormous, but money cannot be better laid out than on purposes of this lasting benefit and national ornament.

"The plan and size of the park, is in every respect worthy of the nation. It is larger than Hyde Park, St. James's Park, and the Green Park together." Here my friend of the Literary Pocket Book is in error, for Hyde Park, even since its robbery of part of its fair proportions by Kensington Gardens, contains 395 acres, St. James's and the Green Park together, at least as many, and the Regent's Park only about 450 acres, exceeding little more than 50 acres Hyde Park alone. But, to proceed: "And the trees planted in it about ten years ago are already becoming umbrageous. The water is very extensive. As you are rowed on it, the variety of views you come upon is admirable; sometimes you are in a narrow stream, closely overhung by the branches of trees; presently you open upon a wide sheet of water, like a lake, with swans sunning themselves on its bosom; by and bye your boat floats near the edge of a smooth lawn fronting one of the villas; and then again you catch the perspective of a range of superb edifices, the elevation of which is contrived to have the effect of one palace. The park, in fact, is to be belted with groups of these mansions, entirely excluding all sights of the streets. One of them is indeed finished;" (it is now five years since this was written), "and gives a satisfactory earnest of the splendid spirit in which the whole is to be accomplished. There will be nothing like it in Europe. The villas in the interior of the park are planted out from the view of each other, so that the inhabitant of each seems, in his own prospect, to be the sole lord of the surrounding scenery.

"In the centre of the park, there is a circular plantation of immense circumference, and in the interior of this you are in a perfect Arcadia. The mind cannot conceive any thing more hushed, more sylvan, more entirely removed from the slightest evidence of proximity to a town. Nothing is audible there, except the songs of birds and the rustling of leaves. Kensington Gardens, beautiful as they are, have no seclusion so perfect as this.

"We cannot recommend a better thing to such of our readers as have leisure, than a day spent in wandering amidst the union of stately objects and rural beauty which constitute the charm of Mary-le-bone Park."

Thus endeth our friend of " the Literary Pocket Book," and so endeth our perambulation round the Regent's Park.

Our next excursion shall be, from this interesting spot, through Regent Street to Westminster ; and till then, gentlemen, adieu.

CHAP. III.

" A Realm gaineth more by one year's peace, than by ten year's war."
LORD BURLEIGH.

" Variety and intricacy, is a beauty and excellence in every other of the arts which address the imagination ; and why not in architecture ?"
SIR JOSHUA REYNOLDS.

———————

PARK SQUARE, FROM THE NEW ROAD—ITS PLANTATION AND PLEASURE GROUND —STATUE OF THE DUKE OF KENT—CLASSIFICATION OF STATUES—PARK CRESCENT—PORTLAND PLACE—LANGHAM PLACE—SIR JAMES LANGHAM'S MANSION —THE LATE MR. JAMES WYATT'S MANSION—ALL SOULS CHURCH—REGENT STREET—THE CIRCUS, OXFORD STREET—ST. GEORGE'S CHAPEL, REGENT STREET —WALK DOWN REGENT STREET—THE HARMONIC INSTITUTION—THE PALACELIKE ROWS OF SHOPS—BUILDINGS, THOSE BY MR. SOANE, MR. NASH, MR. ABRAHAM AND OTHER ARCHITECTS—THE QUADRANT—THE CIRCUS, PICCADILLY—MR. EDWARDS'S MANSION—MR. NASH'S GALLERY AND MANSION— UNITED SERVICE CLUB-HOUSE—WATERLOO PLACE—THE NEW BUILDINGS NOW IN PROGRESS ON THE SITE OF CARLTON HOUSE—REMINISCENCE OF THE VIEW OF THAT PALACE AND ITS ARCHITECURAL SCREEN FROM REGENT STREET.

The morning is again auspicious to our task, which I purpose beginning, where we left off yesterday ; namely, at

PARK SQUARE.

On this spot it was originally intended to have completed the crescent opposite, into a circus, which would have been the largest circle of buildings in Europe. The foundations of the western quadrant of it were even laid, and the arches for the coal-cellars turned. For some reasons, however, this plan was abandoned, and the entire chord of the semicircle left open to the park, instead of being closed in by the intended half circus. This alteration is a manifest improvement of the entire design, and is productive of great benefit to the houses in the crescent and in Portland Place. Park Square is erected in its stead, and consists of two rows of houses, elongated upon the extremities of the crescent, and separated from the New Road, from the park, and from each other, by a spacious quadrangular area,

laid out with planted pleasure grounds, and enclosed by handsome ornamental iron railings.

Having the use of a key for the day, we will, as we are early,
take a stroll among its meandering walks, and enjoy ourselves
among its ambrosial shrubs, its natural symmetry and its trim
beauty; for in an enclosed garden in the neighbourhood of
buildings or other works of art, neatness, symmetry and trim-
ness, approaching to elegance, are the characters that should
be sought after by the landscape or artist gardener. How re-
freshingly cool and soft the velvet turf of this smoothly shaven
lawn is to the feet, after coming from the arid hardness of the
gravelled road; and how delightful to the senses are the fra-
grancy of those gay flowers, the symmetry of those beauteous
dwarf shrubs, and the artfulness of those serpentine walks. I
am not partial to the wild, or what Gilpin calls the natural or
picturesque manner in the domestic garden; but would rather
with Milton,

> " Add to these, retired leisure,
> That in *trim* gardens takes his pleasure."

This smoothness, this dressed gaiety offends against the laws
of the picturesque or Gilpin school. A master in this school,
would turn the velvet lawn into a piece of broken ground,
would plant rugged scrubby oaks instead of flowering shrubs,
would break the edges of these walks, would give them the
roughness of a new made road, would corrugate them with ruts,
would defile the beauty of its whole face by stones and brush-
wood, and by making all rough and dirty, where all is now fair
and smooth, would create what in his vocabulary he would call
the *picturesque*.

So would he act by a gorgeous piece of architecture, if it
were as perfect as the pencil of Callicrates, or the chisel of
Phidias could make it. Let the proportion of its parts, the
propriety of its ornaments, and the symmetry of the whole, be
as exquisite, as ever bore the impress of the mint of genius; in
his eye it is formal, and does not please his picturesque imagination. Therefore, to give it the finishing touch, the master
mark of currency among the people of picturesquiescity, he
would take the mallet instead of the chisel, would beat down
one half of its splendid beauties and throw the mutilated mem-

bers around the rest in heaps, and call exultingly aloud, "be-
hold my work!"   No painter, he would say, could hesitate a
moment which to choose.   The Parthenon in all its glories,
during the splendid era of Pericles, a name deservedly dear to
every lover of the fine arts, would be inferior in his eyes, to the
same fine structure in its demolished state, when blown to
ruins by the bomb-shells of the barbarian Kœnigmarck, and
the villainous gunpowder of the still greater barbarians of
Turks, who desecrated it into a magazine of warlike combus-
tibles.

The rude and undefined masses of the overthrown temples
of Agrigentum, would please his eye more than all the majesty
of the Roman Forum in complete perfection.   He would not
sing with Cowper,

> " Alas for Sicily ! rude fragrants now
> Lie scatter'd, where the shapely columns stood.
> Her palaces are dust"—

but would rather rejoice, if some tasteful-minded earthquake
would topple down St. Paul's Cathedral into a more picturesque
object, than its finely proportioned columns, and ample cupola
built in the form of heaven, now presents to his dilapidating
eye.

Let us pass, beneath these

> ———————————— " Shades,
> And walks beneath, and alleys brown,"

under the New Road into the semicircular gardens of Park
Crescent.

The statue before us is erected by public subscription to the
memory of the late Duke of Kent, a prince of great public spirit,
who at the time of his lamented death, was fast working himself
into the good graces of his countrymen, and rapidly winning the
golden opinions of men.   It is executed in bronze by Gahagan,
and elevated on a granite pedestal.   The Royal Duke is represented
in a standing posture, dressed in a field marshall's uniform, over
which the artist has cast drapery, of his robes and collar of the
order of the garter.   The attitude is simple and unaffected, and
with the bust is very like the royal personage that it represents.

The figure is heroic, that is, between the natural and colossal sizes, being seven feet two inches in height. Its weight of metal is, I understand, about two tons.

This statue of his majesty's lamented brother, is in a manly energetic style; but coarse in execution, and vulgar in conception. As a likeness of a duke, and as an imitation of a British general, of royal rank, there is but little fault to find. As a figure in modern costume it is vastly superior to that of another royal duke (Cumberland) in Cavendish Square; but inferior to Flaxman's Lord Howe, in Westminster Abbey. " Imitation is the *means,*" says Sir Joshua Reynolds, " not the *end* of art; it is employed by the sculptor as the language by which his ideas are presented to the mind of the spectator. Poetry and elocution of every sort make use of signs, but those signs are arbitrary and conventional. The sculptor employs the representation of the thing itself; but still as a means to a higher end— as a gradual ascent always advancing towards faultless form and perfect beauty." The essence of sculpture is correctness, and thus far the artist of this statue has accomplished his purpose; but we look in vain for dignity of character in this mere portrait of the royal duke.

Mr. Gahagan has done well however in abandoning the *lorica* and *thoraca* of the Roman school, and has arranged the military costume of the day with becoming effect. The ducal robe supplies the place of the imperial paludamentum, with appropriateness, and he has arranged it with skill.

The sculptor's art, in the present day, is both a limited and a difficult one; for it will be in vain for him to hope to surpass the splendid relics of Grecian art, that have reached our times. The painter on the contrary has a wider field, and his ancient rivals Zeuxis, Parrhasius and Apelles, live but in the historian's volume. The Apollo, the Venus, the Laocoon and the Phidian marbles of the Parthenon remain as proofs of the perfection to which the genius of the ancients brought this science of abstract form.

As we are upon the subject of drapery,—the Greeks seldom used it in their sculpture, and the Romans almost always; yet did the Greeks surpass the Romans, even in this department of the art. So completely was the naked statue reckoned of Greek workmanship, that Pliny (book xxxiv. chap. 5.) says the

Romans called all the unclothed male statues, *Achillean statues,* on account of the number of statues of which they had of that Grecian hero armed only with his javelin.

The Romans named their draped military statues after the name of the costume in which they were clothed; and the statues belonging to persons of the civil class from the order of vestments in which they were arrayed. They also named them Equestrian, Pedestrian or Curuled, as they were either on horseback, on foot, or seated in the Curule chair.

Thus might we form a classification of modern statues, and, while we repose in this delightful alcove, I will try my hand.

The statue of Charles the First at Charing Cross, we would call Equestrian as to its class, and royal as to its order. That now before us is Pedestrian, and royal. That of his Grace of Bedford, in Russell Square, Pedestrian, ducal from his robes, and agricultural from its attributes and accessories. Charles Fox at the other end of Bedford Place, Curuled and Senatorian. The grand portrait of Lord Mansfield, by Flaxman, in Westminster Abbey, Curuled in class and Judicial in order. But this is not the way to go through our purposed survey of the new buildings of the metropolis, in which I promised to accompany you. Therefore, I must leave it to your future leisure to complete my classification of modern statuary.

Now let us pass round one side of Park Crescent, and, as the sun is darting his hottest beams upon us, the eastern quadrant will be the more shady of the two. The great size of this semicircle of mansions is more imposing in effect than the details are choice in selection, which is the prevailing vice of Mr. Nash's style. He comprehends a whole; he grasps the extremities, he achieves variety—that variety and intricacy which the accomplished Sir Joshua Reynolds considered as a beauty and excellence worthy of being adopted into architecture: but he sees not the detail, he either neglects it or despises it, and certainly does not look at his art with a microscopic eye. He does not finish in architecture like Denner or the Dutch masters in painting; but to pursue the analogy, designs like a painter in fresco, and thinks with Michael Angiolo, that a finished or exquisite detail in architecture is like oil painting in the sister art, fit employment only for women and children.

EAST SIDE OF PARK CRESCENT.

EAST SIDE OF PARK SQUARE, AND DIORAMA,
REGENT'S PARK.

Drawn by Tho. H. Shepherd. Engraved by S. Owen.

WEST SIDE OF LANGHAM PLACE.

Drawn by Tho. H. Shepherd. Engraved by W. Wallis.

PART OF EAST SIDE OF REGENT STREET.

This end of Portland Place is also by Mr. Nash, who has joined his broad style to the finicking finish of the Messrs. Adams, with good effect. No antipodes can be more opposite than the styles of these masters, and yet there is somewhat of resemblance. Both are fond of decoration, and both lay it on with profusion; but the former does not bedizen his exteriors with confectionary so much as the latter, and his style is more bold. It is also more pure, as approaching nearer to the Palladian and ancient Roman, while that of the latter is of the depraved school of the middle and lower empire. The palace of Diocletian, at Spalatro, is the *Magnus Apollo* of the Adams's, as their buildings about the Adelphi, and the centre part of Portland Place, which we are now approaching, are striking proofs. Many of their works, however, are of a more chaste and manly character, as the front of the Duke of Bedford's house, in St. James's Square, the house of the Society for the Encouragement of Arts, &c. in the Adelphi; the office of the Amicable Society in Serjeants' Inn; the street front of Draper's Hall, in Throgmorton Street, and a few others of the same character, whose names I do not at present remember. Nash also aims at more variety and intricacy of form than the Adams's, and has obtained more general beauty; but has been as unsuccessful in the purity of his detail, as the united brethren;* though from a different cause—he, from overlooking it, they from a bad taste, derived from the Roman school of Spalatro.

Portland Place, from its size and the consequence of its houses, is one of the most spacious and magnificent streets in the metropolis, and, in its day, was one of the most architectural that had been erected. Moreover, the novelty of the style, the great width of the street, which is 125 feet in breadth, produced, when first erected, a striking effect. The style of its architecture, however, is feeble and effeminate, and is rendered tame by the bolder executions of more modern architects, with which it is surrounded.

It extends from Park Crescent on the north, to Langham Place on the south, where it was terminated in Adams's days, by Foley House, which has been taken down for Mr. Nash's improvements. The houses are lofty, elegant, and well suited

---

* So they called themselves in that fraternal union of their talents "the Adelphi."

for the more opulent classes of the community, but are, as you may perceive, deficient in boldness and relief.

This isolated mansion on our left, which stands so far behind the others, was the dwelling of that very distinguished ornament of our profession, the late James Wyatt, who designed and built it for himself. The front which now faces Portland Place, was in his time the rear or back front, and looked into the gardens of Foley House, and that which looks up Foley Place, to the eastward, was the principal front. This accounts for the plainness of the elevation, which has had, since the death of its able original proprietor, a Doric portico added to the centre door, by way of some distinction, and also to serve as an occasional entrance from Portland and Langham Places, for it stands on neutral ground between the two.

The front next Foley Place, is well worth looking at, not only as being the work of one of our most tasteful and original architects, but from its own intrinsic beauties. It is also memorable, as being one of the first architectural fronts that was covered with the stucco, first introduced into this country by Mr. Wyatt, and known by the name of Roman cement. It is superior in every way to the oil cement of Adams, which has perished to the core, while the induration of Mr. Wyatt's is perfect to this hour, and appears likely to equal that of the finest stone.

Let us walk round by the new church, and take a survey of this very elegant façade, which is nearly lost to the eye of taste, by the dirt with which it is covered.

It consists of a centre, and two pretty pavilion-like wings, which are decorated with elegant bassi rilievi, and give value, as the painters call it, to the receding front which stands within them. The principal, or entrance story, has three spacious openings covered with segmental arches; the centre of which is occupied by a classically designed door of beautiful proportions, and the side apertures with Venetian windows. The spaces between the chord and circumference of the arches, are decorated with delicate sculptures after the antique.

The drawing-room and chamber stories, are embellished with pilasters or ante of a Corinthian order, selected from the portico at Athens, the horns of whose abacus, contrary to those of every other example, come to points instead of being cut off.

The whole is surmounted by a handsome entablature, blocking course, and balustrade.

For elegance of detail, for harmony of proportion, for good taste, and a chaste suavity of domestic propriety, considering its size, this handsome house is not surpassed by any in the metropolis. It is now the residence of Colonel Mark Wilks, of Kirby, in the Isle of Man, who was governor of the island of St. Helena, before it was occupied by the commissioners for the detention of the Emperor Napoleon.

We must return into Portland Place for a few minutes. The house, that almost immediately adjoins this of Colonel Wilks, with the cupola, balustrade, and Corinthian pilasters of Palladian character, is the residence of Sir Anthony Carlisle, the late professor of anatomy of the Royal Academy. It composes well with the adjoining mansions and small plantations, and although petite in style, from the want of height in the stories, forms a pretty picturesque accessory to the groupe.

The island of houses that stands between Sir Anthony's pavilion and the church, is by Mr. Nash, and in his prevailing style; as are those opposite, which, however, are of better proportions. This is Langham Place, named after Sir James Langham, the worthy baronet who occupies the villa-looking mansion and pleasure grounds at the bottom; Langham House is also by Mr. Nash, and is a very good example of his best style; varied, architectural, and well relieved by appropriate breaks and projections. It carries upon its face, good sense, sound taste, and appropriate character. It is a city or rather a town villa, and not a street mansion, built with a front and no sides, as if waiting for its next door neighbour to be built against its party walls. Whereas, this has side as well as front elevations, stands as if meant to stand, detached with cornices and architectural ornaments and openings on every side, bidding as it were, all loving buildings to keep their distances, and nothing to approach but living creatures and beauteous shrubs. It looks as if the original design was drawn at once in perspective, and the front and flanks designed together with the pencil of an artist, and that the drawing board and formal geometrical elevation had nothing to do with its composition. This is the variety, combination and composition that distinguishes the artist from the artisan.

The view from this tasteful Palladian villa, up Portland Place, is strikingly grand and effective. The vista is one of the finest in this fine part of the metropolis, finished as it is, by the paradisiacal views of the park. It is an inclined plane of architectural beauty, rising from the spot whence we are viewing it, to a climax of scenic perfection, in the distance, that cannot be paralleled in Europe; whether we consider the wealth that it embodies, the salubrity of the site which surrounds it, or the optical beauty which results from this charming combination of architecture, sculpture and landscape gardening.

The season of the year too, adds to the beauty of the passing scene. It is now the middle of the London season, the town is resplendently full, the weather as splendidly gay and exhilirating, the inhabitants all life and bustle, and the circumstance of the last drawing room for the season being held to day, makes this opulent and fashionable quarter of the town as lively as an ant-hill. Every equipage is bearing towards Regent Street, in its way to the palace.

This splendid carriage, with the armed hey-duke behind it, coming out of Duchess Street, is Prince Esterhazy's, which contains diamonds enough to purchase a manor. The crowd now surrounding the carriages and front of the house on the left, just above Weymouth Street, are waiting to see the splendid cortege of the Prince de Polignac the French Ambassador, who is going to pay the respects of his royal master Charles X. to our justly popular sovereign. The Spanish Ambassador on the opposite side, and the newly acknowledged Colombian minister, Count Hurtad, his neighbour, are also preparing to join in the same gratifying ceremony.

I say, gratifying, when I reflect upon the different feelings that actuated our public men, during the last desolating and expensive war, when rivalry in bloodshed and horrors devastated the finest countries in Europe; and now, when our greatest rivalries are in the arts of peace, in commerce, in literature, in the fine arts, in science, in all the elegancies that adorn and support human nature. In these instances all parties are the gainers, for even the unsuccessful for the paramount prize, reap a profit, whilst, in war, the very conquerors are awful losers.

Now let us cross over to the portico of the south-eastern building of Langham Place, and take a look at the singular

Drawn by Tho.ˢ H Shepherd

Engraved by Jaˢ Tingle

ST PANCRASS CHURCH, WEST FRONT.

PL. 8.

Drawn by M.ʳ Shepherd

Engraved by Jaˢ Tingle

ALL-SOULS CHURCH, LANGHAM PLACE.

PL. 7.

Drawn by Tho. H. Shepherd.

Engraved by W. Watkins.

PART OF WEST SIDE OF REGENT STREET.

Published Dec. 21, 1828, by Jones & Cº Temple of the Muses, Finsbury Square, London.

Drawn by Tho. H. Shepherd.

Engraved by W. Watkins.

PART OF WEST SIDE OF REGENT STREET.
CONTINUED.

originality of All Soul's Church. Stay! our station here, if the carriages of the noble ambassadors do not rout us from our post, is one of the best. The portico and wing of that house, with the hatchment over it, bring an agreeable contrast to the church, and with the superb coach manufactory of Messrs. Marks, in the distance, form an architectural picture of no small beauty. *See the print of All Soul's Church, Langham Place.*

The circular perystyle of the whimsical Ionic portico, the capitals of which are composed of winged cherubim, whose heads peer between the volutes with which their wings are intermingling, like owls displayed on the posts of a Dutch barn, have a very good and very original effect from the situation where we now stand. The circular tower within it, that pierces the soffit of the portico, is solid and effective, and where it rises above the balustrade that crowns the cornice, into a circular stylobate to the Corinthian Peripteral temple that forms the bell-tower, it is really productive of beauty, in form and proportion. Nor am I disposed, now my eye has become somewhat used to the daring novelty, to object to the *gothic* innovation of the *impaling* spire, with its sharpened iron apex, placed as a finial to the Dædalian beauty of the campanile, as some have done, who with more of wit than love for originality, have compared it to a flat candlestick surmounted by a thick candle, and a little non-fit extinguisher upon its top.

Elegancies, like the steeples of Bow and of St. Bride's, would cloy, if stuck over every church and chapel in the metropolis, and to omit all the credit due to Mr. Nash for his bold originality in this singular tower and spire, would be unfair, for it really possesses much intrinsic beauty of form, and is no mean ornament to the neighbourhood.

The manufactory of Messrs. Marks and Son beyond it, would have been admired, even for a mansion, in the plain times of the Portman Square architects, but is now lost among the architectural beauties of the new metropolis in the nineteenth century.

The architectural façade to the fronts of the row of stable-offices fronting the coach-maker's is a skilful contrivance to conceal an obvious defect, and is highly creditable to the skill of the architect, as well as an architectural embellishment to the neighbourhood. The little continuous portico of the **Doric** order, appended to the front of the dead wall, is a happy thought, and produces one of those pretty accidental effects that an original design often wants.

There is also much novelty and picturesque effect, in the otherwise clumsy piers and sepulchral arches of the east entrance story to the houses between this part and Margaret Street; and the depth of their recesses affords a solid base for the superstructure of the elevation.

Here we approach the commercial portions of the street; and in no part of Mr. Nash's style is he more happy than in the adaptation of his means to his end. The style of architecture now assumes a different appearance. The portion we have just left, as forming the isthmus between wealth and commerce, is composed of smaller houses, which can be let at smaller rents than either those of the continent of fashion that we are leaving, or those of the great peninsula of commerce that we are approaching. They are also of that dual character that partakes both of the shop and the private house, and can be used for either as circumstances require.

Now, there is nothing doubtful in style; wide handsome fronts, calculated for broad showy shop-windows, wherein goods and manufactured articles of the most splendid description, such as the neighbouring world of wealth and fashion are in daily want of, may be displayed to the greatest advantage; and wide private doors for entrance to the handsome upper apartments, for letting as furnished lodgings to the temporary visiters of the metropolis, are the prevailing characters.

These spots were let to the original builders at heavy ground-rents, and consequently the rents of the houses are proportionably high, and nothing but the costliness of the articles, and the great quantity of them which are sold, could enable the shop-keepers and tradesmen to pay them and procure a living profit. The rivalry of many persons of the same occupations prevent extortion, and keep the goods sold in this splendid mart of retail trade at moderate prices.

The architecture of the shops is various, and sufficiently whimsical in places to please the demon of fashion; but it can be changed as the fashion of the day, or the character of the goods to be displayed within them require: the fronts being supported on slender iron columns within them.

Drawn by Thos. H. Shepherd.

PART OF THE EAST SIDE OF REGENT STREET.

Engraved by Wm. Wallis.

Drawn by Thos. H. Shepherd.

Engraved by Wm. Wallis.

UNITED SERVICE MILITARY CLUB HOUSE, HAYMARKET THEATRE,
& PART OF THE OPERA COLONADE, FROM REGENT STREET.

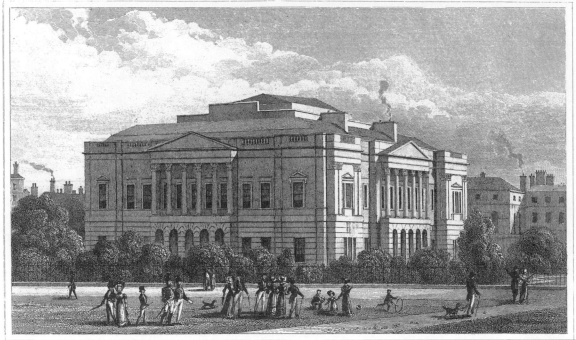

YORK HOUSE, St JAMES'S PARK.

Published Feb 79. 1828, by Jones & Co 3. Acton Place. Kingsland Road. London.

REGENT STREET FROM THE CIRCUS PICCADILLY.

PREVIOUS TO TAKING DOWN CARLTON PALACE.

The style of the elevations above the cornices of the shops, is of the varied character of the Italian school, and of course is highly picturesque; and the domestic arrangements of the dwelling houses are remarkably well adapted to the architectural façades of the exterior. This is indeed a portion of our art in which Mr. Nash eminently excels, and which has rendered his majestic design of Regent Street so much the admiration of strangers and intelligent foreigners. For, as Waller sweetly sung,

> " Glad, though amazed, are our neighbour kings,
> To see such power employed in peaceful things,
> They list not urge it to the dreadful field;
> The task is easier to destroy than build."

The circus which unites, or rather amalgamates Regent Street with Oxford Street, is of a continuous style of architecture with the houses above it; and its form, which takes off the intersectional angles, is one of the best that can be devised for the purpose. It gives an air of grandeur and of space to the streets, and a free circulation of air to the houses. It affords facilities to carriages and horsemen in turning from one street to the other, and is as elegant in form as it is useful in application.

The building on the opposite side of the street, with two turrets and a cupola, just below Princes Street, is the chapel of St. George, a tasteful production of Mr. C. R. Cockerell, whose travels and researches in Greece have added much to our knowledge of the sublime architecture of the ancient Greeks.

As Mr. Cockerell is so classical an architect, he need not fear severity of criticism upon his designs, therefore if you please we will walk over to Welch and Hawes's musical repository, and inspect it leisurely from the northernmost window of their saloon.

In the composition of this church, Mr. Cockerell had that gem of Sir Christopher Wren's, the interior of St. Stephen, Walbrook, in his mind's eye; and as the only difference that ever arose between the tasteful architect of the building before us and myself, was which of us bore the greatest veneration for the memory of Sir Christopher, we shall most likely not differ much as to an application of some of the intricacy and variety of the school of Wren, to the severe simplicity of the architecture of ancient Greece.

The building is of that order of ancient temples which we call prostyle, that is, having columns only in the front; and is the second order of sacred buildings, according to Vitruvius. It is of the Ionic order of columns, and has a portico to the nave, and wings with cubical turrets to the aisles. *See the print of St. George's Chapel, Regent Street.*

The portico is tetrastyle, with columns of that species of the Ionic order, that was used by the ancient Greeks in the temple of Minerva Polias, at Priene, a city of Ionia, near Miletus. Behind the two outer columns are antæ of elegant proportions, flanking a receding pronaos or porch which contains the entrance doorway. This is of antique form, and of just proportions. The portico is covered with a pediment of an extremely elegant and antique form, surmounted by acroteria, which however, at present, support nothing.

The wings are composed of two antæ, one of which supports the epistylium or architrave of the portico, and the other forms the extremity of the building between the front and flank. The entablature is carried through the whole composition, breaking over both portico and flanks. The architrave has three faces, as in the original example; the frieze is plain, the cornice is decorated with dentels in the bed mould, and with lion's heads after the antique in the cymatium.

I know not what the district surveyor would say to Mr. Cockerell, if his lion's heads were spouts to carry the water from the roof after the Athenian manner, casting their liquid odour upon the heads of the beaux and belles that perambulate the broad and handsome pavement from their carriages to the splendid shops on a showery day.

The antæ project sufficiently in either flank, to exhibit its entire proportion and a part of the side walls of the chapel, which are rusticated in square sinkings to mark the courses of stones, in correspondence with those of the front. Between the fronts of the antæ, in each wing, is a very handsome aperture, with Grecian dressings, and relieved from the ground of the wall by sinkings similar to those in the flanks.

On each wing is raised a rusticated attic, surmounted by a cornice of accordant proportions and a lofty blocking course;

St PHILIP'S CHAPEL, REGENT STREET.

TO FIELD MARSHALL HIS ROYAL HIGHNESS PRINCE LEOPOLD OF SAXE COBURG, THIS PLATE IS RESPECTFULLY INSCRIBED.

St GEORGE'S CHAPEL, REGENT STREET.

THE QUADRANT, AND PART OF REGENT STREET.

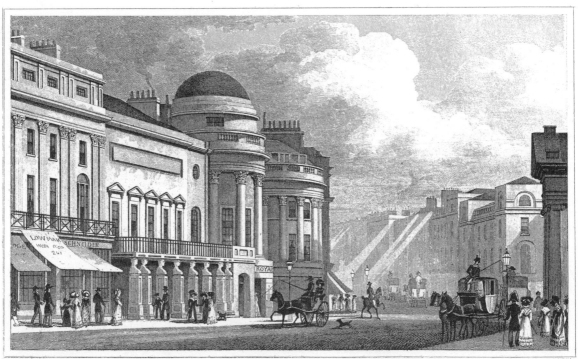

HARMONIC INSTITUTION, REGENT STREET.

which supports a second that forms a base to four antæ, one at each angle of a cubical campanile or bell tower. The order of which these towers are composed, is a species of Doric, somewhat resembling that of the Choragic monument of Thrasyllus, at Athens. The antæ are surmounted by a lofty entablature, consisting of architrave, frieze and cornice in due proportion, crowned by a moulded parapet, which breaks over every part of the centre and conceals the roofs.

The eastern faces of the walls, between the antæ, are divided into ten square panels; the sides are decorated with the two upper panels, the lower part being plain; and the whole of them are ornamented by sculptured bosses. Those of the upper panels are perforated, to serve as a passage for the sound of the bells.

Between the towers (to see which, however, we had better walk a short distance towards Oxford Street), is a lofty capacious hemispherical cupola, with glazed panels for the admission of light to the interior of the church.

This cupola, together with this mode of distributing light to the interior, is more in the Italian style of architecture than in the Grecian. Not that I mean to assert that we have many existing remains of Greek cupolas, or any finer than that of the Pantheon; but that it is not such a cupola as an architect of ancient Greece would have appropriated to such an edifice. Yet it is so recedent from the portico, is so mixed with the architecture of the adjoining houses, and is so little connected with the composition of the front arrangement, that it must be pardoned for the sake of the good effect which it produces in the very handsome interior, which, as I said before, is founded upon that of Wren's graceful example, St. Stephen's, Walbrook.

The effect from this spot, flanked by the well-filled and handsomely displayed shops on each side of the towers, breaking against those buildings beyond it, and relieved by those of the other side of the street, is peculiarly fine and varied. The cupola comes upon the eye like that of an eastern mosque, the glass panels sparkling with the gilding rays of the sun; whilst the circular Corinthian pavilion, on the opposite side of the street, makes a beautiful fore-ground mass for a picture of this original and tasteful building. See *plate of St. George's Chapel.*

The row of Corinthian houses, to the northward of St.

George's chapel, is a great and manifest improvement upon the plain dingy brick elevations of our ancestors. The shops, projecting as they do from the line of the architectural elevations above, serve as a kind of perforated and decorated stylobate to the Corinthian order of the one and two pair stories. The pilasters are arranged in pairs and singly, to accommodate them and their interpilasterings, to the openings of the windows, and the divisions of the party walls.

The entablature, which is complete, after the best Roman specimens, is surmounted by a blocking course, on which is raised a well-proportioned Attic order of dwarf pilasters, with cornice and parapet. The windows of this story are nearly square, and at the same time are both appropriate to their purposes and in unison with the architectural character of the structure. These houses, by being built an entire story loftier than those which adjoin Mr. Cockerell's chapel, create an agreeable variety and a beautiful undulation of form that is highly picturesque and pleasing to the eye.

A cup of coffee, or some other slight refreshment, would, I conceive, be agreeable to us; and after a short repose from our labours, this very hot morning, we can resume our excursion.

This important winding up of our machine, which poor humanity so often requires, and which poor humanity is so delighted to have done, being now accomplished, we will cross over to the chapel, and from the western side of the street take a periscopic view of the eastern side.

That long range of building, which reaches from the corner of Argyle Place to the shop buildings, with a continuous portico of termini, is the Harmonic Institution of Messrs. Welsh and Hawes, which is connected with the establishment formerly called the Argyle Rooms; where the celebrated Pic-nic Society, under the guidance of Colonel Greville, the *Odechorologeïum*, a long-named institution for long winded-spouters, and other musical and oratorical societies were formerly held.

The Harmonic Institution was originally a species of shareholding joint stock company, associated for the publication of musical compositions, and other objects connected with that fascinating art. But it is now conducted entirely by the two eminent musical professors whose name it bears. The portico of termini, with capitals formed of the heads of females, and executed by Mr. J. G. Bubb, produce a pleasing variety next the street; but at the same time an unpleasant darkness in the rooms within. This rises as much from the want of height in the lower story, to which I believe the architect, Mr. Nash, was confined, as from the projections of the portico itself.

The western part of London is as much indebted to the taste for architectural splendour of our present sovereign, as the city formerly was to that of Charles II., in whose father's reign a love for art began to be cultivated by the rich and well educated part of the community.

In this respect the wise measures of our present king are in opposition to the cautious, but perhaps in those days necessary policy of some of our earlier monarchs, who were fearful that the metropolis would grow at the expense of the country, and become as a head too large for the body. With these views, our good old Queen Bess, as she is familiarly called, passed an act (35 Eliz. c. 6) for the restraint of new buildings, converting great houses into several tenements, and for restraint of inmates and inclosures, and from building on any but old foundations, in and near the cities of London and Westminster. But her majesty's taste, which rejected a pictorial prayer book, and commanded Zucchero to paint her portraits without shadows, was never proverbially great, either in painting or in architecture. Her successor too, the cautious James, conceived also that London was increasing in size beyond his conceptions of metropolitan propriety; and that its inhabitants cultivated metropolitan architecture beyond what pleased the British Solomon, who dealt out his wishes like commands, in oracular apothegms and pedantic proverbs. This monarch, as Lord Bacon informs us, was wont to be pressing upon the country gentlemen to abandon London for their country seats; and that he would sometimes say to them, "Gentlemen, in London you are like ships in a sea, which show like nothing; but in your country villages you are ships in a river, which look like great things."

To persons who, like Cobbett, think our vast and increasing metropolis, a *wen* rather than a sound and well-proportioned head, suited to the Herculean fame of the British empire; reply may be made, that LONDON IN THE NINETEENTH CENTURY is not as it was in the fifteenth, the metropolis of England alone; but that it is now the metropolis and mart of the united kingdoms of Great Britain and Ireland, of our immense colonies and territorial possessions in the East Indies: that communications with every part of which, by our improved roads, coaches, the important discovery of the agency of steam, and other means of locomotion, are of ten times the ease and rapidity of former days; and, that vast as has been the increase of buildings in and about the metropolis, the important facts in political œconomy are elicited, that neither is it at present overbuilt, nor inhabitants wanting for the colonies of towns that are now surrounding the ancient capital of England; nor, what is yet of greater importance, has any part of the country, or any provincial town or city, suffered loss or decrease, by the gain and increase of London.

So steady has been the increase of London since the restoration of the ancient power of our kings over every branch of the state, and the consequent expulsion of foreign power over our domestic policy, by the reformation, that its contemplation is almost startling. So great has been the increase of knowledge, by that great diffuser of learning, which no longer debarred the people from instruction, nor made an exclusive *caste* of the priesthood for the benefit of a foreign state, that no memorial of gratitude we can ever raise, would be adequate to the debt we owe to our enlightened and enlightening forefathers, who were instrumental in this vital change in the policy of our country.

The growth of London in the reign of James I. was prodigious. Sir William Petty computes its population to have doubled itself every forty years, from the year 1600; consequently, in 1680 it must have contained four times as many inhabitants as it possessed at the beginning of the century. Although James endeavoured to drive his opulent subjects from the metropolis to their country residences, few of our monarchs had a greater number, or more splendid palaces, than the successor of Elizabeth, whose metropolitan *architectophobia* he seemed to inherit with her crown. Not content with reproving and exhorting his nobles and country magnates, as Lord Bacon records, in imitation of his predecessor, he also issued several proclamations against the increase of new buildings in London and Westminster; yet, at the same time, had both the inconsistency and the good taste to employ Inigo Jones, notwithstanding his staunch papism, to build for him his splendid palace of Whitehall; whose banqueting house and splendid ceiling, by Rubens, together with its entire design, for the preservation and knowledge of which we are indebted to the patriotic liberality of the Earl of Burlington, attest the grand imagination, sound taste and liberality, of both the king and his architect.

Several edicts were, according to old Stowe, the historian, thus issued. One of them forbade all manner of buildings within the city, and a circuit of one mile thereof. Among its enactments was the salutary one to a city built of timber; that henceforward all new buildings should have their fore fronts built of stone or brick; and some offenders were censured in the star chamber for offending against its regulations.

From this period we may date the reformation of the architecture of London, which is also much indebted to the genius and industry of Inigo Jones, the king's chief architect.

Of the principal reformers of taste among the learned and noble men of this period, the great LORD CHANCELLOR BACON stands in the foremost rank; and his published opinions on architecture and gardening, are decisive proofs of the correctness of his taste. His maxim, *that houses are built to live in and not to look on*, should never be forgotten by the domestic architect; and his description of a palace, in opposition to such huge buildings as *the Vatican, the Escurial*, and some others, which he pithily observes, have scarce a fair room in them, is characteristic of the best architectural style of this period, which INIGO JONES, SIR HENRY WOTTON and himself had so much improved.

As we purpose taking a preliminary view of the new palace now building near Buckingham Gate, St. James's Park, previous to its completion, for my hereafter full, true and particular account of its glories; for I hold it a maxim religiously to be observed, that every architect has a right to exclaim to the premature critics, *stay till it be finished;*—a short account of this elegant minded man's idea for a palace may be a good preparative.

He informs his readers (you will find the details in his admirable volume of essays), and his opinions carry weight with men of discernment,—that they could not have a perfect palace

except they had two several sides; one for the banquet, fes-
tivals and triumphs; and the other for the household and for
dwelling. These sides he ordains should be not only returns,
but parts of the front, and should be uniform without, though
severally partitioned within; and to be on both sides of a great
and stately tower in the midst of the front, that as it were
joineth them together on either hand. He desires to have on
the banqueting side, in front, only one goodly room above
stairs, of above forty feet in height, and under it a room for a
dressing or preparing place in times of triumph. How far
Inigo Jones followed this advice, may be seen in comparing it
with his design for the new palace at Whitehall, of which the
present grand and imposing chapel was one of four such buildings, and intended by the architect for the banqueting house.

On the other side, which is the household or dwelling side, the
noble and learned architect would have it divided at the first
into a hall and chapel, with a partition between, both of good
state and ample dimensions. These apartments were not to go
all the length, but to have at the further end a winter and summer parlour; and under these rooms, a fair and large cellar sunk
under ground, and likewise some privy kitchens, with butteries,
pantries and the like. As for the tower, he would have it of
two stories, each eighteen feet high above the two wings, and
handsome leads upon the top, balustraded, with statues inter-
posed; and the same tower to be divided into rooms as shall
be thought fit. The stairs, he directs, to be formed upon a fair
open newel, and finely railed in with images of wood, cast into
a brass colour, and a very fair landing place at the top. I
give you nearly the learned chancellor's own words, for I am
against modernising into fashionable cant, the nervous and
sinewy language of the time of Elizabeth, of Shakspeare and
of Bacon; particularly of the philosophical architect himself,
whose sublime idea for a royal palace I am now repeating to
you, borrowing, not stealing, from the rich storehouse of his
splendid imagination.

His lordship commands, that by no means should the servants'
dining rooms be in any of these lower rooms; for otherwise, he
says, you will have the servants' dinners after your own; for
the steam of it will come up as in a tunnel. And so much for
the front; only he directs the height of the first story to be

sixteen feet, the upper he had before ordered at about forty feet.

Beyond this front he designed a fair court, but three sides of it were to be of a far lower building than the front; and in all the four corners of the court, handsome staircases cast into turrets on the outside, and not within the row of buildings themselves. But these towers were not to be of the height of the front, but rather proportionable to the lower building, He would not have this court paved all over, because it would strike up a great heat in summer; but only some side walks, with a cross, and the quarters laid with grass, kept shorn, but not too close. The row of return, on the banqueting side, was to be divided into stately galleries, in which were to be three or five cupolas in the length of it, placed at equal distances, and embellished with fine coloured windows of several works. On the household side, were to be chambers of presence and ordinary entertainment, with some bedchambers; and all three sides were to be formed as a double house, without thorough lights on the sides, that there might be rooms from the sun both forenoon and afternoon. He would have it so disposed, that there might be rooms both for summer and winter; shady for summer, and warm for winter.

Instead of describing an ideal palace, one would almost think it was the philosophical Pliny the younger, describing his Tusculum or Laurentinum to his friends.

But to proceed with the Chancellor's royal palace: he complains of some fair houses, that were so full of glass, that one cannot tell, he says, where to go to be out of the sun or the cold. Bowed windows he held to be good, except for cities, in respect to the uniformity toward the street; as being pretty retiring places for conference, and at the same time keeping off both the sun and the wind; for that, he observes, which would strike almost through the room, doth scarce pass the window. He would, however, confine them to few in number, not exceeding four in the court on the sides only.

Beyond this court, he would have an inner court of the same square and height, which was to be environed with a garden on all sides; and in the inside cloistered or porticoed on all sides, upon beautiful and well-proportioned arches, as high as the first story. On the under story, towards the garden, it was to be turned to a grotto, or place of shade or estivation; and only have opening and windows towards the garden, and be level upon the floor, and no way sunk under ground, to avoid damps. He proposed also a fountain, or some fair composition of statues, in the midst of this court, which was to be paved as the other court. These buildings were intended for privy lodgings on both sides, and the end for privy galleries; whereof one was to be for an infirmary on the second story, in case the prince, or any special person, should be sick; to have chambers, antichambers, bedchambers &c. joining to it. Upon the ground story he would have a fair gallery, upon columns, to take the prospect and enjoy the freshness of the garden. At both corners of the further side, by way of return, he directs two delicate or rich cabinets to be formed, daintily paved, richly hanged, glazed with crystalline glass, and a rich cupola in the midst, and all other elegancies that might be thought upon. In the upper gallery he wished there might be some fountains running in divers places from the wall, with other conveniencies of that nature.

And thus much, says our philosophical architectural theorist, for the model of the palace; save that there must be, before you come in the front, three courts, and a green court, plain, with a wall about it; a second court of the same, but more embellished, with little turrets, or rather ornaments, upon the wall; and a third court, to make a square with the front, but not to be built, nor yet inclosed, with a naked wall; but enclosed with terraces, leaded aloft, and fairly garnished on the three sides, and cloistered on the inside with columns, and not with arches below. As for offices, he advises to let them stand at a distance, with some low galleries to pass from them to the palace itself.

So far does this " Columbus of the philosophical world" direct the architectural taste of his day; the fruits of which were apparent, and coming to maturity, in the early part of the reign of the unfortunate Charles. This ideal palace would be an excellent task to try the abilities of a young architect to design on paper, and would make an admirable probationary gold medal study for the more advanced students of our Royal Academy. Bacon was not the only philosopher who considered architecture as worthy the attention of an elevated mind. The wise, the enlightened Sir Henry Wotton, who acquired the soundest elements of the art in the school of Palladio, at Venice, (where the only practical English architect of the day, the elegant and accomplished Inigo Jones was then a resident,) also imbibed the purest streams of art, entered still more deeply into its theory, and gave the world his admirable " Elements of Architecture ;" an art which, he says, requires no recommendation where there are noble men or noble minds. He modestly admits that he is but a gatherer and disposer of other men's stuff; he yet gives to the world the soundest doctrines of practice, and the purest of taste.

Inigo Jones was the great practical architect of this brilliant period of our history ; the Lord Chancellor Bacon, the philosophical director of the public taste; Sir Henry Wotton, the learned theorist; and king James, with his son and their enlightened and brilliant courts, the truly royal and noble patrons of architecture and the rest of the fine arts. These eminent architectural masters acknowledged Vitruvius for their principal legislator, and estimated the learned labours of Palladio at their due value. When monarchs, like James and Charles, patronize architecture ; when statesmen, like Buckingham, Richlieu and Colbert; when magnates, like Pembroke and Bedford, encourage its productions from love of its beauties, from principle, and from a studious conviction of its importance ; when legislators and philosophers like Bacon, ambassadors like Wotton, and architects like Jones, study, practice and write upon it and its principles—the art is both ennobled and ennobles, and it must flourish abundantly. Jones and Wren, two of the greatest names in English art, loved architecture *as an art*, practised it *as a profession*, but despised it *as a trade*. When architecture is so patronized, so studied, and so practised, it will rise to a level with the best days of Greece and Rome ; but not till then. It will be in vain that details are only sought for from books, unless the spirit and the mind of the great geniuses of antiquity animate the artist. Vain will it be, if he should

" Line after line, with painful patience trace,
This *Roman* grandeur, that *Athenian* grace ;
Vain care of parts ; if, impotent of soul,
Th' industrious workman fail to warm the whole."

TICKELL.

What a community of master-minds were cotemporaneous in the period upon which I have just been dilating! Paterculus observes, with much judgment, that great men generally are cotemporaries. The spark given by one, is caught by the others, and poets, painters, architects and philosophers, are elicited into one bright blaze of cotemporary and universal intellect.

Now let us continue our peregrinations, and examine that circular building of the Corinthian order, which I before noted, as forming so excellent a foreground piece to the view of St. George's Chapel. See *the print of St. George's Chapel, Regent Street*, and that of *part of the east side of Regent Street*. It stands at the south-west angle of Argyle Place, and breaks, by its agreeable circular form, the monotony of perpetually recurring salient angles at the corners of the streets which intersect the main body of Regent Street. Its rotund convex form, also contrasts, in a very picturesque and satisfactory manner, with the rotund concave forms of the four corners of the intersection of Oxford Street and Regent Street, and shews the fecundity of the artist's mind who has produced so much variety in similar situations. The main feature of the building is a peristyle of coupled columns of the Corinthian order, raised on a stylobate, and surmounted upon a basement of piers and camber arches, which form the windows and door of the ground floor, or shop story. The columns are covered by a proper entablature of the order, of rather a feeble character, with a blocking course, piers, and balustrades over the intercolumniations. Between the columns are the lofty windows of the one pair floor, or principal story, and behind the balustrade is elevated a well proportioned attic story, with windows over those below. This story is crowned by a circular unbroken cornice and scamilli, which are covered with a hemispherical cupola by way of roof.

The design of this building, whether regarded as a portion of the entire arrangement of the architecture of the street, or independently of it, deserves approbation; since it displays utility as a commercial building, with beauty as an architectural composition.

A slight turn from the continuity of the street, brings us to a row of handsome shop buildings, which reach from the circular building on the north to the corner of the next street southwardly. This is as picturesque a range of buildings as any between Portland Place and Pall Mall, and exhibits the peculiar talent of its architect in a striking manner. The shop, or ground story, forms one straight continuous line, of a simple unbroken entablature from end to end, covering with its broad frieze the upper parts of the windows. The epistylia of the centre buildings are supported by antæ or pilasters, and of the wings by stylagalmatic termini of female heads. The shop windows and doors intervene, and with a well-proportioned balustrade elevated on a blocking course above the cornice, complete the composition; which forms an appropriate, useful and handsome basement for the architectural elevation of the dwelling part of the houses.

The superior elevation consists of five parts, namely, a centre, two wings, and two receding parts of the main body of the composition. The latter part consists but of two stories above the shop entablature, whilst the centre and the two wings have three; and project boldly before the main body of the building :—indeed sufficiently so, as you may perceive by turning a little this way, to hold windows for the centre house, and returns of the panels in flanks for the wings, which produce a good effect in the returns, and show a composition in perspective. See the print of *part of the east side of Regent Street*, with a view of All Soul's Church in the distance.

I have before mentioned this mode of architectural composition, when we were examining the villa of Sir James Langham, in Langham Place, and endeavoured to show its superiority over the geometrical board and square elevations of the carpenter's drawing schools, which omit all consideration of the flank in their mode of composition.

The central building of this pleasing structure, to which I crave leave to call your particular attention, as comprising all merits and many of the defects of the school of the able architect who designed it, is composed of an inverted tetrastyle portico of the Ionic order, inclosed between large panelled piers which support, with the columns, the entablature. The wings are similar, except that they are not so wide, and the porticoes have but two columns included in the openings between the piers. The main receding building has no columns, but the cornice of the wings and centre is carried through without any break, except at the angles of the building.

In the intercolumniations are two stories of windows, the upper tier of which rests upon a string which is carried through the whole elevation, and forms a connecting tie, as well as an appropriate division of the stories. The lower tier of windows in the main receding building, is composed of six wide and handsome Palladian windows with pediments; and the upper tier has dressings of architrave and cornice round each window. This portion of the elevation is finished with a lofty blocking course over the cornice, which elevates and serves as a base for a handsome balustrade that crowns the whole, and forms a light and handsome finish to the roofs.

The centre and wings have long attic windows over the whole openings, formed by the piers beneath them, and a sort of grotesque antæ-baluster supports the upper part. Its square panels formed of square sinkings in the stucco, serve as embellishments to the piers both in face and in flank, over the long panels with Grecian angular frets in the corners of the principal story. These are surmounted at a proper height by a small sub-cornice and blocking course, with immense ill-proportioned semicircular acroteria, ornamented with caricatures of the Greek honeysuckle, which I heartily wish the first bricklayer's labourer who may be employed next winter to throw the snow out of the gutters, would have the good taste to pitch over with the rest of the rubbish, to Macadamize the street with.

Thus much for the elevation, which, as a whole, shows a mind alive to picturesque composition, to light and shade, to agreeable form, to proportion, and to most of the loftier features of architectural composition; but, in the minor graces of detail, in which our masters, the Greeks, so eminently excelled all that preceded or succeeded them, an eye, either cold to beauty or contemptuous of its charms. The Ionic order of the principal stories is robbed of its frieze, and therefore wants height. This grammatical error gives the building the appearance of being constructed like some of the churches in modern Rome, with the columns of their predecessors; which being too lofty to admit of a perfect entablature, and, therefore the frieze, an integral part of every order, is omitted by virtue of that law, " compulsion," which even Falstaff himself would not submit to.

Again, the cornice of the Attic order is too small and trivial for its place, and the moulded semi-Gloucester cheeses on the blocking course most outrageously too large. The stylagalmatic termini, which support the shop cornice, are any thing but in good taste; and yet the whole, not *because*, but *in spite* of these deficiencies in taste and selection of detail, presents a bold and highly picturesque composition. The depth of the receding parts between the centre and the wings, is productive of great variety of light and shade, and the entire design forms a pleasing composition, of which the combination discovers both judgment and skill, with a very considerable share of novelty.

An amiable friend of mine, who, a few years since, occasionally aided me with his friendly pen in " *the Annals of the Fine Arts*,"* has some opinions so completely in accordance with my own views on this head, that I cannot resist the pleasure of calling in his aid. " Works of architecture," says my friend, " are not to be judged by precisely the same rules by which we appreciate the productions of the poet, the painter and the sculptor. These, indeed, require no external assistance in order to enable them to embody the conceptions of their minds. With the architect it is different; he is dependant upon circumstances, over which he possesses but small control; and is perpetually subjected to restraint arising from the caprice and interference of others. To these causes, in conjunction with others of a pecuniary nature, is to be attributed the vast disproportion, both as to number and excellence, between buildings which have been executed and those which have been merely projected."

In estimating the merits of a piece of architecture, the true question is, Has the artist availed himself to the fullest extent of all the capabilities of his plan? Has he effected as much as it was possible to accomplish in the allowed extent? Has he obviated the peculiar difficulties with which he has had to contend? After mature examination, and in spite of the prejudices which my unbounded admiration of the beauties of the Greek school may have fastened upon my mind, I have often been led to admire, not only the skill by which *the Architect of Regent*

* Vol. 4, p. 512.

Street (and that is a title that will always distinguish and honour his name), has surmounted many obstacles, but also the happy contrivances by which in effecting these he has elicited positive beauties.

The street that we are now surveying is replete with such qualities; and when it was commenced, I took the opportunity afforded me by my situation as Lecturer on Architecture at the Surrey and Russell Institutions, where criticisms on the buildings of the day were required of me, to state publicly, that " the new street now in formation from Pall Mall to Portland Place is a great and useful undertaking; possessing as a whole a grand and commanding character, with more architectural features and variety than any large work that we have seen since the rebuilding of London after the great fire. Yet it has many blemishes ;"* I thought so then, and the many and very particular examinations that I have given of its various buildings from then till now, confirm me in this opinion ; and to borrow an apology from my before-quoted friend of " the Annals" in the same article, if I have at times presumptuously ventured to cavil at slight imperfections, it is not because I consider them sufficient to detract from the obvious and aggregate excellences of the design ; but because I am of opinion that the criticism which would really instruct, ought to discuss candidly both defects and beauties ; and not actuated by sinister motives either invidiously disparage, or puffingly extol. Above all, it is my object to avoid that nauseating sycophancy, which is generally found to characterize the labours of those cicerones who, professing to furnish the stranger with a *guide*, too often mislead the judgment. Men, who hardly dare to " hint a fault, or hesitate dislike," and their unqualified commendations, says my friend, are not likely to assist in arriving at the ninth beatitude, " Blessed are they who expect nothing, for they shall not be disappointed."

Therefore, as I before hinted, with all these merits, I consider Regent Street to possess many blemishes; some of the architectural specimens being in a taste absolutely barbarous, and mixed with others equally pure and refined. Its masses, great parts and divisions, are grand and effective ; and its breaks and

* Lectures on Architecture, by J. Elmes, p. 403.

general outline productive of an agreeable variety of light and shade, whilst at the same time it is entirely free from that dull monotony of elevation which is so wearisome in many of our new streets. It is also, I there said, the finest work now in progress, and has given an architectural feature to the metropolis, that was so much wanted as a relief from the eternal *two windows iron railing and a door,—two windows iron railing and a door,*—of the (then) new streets and squares of St. Mary-le-bone.

Until this great undertaking, our architecture seemed selfish and internal. Windows undecorated externally, and made solely to give light and air to the interior; and doors placed in square brick holes, whose only service seemed to be to exclude strangers, were the prevalent features of modern English domestic buildings; whereas architecture, on the contrary, should exhibit the taste and wealth of the master of the mansion, by its exterior to the observing *stranger;* as well as contribute to the internal comfort and splendour of the family and its immediate *friends.*

All the buildings in this street are not, however, designed by Mr. Nash, who is entitled to the honour of being its first projector, its indefatigable continuer against obstacles almost insurmountable, and its successful completer against numerous prophecies of its failure and ruin. The row below that which we have just been examining, belongs to the eminent wine merchant, Mr. Carbonel, who figures in the history of Brinsley Sheridan. It was designed by Mr. Robert Abraham, who is also the architect of the County Fire Office; but he must give way for the present to Mr. Soane, the classical professor of architecture in the Royal Academy, who designed that long and lofty row of buildings on the opposite side of the way.

How thronged the street is! we must wait till this regiment of Life Guards, and this, almost army of carriages, horsemen and foot passengers have passed, before we can catch a glimpse at it. Who, judging by this never ending throng, which, as a moving mass, reaches from Hyde Park Corner to Whitechapel Church, can think London too large for its wants; although its amazing enlargement on every side is almost a miracle. If honest Tom Freeman, the Gloucestershire man, who published, in a collection of epigrams, in 1614, one called

" London's Progresse," were permitted to have a day or two to witness its progress in 1827, he would have far more reason to exclaim now than in his day,

> " Why, how nowe, Babell, whether wilt thou build?
> I see old Holborne, Charing Crosse, the Strand,
> Are going to St. Giles's in the field.
> St. Katerne she takes Wapping by the hand,
> And Hogsdon will to Hygate ere't be long.
> London is got a great way from the streame,
> I thinke she means to go to Islington,
> To eate a dish of strawberries and creame.
> The citty's sure in progresse I surmise,
> Or going to revell it in some disorder
> Without the walls, without the liberties,
> Where she neede feare, nor mayor, nor recorder.
> Well, say she do, 'twere pretty, yet 'tis pitty,
> A Middlesex bailin should arrest the citty."

St. Katherine, however she may once have taken Wapping by the hand, has now left her dingy spouse, and taken refuge under the protection of the more fashionable and better dressed Regent's Park; buying her liberty by largesses of docks and warehouses to her mercenary old yoke-fellow of Wapping old stairs.

As we cannot yet obtain a favourable view of Mr. Soane's structure, let me call your attention to that well-proportioned arched gateway in the Italian style of architecture, with a window and cornice over it. It is the new entrance front to Archbishop Tennison's chapel, built in 1823, after the designs of Mr. C. R. Cockerell, the architect of St. George's Chapel in the upper part of this street, that we examined a short time since.

The front next Regent Street consists of a wide and lofty arch, with channelled rusticated piers and voussoirs. Over the key stone is a string course of solid masonry, a dressed window, and a cornice and blocking course by way of finish. The arched gateway leads to the vestibule of the chapel, which spreads behind the houses in the street. There is not in the whole street a design more chaste in decoration, more harmonious in proportion, or more judicious in appropriation. Simplicity, and consequently modest dignity, distinguish this harmonious elevation, which possesses, notwithstanding its narrow limits, a general symmetry and proportion as delightful to the eye as it is creditable to the taste of its author.

Now that the cloud of human beings, horses, carriages and the dust of Mr. Loudon M'Adam has somewhat dispersed, and permits us to have a glimpse at Mr. Soane's row of buildings, let us walk on and consider it in flank from the north, in front, and again from the south. There are many reasons for this peculiar consideration of this very original and singular composition. *First,* because the tasteful architect of the pile is accused of having attempted in it what he himself calls " the philosopher's stone of architecture," *a new order : next,* because he was ridiculous enough to suffer himself to be persuaded, while suffering under a painful disease of the eyes, to bring an action against the critic for thus libelling him : and *also,* because he has in one or two instances deviated from those sound rules of Grecian architecture, which are not too lightly to be sacrificed, or deviated from, only by a great master, who is thoroughly conversant in the nature of all the combinations of his art.

Mr. Soane, I consider to be such a master, and therefore, has by prescription, a right to make such deviations and to take such liberties, as long as he keeps within the bounds of good taste, and runs not into a capricious riot of doubtful vagaries.

Let us take a stand in this quiet angle, and survey his composition, one of the largest examples of domestic architecture, except perhaps his Bank Buildings in Lothbury, that he has executed ; and as he is one of the master-spirits of his art in our days, an investigation of such a design from the hand of such an artist cannot be a loss of time.

First, Mr. Soane was offended at the critic, for accusing him of the crime of endeavouring to invent a new order of architecture, although he has introduced a novel description of columns as supporters to his balconies, which we will examine in detail presently, when we cross the street.

On this subject, I remember hearing Mr. Soane declaim in the Royal Academy to us of his students in the spring course of lectures in 1819, when he said, that the ignis fatuus of philosophy,* the search after the philosopher's stone, occupied the attention and bewildered the minds of the learned for ages ;

* From manuscript notes taken by me in February 1819, and reported in the Annals of the Fine Arts, vol. 4, p. 289.

and some followers of architecture have also wandered out of their paths in the endeavour to discover or invent a new order, *the philosopher's stone of architecture.* The architects of Italy in the fifteenth and sixteenth centuries made many attempts of this kind, and in the reign of Louis XIV. the fancy extended to France. Would it had stopped there ; but unfortunately the mania attacked this country also, and various futile attempts were made in this way. In France a sixth order, absolutely new in all its parts, mouldings and ornaments, was reported to have been invented by Pierre de la Roche. In the reign of our Edward III. his son, the black prince, in consequence of his victory over the French at the battle of Cressy, adopted the crest of ostrich feathers worn by the king of Bohemia, who was killed in that battle, and it has been retained by all succeeding princes of Wales. With this beautiful badge, says Mons. de la Roche, I adorn the capital of my new order, and from the beauteous and graceful delicacy of the nodding plumes, from their enlarged size and bold projections, they must, when thus applied, rank far above the Corinthian order ! We are further told, that this order was absolutely new in all its parts, and that it must eventually and infallibly supersede the Corinthian, as it only required the sanction of antiquity to make it generally adopted ; and, says Pierre de la Roche, when " *my order* " shall be hereafter found among the ruins of palaces and cities, the effects of cotemporary jealousy having subsided, then will posterity give the honour due to my invention ! How far the inventor's anticipated idea of the opinions of posterity upon the design may be justified, said our able professor, I know not, for as yet this new order has never been executed in any single instance.

Other architects, besides the one that Mr. Soane has cited, have tried their hands upon a new order. In Sir William Chambers' valuable treatise on civil architecture, there are no less than six. One of *Flora* composed of leaves and tendrils, which is but a *species* of the *genus* Corinthian, although Sir William terms it Composite. A second of *Mars,* composed of Amazons, with curved draperies over their elbows, supporting the abacus at the angles for the volutes and caulicolæ, an armorial trophy with shields, and an empty helmet for the rose in the centre. A third of *Apollo,* with a sphinx at every corner, peeping out over the second tier of Corinthian leaves, under the pent house of the abacus. A fourth, which he calls *the French order*, composed of palms for the volutes, a cock for the central flower, and tasteless lyres between the palm branches, which serve as stems to the caulicolæ. A fifth of *Venus*, the lower part of which, the abacus and central volutes, are strictly Corinthian, whilst the caulicolæ and angular volutes are formed of dolphin's tails, the heads of these loving fish nearly meeting under an escallop shell, which supports the central volutes. And the sixth is of *Mars*, which resembles that of his paramour in the lower half, but has ram's heads and horns in the upper, which, by the way, would be a more characteristic appendage to the capital of the injured spouse of the goddess.

Yet of this attempt to make a new order, Sir William says,* "the ingenuity of man has, hitherto, not been able to produce a sixth order, though large premiums have been offered, and numerous attempts have been made, by men of first rate talents, to accomplish it. Such is the fettered human imagination, such the scanty stores of its ideas, that Doric, Ionic and Corinthian, have ever floated uppermost; and all that has ever been produced, amounts to nothing more than different arrangements and combinations of their parts, with some trifling deviations scarcely deserving notice; the whole generally tending more to diminish than to increase the beauty of the ancient orders."

Sebastian le Clerc, a French artist of some ability, who wrote and published a treatise on architecture, that was translated into English by Chambers in 1732, and is much cited by him in his own larger work, has also given two new orders. One he names *the Spanish order*, and pronounces it to be more elegant than the Roman or Composite, both in the whole and in its parts. The leaves are plain, such as are often called water-leaves, with grenate stalks rising among them. The horns of the abacus are supported by small volutes, and the centre is decorated with a lion's head instead of a rose, which noble animal, the author says, he need not mention, is the symbol of Spain; and that it expresses the strength and gravity as well as the prudence of the people of that nation. He also gives a

* Page 153 of Gwilt's (that is the best modern) edition of 1824.

second design for a Spanish order, and leaves the architect at
liberty to choose which of them he likes best, flattering himself
that either the one or the other will do very well, if executed
by a good sculptor.   Further, in the frieze, he says, over this
capital may be added a terrestrial globe with cornucopias,
palms and laurels, which are significant ornaments, he observes,
that explain themselves.   To the globe in the frieze, he has appended the heraldric ornament of the knightly collar of the
golden fleece which hangs down on to the architrave.   The other
he calls *the French order,* which he conceives to possess as great
a share of delicacy, richness and beauty as is practicable without running into excess.   The ornaments of the capital are three
fleurs de lis on each side, with palms, and the badge of France,
a cock; arms underneath, and a lyre in the shade of the
palms under each horn of the abacus, which are so many sym-
bolical ornaments, he adds, that persons of understanding will
conceive without any difficulty.   Crowns are introduced as ornaments in the frieze, and a sun shining in the middle ; whence
it will be easily apprehended, he says, " that this order is consecrated TO THE GLORY OF THE GRAND MONARQUE."   *Cock a
doodle doo!* "This order," he exultingly exclaims, " will have the
noblest, the most beautiful, and agreeable effect imaginable:
I have made," he continues, clapping his wings, " a little model
of it in rilievo, *which I never see without pleasure.*"

Although Sir William Chambers translated this balderdash
in 1732, yet when he published his own matured treatise in
1759, in animadverting upon such vagaries, he says, " the substitution of cocks, owls, or lion's heads &c. for roses; of trophies, cornucopias, lilies, sphinxes, or even men, women and
children for volutes; the introduction of feathers, lyres, flower-
de-luces, or coronets for leaves; are more alterations than improvements; and the suspension of flowers, or collars of knight-
hood, over the other enrichments of a capital, like lace on
embroidery, rather tends to complicate and confuse the form,
than to augment its grace, or contribute to its excellence."

You may remember, that I have more than once during our
survey, spoken of the propensity of some of the architects of
this street and neighbourhood to despoil the orders of distinctive parts, such as the omission of friezes, or architraves, and
sometimes both, and other similar violations of propriety.   Of

Drawn by Tho. H. Shepherd.   Engraved by M. Barrenger.

PART OF EAST SIDE, REGENT STREET.

Drawn by Tho. H. Shepherd.   Engraved by M. Barrenger.

PART OF WEST SIDE OF REGENT STREET.

Drawn by Thos. H. Shepherd.
Engraved by W. Tombleson.

WATERLOO PLACE, & PART OF REGENT STREET.

TO HIS GRACE THE DUKE OF WELLINGTON THIS PLATE IS RESPECTFULLY INSCRIBED.

Drawn by Thos. H. Shepherd.
Engraved by W. Tombleson.

REGENT STREET, FROM THE QUADRANT.

Published March 1, 1828, by Jones & Co. 3, Acton Place, Kingsland Road, London.

this practice, Sir William says with the greatest truth, that " the suppression of parts of the ancient orders, with a view to produce novelty, has of late years" (one would think that the worthy knight of the Polar star was peeping down upon some of our new mansions and palaces), " been practised among us with full as little success. And though it is not wished to restrain sallies of imagination, nor to discourage genius from attempting to invent; yet it is apprehended, that *attempts to alter the primary forms invented by the ancients, and established by the concurring approbation of many ages*, must ever be attended with dangerous consequences, must always be difficult, and seldom, if ever, successful. It is like coining words, which, whatever may be their value, are at first but ill received, and must have the sanction of time to secure them a current reception."

As we have now taken a general view of the origin and progress of the Metropolitan Improvements, let us proceed to a brief view of such subjects that we have hitherto passed over, which are of sufficient importance to require our investigation and the pencil of our artist.

We will therefore proceed to Pall Mall, and take a view northwards up the street, which is approached, from the new opening into the Park, by

WATERLOO PLACE.

This grand opening is formed by the removal of sundry old dismal looking houses on the north side of Pall Mall, opposite the late Carlton house; and consists of two sides of a large square, or *piazza*, open to Pall Mall, and the new opening into St. James's Park. The third or north side is perforated in the centre by Regent Street, to which *Waterloo Place* forms a capacious opening, like that of a fine estuary opening from the sea, and forming the mouth of a great river.

The east and west sides of *Waterloo Place*, are similar in design and elevation. They consist of a centre formed by an Ionic portico raised on a basement which forms the entrance story, and two flanks of Ionic pilasters corresponding with the columns, and raised on a similar basement. On the top of the entablature is raised an attic order, perforated by the windows of the upper story.

The north side is similar in height, and consists of an Ionic tetrastyle portico, projecting from the plain flanks of the first row of buildings up Regent Street. These porticoes are crowned by a blocking course and balustrades between solid pedestals over each column. The ground story of these pavilion-like buildings are perforated by three windows, under the intercolumniations of the order above it, decorated with architraves to the sides and entablatures over the lintels.

The line of the principal story, is here well marked by a broad and very effective string course, on which the order of architecture that gives character to the design, and which embraces the entire height of the principal and two pair stories, is elevated. The upper stories of this edifice are in the roof, and lighted by the balusters.

The principal story has semicircular headed windows, with archivolts springing from moulded imposts, and the chamber story has plain square windows without decorations.

The sides, or rather the principal fronts of these pavilions next Regent Street correspond in elevation, except that the projecting porticoes have a greater number of columns, and the receding sides are perforated by windows, which are necessary in this instance for the interior use.

Waterloo Place, and this portion of Regent Street, which is immediately attached to it, embrace all the beauties and all the defects of Mr. Nash, their ingenious architect's style. Grand and effective as a whole, rich in composition and mind, but sadly defective in elegance and correctness of detail. It is a reformed Italian, but still below Grecian purity.

Before we leave this spot, let us turn round, and take a farewell leave of the remains of Carlton House, which once formed the southern termination of this magnificent street. See plate of *Regent Street, from the Circus, Piccadilly*. When Carlton House, or Palace, stood on the southern side of Pall Mall, with the before mentioned ordinary dismal looking dwelling houses only in front of it, its then splendid portico and beautiful wings looked of sufficient importance; but when these houses were pulled down and the loftier houses of Waterloo Place erected, and the rising ground of Regent Street opened, so that we looked down upon and saw the majestic towers of Westminster rising above it, it assumed a mean and low appearance. Its removal therefore is by no means to be regretted, and the fine opening that is made in its stead, is one of the greatest improvements in this spot of almost magical transformations.

We will now take a cursory view of

YORK HOUSE, ST. JAMES'S PARK,

built for his Royal Highness the late Duke of York, and purchased of his executors by the Marquess of Stafford.

This splendid palace is quadrangular and insulated, presenting four architectural elevations of great beauty and grandeur.

Its principal front, which has a projecting portico for carriages to drive under, is to the north, next Cleveland Place; the next in point of decoration faces the east, and is entered from the stable yard, opposite the new palace of his Royal Highness the Duke of Clarence; the park front is to the south, and overlooks St. James's Park and its own private grounds, and

Drawn by Tho. H. Shepherd.   Engraved by H. W. Bond.

THE NEW OPENING TO ST MARTIN'S CHURCH.
FROM PALL MALL EAST.

Drawn by Tho. H. Shepherd.   Engraved by H. W. Bond.

SUFFOLK STREET, PALL MALL EAST.

Drawn by Thos. H. Shepherd.

Engraved by Thos. Barber.

THE NEW COLLEGE OF PHYSICIANS, PALL MALL, EAST.

TO ROBERT BREE M.D. THIS PLATE IS MOST RESPECTFULLY INSCRIBED.

Drawn by Thos. H. Shepherd.

Engraved by Thos. Barber.

IMPROVEMENTS, CHARING CROSS.

TO THOS. HOPE ESQ: THIS PLATE IS RESPECTFULLY DEDICATED.

the western front faces the Green Park and His Majesty's new palace, now building on the site of Buckingham House.

This beautiful mansion, which is hereafter to be the residence of that munificent patron of the fine arts and artists, of his native country, the Marquess of Stafford, is designed by the brothers Benjamin and Philip Wyatt, Esqs., sons of the late James Wyatt, and is worthy of the name.

The character of the building is palatial and splendid; it is composed of hexastyle porticoes of the Corinthian order, which occupy the height of the principal story, raised on piers and the openings between them covered with semicircular arches. On the roof is a raised story which lights a spacious picture gallery. The house stands in its own grounds, which form a beautiful horticultural accessory to the architecture.

The next recent great improvement is

THE NEW OPENING TO ST. MARTIN'S CHURCH,

the best view of which is from *Pall Mall East*.

The want of this opening was complained of so long ago as in 1734, by Ralph, an architectural critic of some consideration, who has the credit of first suggesting this manifest improvement, which forms an architectural picture of great beauty. The building on our left is called the King's Mews, and were formerly the royal stables. It is now used for an exhibition of works of art, manufactures, &c. and was designed by the great Earl of Burlington. That on our right is the portico of the College of Physicians, a new building by Mr. Smirke, and forms, with its illustrious opponent, a fine architectural frame to Gibbs's beautiful portico of the church of St. Martin in the Fields, which is now seen to its deserved advantage. The portico is fine, but the spire and tower, though far surpassing many of more recent date, is, compared with those of Sir Christopher Wren, mean and inefficient.

We will now take a look at

SUFFOLK STREET, PALL MALL EAST,

a street inhabited by architects, and replete with many architectural beauties. Among these is the Italian Ionic house on our right, an appropriate design enough for an Italian warehouse, whose purposes are farther indicated by the oil jars on the acroterium of the entablature. Another, the residence of Mr. Cresy, the architect, is a fac-simile of Andrea Pallacho's house at Vicenza, and a third, on the same side of the way, the house with a projecting Roman Doric portico, elevated on three semicircular arches, is the house and spacious galleries of the Society of British

Artists, the portico of which is designed by Mr. Nash, and the suite of six octagonal galleries, all on one floor, and lighted from above, were designed by and erected under the directions of your humble servant.

Mr. Lewis Wyatt and Mr. H. Kendall, both architects whose talents have tended towards the embellishment and improvement of the metropolis, have houses in this classical little street, in which also is the stage entrance and green room of the Haymarket Theatre.

Another great improvement, and classical ornament to this portion of the metropolis, is

The New College of Physicians, Pall Mall East,

another design of Mr. Smirke's, and which forms part of a fine group with the Union Club House. The principal front of this substantial and elegant structure is next Pall Mall East, and is composed of an hexastyle projecting portico of the Ionic order, which supports a well-proportioned pediment. The front is elongated by two antæ, one on each side of the portico, which are repeated with a break between them, in the flank or eastern front, and has a distinguishing centre-piece, of two slightly-projecting antæ, and an elevated attic, with a balustrade in each wing.

The building is divided into two stories, and the windows are decorated with architraves and sub-cornices. The columns are beautifully wrought with a delicate *entasis*, or swell, so characteristic of the pure Greek school, of which its architect, Mr. Smirke, is so distinguished a disciple. The architrave, however, is disfigured by three faciæ, which should never be allowed to enter (in spite of ancient precedent) into any order but the Corinthian, in order to keep the characteristics of each distinct.

The effect of this portico, in the latter part of a fine summer's day, is beautiful; diversified, as it is, by the deep and broad shadow cast from the entablature and pediment; the perpendicular lines of the fluted columns, and the contrast of the shadowed eastern front, which continued, forms with a corresponding wing, and a receding portico of the same order, the principal front of the Union Club House. In our view of the new opening to St. Martin's Church, this portico now so beautiful in light, forms in shade an equally beautiful forepiece to the picture.

We will now cross over to the other side of King Charles's statue, and take a general view of the

Improvements, Charing Cross.

Foremost in this view is the statue of the unhappy and unfortunate Charles the First, which is of bronze, and cast in 1633, by Le Sueur, a French sculptor of great talent, who wrought the beautiful brass monument

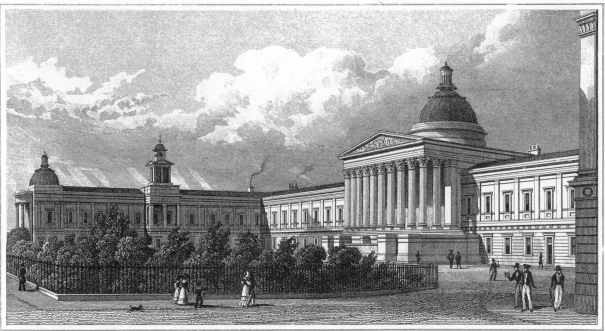

Drawn by Tho. H. Shepherd. Engraved by W. Wallis.

THE LONDON UNIVERSITY.

TO HENRY BROUGHAM ESQ. M.P. AND THOMAS CAMPBELL ESQ. TO WHOSE UNITED EXERTIONS,
LONDON IS INDEBTED FOR HER UNIVERSITY, THIS PLATE IS RESPECTFULLY INSCRIBED.

Drawn by Tho. H. Shepherd. Engraved by W. Wallis.

TEMPLE OF THE MUSES, FINSBURY SQUARE.

TO HENRY BROUGHAM ESQ. M.P. FROM WHOSE SUGGESTION THE SERIES
OF "JONES' UNIVERSITY EDITION OF BRITISH CLASSIC AUTHORS" WAS COMMENCED, THIS PLATE IS RESPECTFULLY
INSCRIBED BY THE PUBLISHERS.

Drawn by Tho.ˢ H. Shepherd.

Engraved by W.ᵐ Deeble.

ST PAUL'S SCHOOL.

INSCRIBED TO THE R.ᵗ REV.ᴰ THE LORD BISHOP OF LLANDAFF, &c. &c. DEAN OF S.ᵗ PAULS, BY HIS OBLIGED SERV.ᵗ

JAMES ELMES.

Published Sep. 29, 1827, by Jones & C.º 3, Acton Place, Kingsland Road, London.

Drawn by Tho.ˢ H. Shepherd.

Engraved by W.ᵐ Deeble.

THE LONDON INSTITUTION, FINSBURY CIRCUS.

DEDICATED TO PROFESSOR MILLINGTON, WHOSE LECTURES HAVE OFTEN ENLIGHTENED HIS HEARERS WITHIN THESE WALLS.

BY HIS SINCERE FRIEND THE EDITOR.

of the Duke of Buckingham, in Henry the Seventh's Chapel, for the Earl of Arundel. After the execution of the king, the parliament ordered it to be sold by auction, when it was purchased by a cutler in Holborn, of the name of Revett, who pretended to melt it down and make handles for knives of it. He, in fact, caused knives with bronze handles to be exposed to sale in his shop, by which he soon made a fortune; the faction which opposed the king being all desirous of having some part of his statue debased to a knife-handle. The loyal cutler, however, concealed it till the restoration of Charles the Second, when he presented it to that king, who caused it to be erected in its present situation.

The large building, directly opposite, is the Union Club House and the Royal College of Physicians, the white house, in the middle distance, the bank of Ransom & Co. and that with the colonnade, in the extreme distance, crowned with a lofty slated roof, the King's Theatre, or Italian Opera House.

THE LONDON UNIVERSITY,

is erected upon the eastern side of an area of about seven acres of freehold ground, between Upper Gower Street, Bedford Square, and the New Road. The council obtained designs from several architects of eminence, and after due deliberation, finally adopted that of William Wilkins, Esq. R.A. a selection in which their own judgment coincided with that of almost every proprietor who inspected the drawings. The building in its execution had the benefit of the superintendance of Mr. J. P. Gandy Deering, A.R.A., the author of the well known Work on Pompeii, in conjunction with Mr. Wilkins, and consists of a central part (see plate of *the London University)* four hundred and thirty feet in length, with two wings, forming together three sides of a quadrangle, the central portico looking westward.

That part of the edifice which is now finished, contains four theatres for lectures, each capable of containing four hundred and forty students; two lecture rooms that will accommodate two hundred and seventy students each; five lecture rooms that will accommodate about one hundred and seventy each; a library and museum, each one hundred and eighteen feet in length, by fifty feet in breadth, and twenty-three feet in height; a hall for public occasions, ninety feet in length, by forty-five feet in breadth, and twenty-three feet in height; an anatomical museum; a complete suite of rooms for the professors and students of anatomy and surgery; a laboratory and apparatus room for the professor of chemistry; rooms for the reception of the apparatus of the professor of mechanical philosophy, and several smaller apartments for the accommodation of the council, the professors and officers of the establishment.

The London Institution.

The gound story of this building is divided into an entrance hall, vestibule, stairs to the library and corridor leading to the lecture room, laboratory, &c., besides reading and newspaper rooms, the librarian's private apartments, &c. The upper story is the library, which occupies the whole front.

The elevation, which faces the south, and catches great picturesque variety from the sun, is divided perpendicularly into three principal parts or features; namely, a projecting portico of two stories, and two wings or continuations laterally of the front, with two minor sub-wings, corresponding with the lower order of the portico; and horizontally into two principal orders and three stories. The lower order is appropriated to the ground or entrance story, and is composed of a portico in antis of the Doric order, after an ancient example of very sturdy proportions. The entablature is carried through the whole line of front, and has wreaths of laurel leaves in the frieze substituted for the more characteristic triglyphs, which belong to the order. The front on each side of the portico is rusticated, and the apartments are lighted by windows, with semicircular heads.

The upper stories are supported by the ground story, in the manner of a basement or pedestal story, and consist of a tetrastyle portico, of that species of the Corinthian order which Mr. Soane first used at the Bank of England, copied from the beautiful circular temple, called the Sybils, at Tivoli.

The sides are supported by antæ between the windows, and an entablature surmounted by a balustrade, the piers of which are ornamented by heads of sarcophagi. The whole front is in good proportion, and harmonizes with the adjacent buildings remarkably well.

St. Paul's School.

This building is composed of three principal parts, a centre and two wings, connected by a continuation of the main body. The centre is a hexastyle portico of the Tivoli-Corinthian order, elevated upon a rusticated basement of solid piers, one of which stands under every column, and leaves a footway for passengers between them. The wings are elevated on a similar basement, the apertures between the piers being converted into doors and windows. On these are raised an attached portico of two three-quarter columns in antis. The wings project the width of an antis, but the centre projects an entire intercolumniation more, and finishes with antæ against the wall to support the entablature. The basement or entrance story is a continuation of the same arrangement as the wings and

SOUTHWARK BRIDGE, FROM BANK SIDE.

WATERLOO BRIDGE.

NORTH & WEST FRONT OF THE BANK OF ENGLAND, FROM LOTHBURY.

TO JOHN SOANE, ESQ.S THE ARCHITECT, THIS PLATE IS RESPECTFULLY INSCRIBED.

EAST FRONT OF THE BANK OF ENGLAND, AND NEW TOWER OF
ROYAL EXCHANGE, FROM ST. BARTHOLOMEW LANE.

centre, the openings between the rusticated piers being used for windows and entrances to the master's houses. The centre is appropriated to the school, and has lofty windows between the columns. The same height in the wings and intermediate portion of the building is divided into two stories, the lower of which has lofty windows, dressed with architraves and surmounted by entablatures, and the upper, square attic windows, with architraves on the tops, sides and sills. The wings are surmounted by blocking-courses and acroteria upon the cornices, and the centre by a low attic and acroteria, upon the summit of which rises a cupola, in too fragile a style of decoration to accord well with the manly proportions of the rest of the building.

SOUTHWARK BRIDGE.

This bridge was designed by the late John Rennie, Esq. and executed under his direction. The magnificent centre arch is composed of a segment of a circle, whose chord or span is two hundred and forty feet, its versed sine or height twenty-four feet, and the diameter of the circle of the curvature at the vertex or crown of the arch six hundred and twenty-four feet, the side arches being two hundred and ten foot in span.

The arches are composed of eight ribs of solid masses of cast iron, in the form of the voussoirs of stone bridges. These ribs are rivetted to cast iron diagonal braces to prevent racking. The frames of the arches are six feet in depth at their vertices, and the extrados of the voussoirs extend to eight feet at the springing of the arches. Many of the single pieces of this gigantic skeleton are of the enormous weight of ten tons each, and the total weight of the iron employed in its construction is between five and six thousand tons.

This fine bridge, which is as elegant in its form as it is scientific in construction, was entirely built at the expense of a joint stock company. Its cost, including its present inefficient approaches, amounted to about eight hundred thousand pounds. The preparatory works were begun on the 23rd of September, 1814, and the first stone was laid by Admiral Lord Keith, on the 23rd of May, 1815. On the 7th of June, 1817, the first stone of the northern abutment, on the site of the ancient Three Cranes Wharf, was laid by Alderman Wood, the Lord Mayor, and the bridge was opened to the public in April, 1819.

WATERLOO BRIDGE,

was erected by the late John Rennie, from the designs, it has been said, of the late Mr. Dodd; but that great schemer only projected the work, and took the design from Perronet's bridge over the Seine at Neuilly near Paris.

The design as executed, consists of nine elliptical arches, with Grecian Doric columns in front of the piers, covered by an entablature, and surmounted by the anomalous decoration of a balustrade upon a Doric cornice. The road way upon the summit of the arches is level, in a line with the Strand, and is carried by a gentle declivity on a series of brick arches, some of which are used as warehouses, over the road-way on the Surry bank of the river, to the level of the roads about the Obelisk by the Surry Theatre. The width of the river in this part is 1326 feet at high water, which is covered by nine semi-elliptical arches, of 120 feet span, and thirty-five feet high, supported on piers thirty feet thick at the foundations, diminishing to twenty feet at the springing of the arches. They are eighty-seven feet in length, with points in the form of Gothic arches as cutwaters towards the stream. The dry or land arches on the Surry side are forty in number; thirty-nine of which are semi-circular, sixteen feet in diameter, and one semi-elliptical, over the road-way of Narrow Wall, of twenty-six feet diameter. The entire length of the bridge and causeways is 2426 feet, made up of 1380 feet for the entire length of the bridge and abutments; 310 feet, the length of the approach from the Strand; and 766 feet, the length of the causeway on the land arches of the Surry side. The first stone was laid on the 11th of October, 1811.

We will now proceed to that great national, and tasteful building,

The Bank of England;

and first, we will begin with the principal front next Threadneedle Street. Our best position to see this richly variegated, picturesque and beautiful front, will be from Bank Buildings: from which spot the circular corner next Princes Street forms a striking foreground; the Royal Exchange on the right forms a good middle distance; the old church of St. Bartholomew a capital object, from its singular antique tower, for the distance; and the far-famed lucky lottery office of Richardson, *Goodluck*, and Co., from its solid form, and true Italian proportions of its Doric entrance story, (a design of Sir Robert Taylor's), and which is now in strong shadow, for a powerful relief and contrast in the foreground. Thus have we in one architectural picture, compositions by three great masters in our art, Sir Christopher Wren, Sir Robert Taylor and Mr. Soane.

The establishment of this great and important corporation is principally owing to the exertions of Mr. William Patterson, a native of Scotland, and Michael Godfrey, Esq. These two gentlemen, after labouring with great assiduity for nearly three years, at last obtained the sanction of government, and in the spring of the year 1694 the Company of the Bank of

England was incorporated by act of parliament. Sir John Houblon was its first governor, and Michael Godfrey, Esq., one of its founders, its first deputy governor.

This great national structure, which has now become so great an ornament to the heart of the city, was erected at various periods, and without due regard to the uniformity of the exterior. The first stone of the original building on the present site, then the dwelling-house and garden of Sir John Houblon, was laid in 1732, and finished in 1736, from the designs of Mr. George Sampson, in the Palladian style of architecture. This building comprised the original centre next Threadneedle Street, that has been recently pulled down by Mr. Soane, and the present pay-hall, which is a spacious room seventy-nine feet in length and forty in breadth, with a statue of King William, in whose reign it was founded, sculptured by Cheere. The wings next Threadneedle Street, the exterior of the Rotunda, stock offices, &c., next Bartholomew Lane, and of the dividend and other offices next Princes Street, were designed and erected between the years 1765 and 1788, by Sir Robert Taylor, from a design in imitation of the celebrated garden front of the pope's palace in Rome, which is published in Sir William Chambers's Treatise on Civil Architecture, as a design of Bramante, one of the architects of St. Peter's at Rome.

The Rotunda was rebuilt in 1795, by Mr. Soane. It is a circle of fifty-seven feet diameter in plan, and about the same in height. It is covered by a hemispherical cupola, and lighted by a lantern light, supported and divided by caryatides, constructed upon the central aperture or eye of the cupola. The perpendicular walls are divided at regular intervals by semicircular headed recesses, three of which serve for entrances, and the other for desks, &c. for the accommodation of the public. In this vast rotunda, the cupola of which from the outside has so striking and elegant an appearance, the general and preparatory business for the purchase and sale of stock is transacted ; and the various offices appropriated to the management of each particular stock branch out from it, and from its classical vestibule, which opens from Bartholomew Lane.

In the year 1800 the widely increased concerns of the Bank made an increased establishment, and more space for the transaction of its business, necessary. The directors therefore made application to parliament for powers to enlarge their building. This was a favourable opportunity to render the exterior of the Bank one uniform pile, and Mr. Soane lost no time to embrace it. He therefore submitted to the committee of directors a series of designs, to extend the north or Lothbury front westward, and to connect together the whole of the old offices and those which they then required to be erected, in order that the exterior of the Bank might thereafter form one uniform appearance, which design they have just accomplished. The committee approved this design, which, I remember, at the time, made a considerable figure in the Royal Academy exhibition, and a great impression upon the cognoscenti of the day, from the novelty of its arrangement and style of architecture, which was altogether new to the critics. This design has been acted on, without any deviation, excepting in the Lothbury front, where, after the old houses had been pulled down and the site cleared, the space being found insufficient for the portico which Mr. Soane originally proposed for the centre, it was unavoidably contracted to meet this unforeseen circumstance, and to its great detriment. See plate of *the Bank from Lothbury*. Had a portico of six columns of Tivoli Corinthian been added to this front, as the architect intended, it would have been one of the grandest and chastest elevations in modern executed architecture. In other respects I have the architect's own authority for stating that his general plan then submitted to the committee has been followed. The whole of the exterior now presents as much uniformity as could possibly be expected in a building of such extent, continued progressively, as Mr. Soane observes in his new work, as circumstances required, during a period of upwards of thirty years.

When Mr. Soane was appointed to the important office of architect to this wealthy corporation, the frivolous wings and petty style of Sir Robert Taylor were comparatively new, having been recently erected at a very considerable expense. Mr. Soane, as I have just mentioned, began his operations by producing a design for an amalgamation of the heterogeneous fragments of his predecessors, with a foresight that a long life and perseverance have just accomplished; and in a style of architecture at once masculine, appropriate and novel.

Mr. Soane, in the structure before us, which, like the villa of Hadrian at Tivoli, comprises many buildings, introduced into this country the manly and beautiful order of the circular temple at Tivoli, which he measured and delineated during the completion of his professional studies in Italy with praiseworthy care and accuracy. In this grand edifice the architect has given a beautiful adaptation of a portion of this exquisite architectural gem (which Claude has introduced for its endless beauties in many of his works) in the round corner between Princes Street and Lothbury; and has carried on his bold design upon a lofty base, emulating the beauties of his predecessor Vanburgh, whose talents Mr. Soane has often honoured in his lectures.

The general character of the entire building, as now completed, is that of stability and strength, harmony and apt decoration, and above all, appropriateness, or fitness of means to its ends. It is an irregular rhomboidal figure, measuring about three hundred and sixty-five feet on the south or principal front, four hundred and forty on the western side, four hundred and ten on the northern or Lothbury front, and two hundred and

Drawn by Tho. H. Shepherd.

Engraved by J. Carter.

THE TEMPLE CHURCH, AS RESTORED.

Drawn by Tho. H. Shepherd.

Engraved by J. Carter.

THE RUSSELL INSTITUTION, GREAT CORAM STREET.

TO LORD JOHN RUSSELL, THIS PLATE IS RESPECTFULLY DEDICATED.

Drawn by Tho. H. Shepherd.

Engraved by J. Henshall.

THE NEW CORN EXCHANGE, MARK LANE.

Drawn by Tho. H. Shepherd.

Engraved by J. Henshall.

THE CUSTOM HOUSE, FROM THAMES STREET.

forty-five on the eastern flank, next Bartholomew Lane. This area comprises nine open courts—the rotunda, numerous public offices of spacious dimensions and elegant architecture, a court room, committee room, directors' parlour, an armoury, a printing office, and private apartments for the residence of officers and servants of the establishment. The principal apartments are on the ground floor, and there is no upper story over the chief offices, which are all lighted from above. In the basement story are numerous rooms, and fire-proof vaults for the conservation of bullion, coin, notes, bills and other securities.

THE TEMPLE CHURCH AS RESTORED.

This ancient and very beautiful church was founded by the Knights Templars in 1185, when the western or circular part was built, and dedicated to the Virgin Mary. It was re-dedicated in 1240, when the other part is generally supposed to have been erected by the Knights Hospitallers.

The western or circular part is peculiarly interesting, from its age, and from being one of the earliest specimens of the pointed style of architecture in this country. It has a circular external wall, with twelve openings, which serve as doors and windows, with dwarf buttresses between them. See plate of *the Temple Church as restored.*

The interior is formed by a series of six clustered pillars, with Norman capitals and bases, which support the same number of pointed arches, over which is a triforium and clerestery with semicircular intersected arches, that form by their intersections the probable origin of the lancet-shaped or pointed arch. The monuments of this church are all interesting and valuable for their antiquity and the celebrity of the personages whose fame they celebrate. The most remarkable of them are the recumbent statues of knights templars on the pavement of the circular church, in two groups of five each, lying north and south of the passage way to the choir.

The choir, or present church, which is now used in common by the Societies of the Inner and Middle Temple, consists of a nave and two aisles of nearly equal height, but differing in width, the nave being the widest of the three divisions. It has four pairs of clustered pillars, which support, with the addition of the eastern and western walls, six pointed arches, which are supported laterally on the north and south sides by strong dwarf stone buttresses. Between the buttresses are a series of lancet-shaped pyramidal windows, with isolated columns, which add great lightness to the building.

The walls of this church are of stone, strengthened by massive dwarf stone buttresses, and a triple roof, one over each aisle, and another over the nave, covered with lead of great thickness. The whole edifice was repaired in 1682, in 1811, and again in 1827 and 1828, under the direction of Mr. Smirke, who has restored it in a masterly style.

THE RUSSELL INSTITUTION,

in Great Coram Street, Russell Square, was originally erected by and from the designs of James Burton, Esq. whose elegant villa, the Holme in the Regent's Park, occupied our attention in the early part of this work. The original intention of this substantial-looking building was for an assembly, concert and card rooms. It was built about the year 1800, and in 1808 was purchased by a company of proprietors, and appropriated to its present purpose,—*literature.* It contains an extensive library, of which the present librarian, Mr. Brayley, has recently published a systematized catalogue, consisting of a very select collection of the most useful works in ancient and modern literature.

The reading rooms and library are also provided with all the leading periodical publications, and the current pamphlets of the day. The library is a spacious room, the whole length of the front, and there are also convenient newspaper rooms, a theatre for lectures and private rooms for the librarian.

The front next Coram Street is distinguished by a tetrastyle portico of the Doric order, with triglyphs; the cornice and frieze of which runs through the wings and flanks, divested of the triglyphs. See plate of *the Russell Institution, Great Coram Street.* There are also two low subporticoes which descend to a suite of baths; but, as they are recent additions, they must not be considered in estimating the value of this imposing and chaste elevation.

THE NEW CUSTOM HOUSE.

The first building ever erected for the purpose of transacting the business of the Customs was in the reign of Queen Elizabeth, and near to the site of the present extensive edifice. In the great fire of 1666 it was destroyed, with all the surrounding neighbourhood and the greater part of the city, and was rebuilt on a more extensive scale than before this calamity in the reign of Charles the Second, by Sir Christopher Wren. That building also met the same fate in 1718, and was rebuilt upon much the same plan. It was again consumed by fire in February, 1814, and was rebuilt upon a still larger and more extensive scale, from the designs and under the superintendence of David Laing, Esq. the architect to the Board of Customs.

In consequence of defects in its construction, which threatened a downfal to a considerable portion of the building, the long room was shored up, the front next the river taken down, and the present river front, which differs much from the preceding elevation, was erected in its stead by Mr. Smirke.

The south or river front is four hundred and eighty-eight feet in length, and the east and west fronts, or depth of the building, are each one hundred and seven feet. These three fronts are faced with Portland stone, and the north front, which is next Thames Street, is faced with brick and has ornamental stone dressings. The first stone of the new building was laid on the 25th of October, 1813, with the usual ceremonies, at the south-west corner, by the late Right Honorable the Earl of Liverpool, then first Lord of the Treasury, and the Right Honorable Lord Bexley, then Chancellor of the Exchequer, attended by the Commissioners of His Majesty's Customs, and in the presence of a great concourse of spectators. The new building was opened for public business on the 12th of May, 1817.

THE STATUE OF ACHILLES

was erected in Hyde Park, by a public subscription of ladies to the memory of the great and important victories of the Duke of Wellington. The inscription on the massive granite pedestal records the history of this singular statue. See print of the *Statue of Achilles in Hyde Park*.

The colossus before us is a restoration in bronze of one of the celebrated groupe on the Monte Cavallo at Rome, the first cast of which was brought into this country by Mr. Charles Day, and exhibited by him first at the King's Mews, Charing Cross, and since at the Egyptian Hall, Piccadilly.

This fine cast, which for some reason, is called Achilles, was executed by Mr. Westmacott, the Professor of Sculpture in the Royal Academy. The original statue has the straps of a shield on its left arm, which the artist has restored to a perfect *discus*, or circular shield; but has not given him a sword. The original is placed by the side of a horse, as if in the act of reining him in; but the action would have been obscure in the isolated statue without the shield, which is, therefore, in this case, both explanatory and appropriate.

ENTRANCE TO THE KING'S PALACE, HYDE PARK CORNER.

This splendid triumphal arch, is of elegant proportions, florid decorations, and exquisitely finished workmanship. It is executed from the designs of Mr. Decimus Burton, being one of the finest modern triumphal arches in existence.

The triumphal arches of Rome, that are now in existence, are of three very distinct species, if I may so call them. First, those with a single arch, like that of Titus of Rome, of Trajan at Ancona, and this before us. See print of the *Entrance to the King's Palace, Hyde Park Corner*. Secondly, those which are formed of two arches or arcades, such as those of Verona, &c., which appear also to have served for entrance gates to the city; and, thirdly, the species composed of three arches, the centre being the principal or grand arch for cavalcades, chariots, &c., and the outer two smaller, as posterns for foot passengers.

The arch before us is of the first species, consisting of a single arch and suitable architectural decorations. The aperture, covered by the arch, has an architrave, surmounted by an archivolt without a sculptured keystone, which is an innovation by no means pleasing. The sides are decorated with Corinthian pilasters, and the space on the wall which corresponds in height with the capitals, have sculptured wreaths of laurel enclosing the initials G. R. IV., and crowns alternately.

From the four central pilasters, a portico of four columns projects on two solid plinths, each of which support two columns of the Corinthian order. The entablature is lofty and elegant, with a richly sculptured frieze, and a row of boldly projecting lions' heads on the cymatium, marking the centres of columns and other sub-divisions of the order. Above the entablature, on a lofty blocking-course, is raised an attic, the body of which is embellished with a sculptural representation of an ancient triumph. On each of the columns is a statue of a warrior, and on the summit of the acroterium which surmounts the attic, is a figure in a quadriga or ancient four horse chariot.

The design of this very beautiful palatial entrance, is classical and appropriate, is one of the most distinguished ornaments of our metropolis, and possesses an originality of thought, that is rarely met with, in modern compositions of this kind. The masonry and sculpture are beautifully executed, and tend by their perfection to the unity of appearance between the artist's design and the artisan's execution, which is alike creditable to both.

SURRY THEATRE.

This place of amusement was originally called "Hughes's," after its proprietor, and like Ducrow's Royal Amphitheatre near Westminster Bridge, was appropriated chiefly to horsemanship, and therefore named the Royal Circus.

Like many of its betters, this Theatre has been the victim of the god of fire, and was burned down about three and twenty years ago. It was then rebuilt from the designs of Signor Cabanel, an Italian artist of great

Drawn by Thos. H. Shepherd.   Engraved by S. Freeman.

STATUE OF ACHILLES.
IN HYDE PARK.

Drawn by Thos. H. Shepherd.   Engraved by J. Cleghorn.

ENTRANCE TO THE KINGS PALACE.
HYDE PARK CORNER.

SURRY THEATRE, BLACKFRIARS ROAD.

THEATRE ROYAL, DRURY LANE.

knowledge in theatrical buildings, under the directions and immediate super-intendence of the late Mr. James Donaldson the younger, son of James Donaldson, Esq., architect of Bloomsbury Square, and the brother of Thomas Leverton Donaldson, Esq., the able author of the History of Pompeii. This amiable young man fell a sacrifice to his great exertions and anxiety to get the theatre finished within the time that he had en-gaged; and his fatigue, having to direct and control two gangs of work-men, one by day and the other by night, was too much even for his young and powerful frame.

The front, as you will see by a reference to the print of the *Surry Theatre, Blackfriars' Road,* is more theatrical and scene-painter-like than architectural; but it is appropriate, and does not offend the canons of taste, more than some prouder edifices that affect a greater state.

When Elliston first took this theatre he removed the ride, which he con-verted into the best pit in London (as the seats rise so much from front to rear), and from a theatre of buffoonery and balderdash, into one of a much more rational character. He performed in it himself, introduced well painted scenery, and as good a version of Shakspeare as the law would allow. The public encouraged him, and he gained wealth in his well-managed speculation, and gave it a new and better name,

" 'Twas called *the Circus* once, but now *the Surry.*"

Elliston then became the lessee of the immense establishment of Drury Lane, when the Surry Theatre devolved to that clever manager and excel-lent light dramatic writer Thomas Dibdin, who acquired far more reputa-tion than profit in his speculation.

It next fell under the management of his brother Charles, who con-ducted it with ability, and I have heard with profit; but it has again returned under the control of Elliston, who has resumed his station in the Drama in this pretty theatre with unrivalled success. Elliston first set the example in this theatre of improving the style of performance in the minor theatres, and he has been followed to the manifest improvement of the public taste, by all the others.

DRURY LANE THEATRE.

The principal front next Brydges Street is two hundred and thirty-one feet in length, and, before the addition of the present ugly portico, con-sisted of two slightly projecting wings, from which an elegant tetrastyle portico of the Ionic order, the whole height of the building, was to have projected. See print of the *Theatre Royal, Drury Lane.* These wings are formed of four antæ, surmounted by an entablature, the architrave of which is very properly omitted in the central part, and in the sides which extend beyond the wings. This central part or entire façade is plastered with Roman cement in imitation of Portland stone, and joins on to the north front in little Russell Street, (so named after the Duke of Bedford, its ground landlord,) with great ingenuity and pleasing effect. The cornice is surmounted by a lofty blocking-course, breaking into piers over the antæ. The capitals of the antæ are of the pure Greek Ionic, after those of the temple of Minerva Polias at Priene; the echini of which are embellished with eggs and tongues, and the hypotrachelion with the beautiful foliage of the Grecian honeysuckle. Between the shafts of the antæ in each wing is a window, constructed upon a deep stone sill, which corresponds in lines and height with the string-course of the north and south front lines. The division of the stories is properly marked by a larger or principal string-course, which runs through, and pervades the whole composition.

The windows in the wings have dressings, consisting of architraves up their jambs, with spreading shoulders near their summits, which are carried along the head, and support an architrave and appropriate cornice. The three centre windows have similar dressings; but as a distinctive mark, and not being protected like the others by a projecting epistylium, they have triangular pediments, which create both variety and beauty, arising from utility, in the composition.

Had this front been decorated, as originally intended by its architect, Mr. Benjamin Wyatt, with an Ionic portico of columns in accordance with the preparatory antæ, its effect would have been extremely beautiful, and produced as harmonious a composition as any in the metropolis.

The New Bridge over the Serpentine, Hyde Park.

This very elegant bridge was designed and executed by Messrs. Rennies, and forms a beautiful object from either side. A good view is obtained from the southern bank of the water, where the rich and luxuriant foliage of the plantations in Kensington Gardens forms a fine back-ground over its summit; and the walks round the margin of the lake a lively contrast to the dark shadows of the arches, which cast their reflexes on the surface of the silvery waters. See the *Print*.

The bridge itself, which is the object of our investigation, consists of five water arches and two land arches. Its upper surface is level, and connects by its roadway the northern and southern banks of the canal. The river arches are segments of circles, with archivolts and key-stones, surmounted by a block cornice, and a balustrade with equidistant piers. The spandrels of the arches are filled by level courses of masonry, and no projecting piers above the cut-waters.

THE NEW BRIDGE, OVER THE SERPENTINE, HYDE PARK.

TO MESSRS RENNIES. ENGINEERS. THIS PLATE IS RESPECTFULLY INSCRIBED.

RICHMOND TERRACE, WHITEHALL.

TO R. WILMOT HORTON, ESQ. M.P. &c &c THIS PLATE IS RESPECTFULLY INSCRIBED.

Drawn by Thos. H. Shepherd.   Engraved by W. Wallis.

GRAND ENTRANCE TO HYDE PARK, PICCADILLY.

TO DECIMUS BURTON ESQ: THE ARCHITECT, THIS PLATE IS RESPECTFULLY INSCRIBED.

Drawn by Thos. H. Shepherd.   Engraved by W. Wallis.

ONE OF THE NEW LODGES, HYDE PARK.

The land arches are semicircular between the projecting piers, and have also a balustrade over them, the width of the aperture below. These arches are also dressed with archivolts, that descend as architraves to the plinth, at the level of the springings of the larger arches and key-stones. The parapet of the road-way is plain and of the same height as the balustrade of the bridge. The entire design of the bridge is light, elegant, and particularly well adapted to its situation. Its material is a durable sand-stone, from Yorkshire, called Bramley Fall, which is esteemed by many competent judges as less liable to be acted upon by the changes of the atmosphere than even granite.

RICHMOND TERRACE, WHITEHALL.

The design of this terrace is common-place, and exhibits neither taste nor fancy. See print of *Richmond Terrace, Whitehall.* The order is Ionic, of no peculiar beauty; the antæ not in character nor accordance with the columns, and the entrance or ground story is of most veritable carpenters' architecture. The whole is imposing from its size, and the good finish of the workmanship.

The composition is divided into two parts, a centre and two wings, raised upon a rusticated basement, which forms the entrance or ground story, and projects under the centre and wings. The centre is a hexastyle portico of three-quarter, or attached columns, surmounted by a pediment and blocking-course. The wings are composed of two similar columns between two antæ, in imitation of the ancient tetrastyle portico in antis. The whole entablature is continued through the whole front, which is productive of heaviness in the parts between the wings. The cornice is surmounted by a balustrade, and a continued balcony at the basis of the columns runs along the entire front.

The terrace itself, that is, the part which is raised above the level of Privy Gardens, and separated therefrom by a very pretty stone balustrade and coping, elevated in the centre and with circular and scroll ends, accommodated to the form of the carriage road, is both ornamental and useful to the houses.

ONE OF THE NEW LODGES, HYDE PARK.

Its composition consists of a centre and two flanks: the former projecting slightly, is embellished with an opening, which forms an inverted portico of two columns, within which the entrance door is perforated. No other opening breaks the simplicity of this front, the manly character of which is increased by the continuance of the bold entablature on each face of the building; but the roof is crowned by a square chimney shaft, rising above the slated roof, which adds much to the architectural effect of the picture.

THE GRAND ENTRANCE TO HYDE PARK.

This elegant composition, designed, like the preceding, by Mr. Decimus Burton, is divided into five leading parts, namely, three arched entrances, and two connecting colonnades. The centre or principal arcade (See plate of *the Grand Entrance to Hyde Park, Piccadilly)*, is wider than the side entrances, and decorated by coupled columns of the Ionic order, which is the pervading character of the whole composition.

The side entrances have two columns in antis, and the antæ are repeated in the profile or ends of the structure. The colonnades are open and support a beautiful entablature, in which the able architect has committed the anomaly of introducing an architrave of three faces, which ought to be exclusively confined to the Corinthian order. The entablature is carried through the entire composition, the side entrances having a blocking-course with a raised and projecting centre, as if designed as a base for a group of statues or a trophy. This feature, the blocking-course, is omitted over the colonnade, and elevated into an attic or stylobate over the principal arch. The pedestal or frieze of this portion of the design is embellished with *bassi-rilievi* in the Athenian style of sculpture, representing a triumphal procession of equestrian warriors. Side or postern entrances for foot passengers only, formed between stone piers, add to the convenience of the public and to the picturesque beauty of the design, by carrying the composition beautifully into a pedimental form. The iron railing is of a very novel, beautiful and solid form, and the whole composition grand and effective. The sculpture of this beautiful ornament to the western part of the metropolis was executed by Mr. Henning, and the masonry by Messrs. Bennett and Hunt.

FURNIVAL'S INN, HOLBORN.

The composition of the front of this Inn of court, is, like that of Richmond Terrace, of three parts, a boldly projecting centre and two slightly projecting wings. In height, it has four stories, the lower of which, the entrance or ground story, is rusticated, and perforated by windows with semicircular heads. The centre opening is a large gateway, covered by an elliptical rusticated arch, and leads to the inner quadrangle. The one and two pair stories have windows arranged according to interior convenience, and decorated by architraves. Those in the wings have pediments, but for what reason they are so protected, standing under a cornice of

FURNIVALS INN, HOLBORN.

NEW GOVERNMENT MEWS, PRINCES' STREET, STORY'S GATE,
WESTMINSTER.

NEW CHURCH, STEPNEY.

THE NEW HALL, CHRIST'S HOSPITAL.

equal projection as the others, whilst the others have only horizontal cornices, it would puzzle a critic to tell.

The centre part of this principal division is decorated by what is meant for a tetrastyle portico of the Ionic order; but owing to the extraordinary and unprecedented width of the centre intercolumniation, it looks more like two sets of coupled columns, after the method of Perrault, than a well arranged columniation of a Grecian order. In consequence of this mal-arrangement of the columns, the epistylium over the centre opening looks weak and frangible. See print of *Furnival's Inn, Holborn*.

THE NEW GOVERNMENT MEWS, PRINCES STREET, STOREY'S GATE, WESTMINSTER.

The front of this chaste and classical building from Mr. D. Burton's design, is composed of three parts, a centre and two wings, inclosing the body or leading feature of the composition, which is pure Doric. The centre has a carriage way, and two posterns, the former being covered by a semicircular rusticated arch, and the latter by lintels reaching from antæ to antæ. It has two columns between the antæ after the manner of the ancient order of temples called *in antis,* and the angles guarded by a pair of coupled antæ, making the composition in a manner octastyle. See print of *New Government Mews.* The entablature is continued through the whole composition; the antæ are continued at regular intervals of two triglyphs and three metopes distance, in the main body of the front; and the wings are distinguished by inverted porticoes of two columns *in antis,* and covered by triangular pediments.

This length of entablature, unbroken except in the centre and the two wings, is surmounted by a plain and lofty blocking-course, eminently in character with the order of the building. The centre is marked by an attic, which is not an unmeaning screen, but a solid building, the full depth of the gateway below.

From the place in which we are now standing, this elegant and classical composition has a charming effect, which is much increased by the venerable turrets of Westminster Abbey, that tower above its centre in picturesque grandeur.

THE NEW CHURCH, STEPNEY,

is from a design of the late John Walters, Esq., and erected by private subscription in 1819. It is one of the best designs in the later pointed style of English architecture that has been recently erected. The western front (see plate of *the New Church, Stepney*) is composed of a lofty centre, forming the nave, and two wings which form the aisles.

The centre part has a low entrance door, with a flat pointed arch in a square moulded frame, below a wide and lofty transom window, covered by a gable. At the angles are octangular buttresses surmounted by pinnacles.

The aisles have also low doors with obtuse pointed arches, and angular buttresses surmounted by pinnacles, which are repeated between every window in the north and south sides. The parapets in the west front are perforated, and in the others plain, and the spaces above the doors which lead to the aisles are handsome canopied niches, with pedestals for figures. The whole composition has a very striking English and ecclesiastical character.

The New Hall, Christ's Hospital.

The exterior of this building is raised upon an arcade of flat pointed arches, which form a cloister for the boys to play under in wet weather, and is terminated at each end by two large and lofty octagonal turrets finished on the top with panels and embrasures. The hall, which is erected above the cloisters and separated by an ornamented string course, consists externally of nine lofty and spacious windows of the pointed style, divided into three heights, and four widths by moulded stone mullions. The windows are divided by buttresses that support the principal trusses of the roof, and are finished by lofty octagonal pinnacles and foliated finials. The centre of each window is again marked by intermediate pinnacles supported by sculptured corbels, and the parapet is formed between them of moulded embrasures.

This beautiful elevation is constructed with fine Heytor granite, of a close compact nature, and of a beautiful gray colour, which harmonizes well with the architecture.

The interior is two hundred feet in length by fifteen in width. A spacious gallery runs along the side opposite to the windows and the two ends, from which the public at certain times of the year are admitted to hear the children sing anthems and other pieces of sacred music, and sup in public. At one end is a fine organ, and a pulpit is affixed under the centre window for the purposes of divine service. The decorations are bold and massive, the brackets of the ceiling, the beams, and the galleries of oak, and walls finished a plain light stone colour.

Crockford's Club House, St. James's Street.

This building, of great extent and expensive execution, is from the designs of Messrs. Benjamin and Philip Wyatt, and does great credit to their well known name. It consists of a lofty ground story, lighted by

Drawn by Tho. H. Shepherd.

Engraved by Wm Tombleson.

CROCKFORD'S CLUB HOUSE, S^T JAMES'S STREET.

Drawn by Tho. H. Shepherd.

Engraved by Wm Tombleson.

BURLINGTON ARCADE, PICCADILLY.

WHITTINGTON'S ALMS HOUSES, HIGHGATE.

BREWER'S ALMS HOUSES, MILE END.

five spacious Venetian windows, and a magnificent upper or principal story, with an equal number of French casement windows decorated with proper entablatures. The two outermost of these upper windows, being without the pale and protection of the central projecting part, have the additional embellishment of pediments. See plate of *Crockford's Club House, St. James's Street.*

The entrance is by way of the lower central window, up a flight of stone steps to the elevated ground floor, under which is a lofty, airy, and extensive basement story, containing the kitchen and other offices and domestic apartments. This story is lighted by a wide area, which is separated from the street by an elegant stone balustrade. On the pedestals of this balustrade are raised a series of bronzed tripods, that support as many elegant octagonal lanterns.

The front is composed of a centre, formed by a slightly projecting tetrastyle portico of Corinthian pilasters or antæ, which support an entablature, and two slightly receding wings, in which the epistylium is properly omitted, being supplied by the wall itself. On the upper part of the cornice is a raised blocking course, with a lofty balustrade, and piers over each pilaster, as well as beneath them.

In the order of which this elevation is composed, the brother architects have followed the heresy of Mr. Nash, by giving an Ionic entablature, strictly so in every respect, to Corinthian pilasters; or, *rice versâ*, have given Corinthian pilasters to an Ionic entablature, instead of the rigid orthodoxy of their father, whose beautiful façade (Brookes' Club House) just below this, stands in awful rivalry of their defection from the true faith. Yet it is a pleasing, and from its magnitude a grand composition; and the interior, which is finished in all the rich and gaudy style of Louis XIV., is a fine specimen of that overloaded but magnificent style of domestic architecture.

BURLINGTON ARCADE, PICCADILLY,

a design of Samuel Ware, Esq., the author of a very scientific volume of tracts on vaults and bridges, and architect to many excellent buildings in Ireland, the splendid alterations at Chatsworth, at Northumberland House, and other places for the Dukes of Devonshire and Northumberland.

WHITTINGTON'S ALMS HOUSES, HIGHGATE,

is a building of English domestic architecture, by Mr. George Smith, the architect of St. Paul's School, the New Corn Exchange, and other works noticed in these pages. It is a handsome and collegiate looking building (see plate of *Whittington's Alms Houses, Highgate)*, as indeed it should be; for it is in lieu of that benevolent and munificent citizen's ancient college on College Hill, near Queen Street, Cheapside, which was by license from King Henry IV., in the year 1410, made a college of the Holy Spirit and Saint Mary, by Sir Richard Whittington, four times Lord Mayor of London, for a master, four fellows, clerks, choristers &c. Contiguous to which was erected an alms house, denominated God's House, or hospital, for the accommodation of thirteen persons, one of whom is the chief, with the appellation of tutor. It is still under the management of the worshipful Company of Mercers.

Every city apprentice must remember the legend of the poor truant Dick Whittington, sitting disconsolate on a stone at the rise of Highgate Hill, and fancying the city bells ring—

> "Turn again Whittington,
> Thrice Lord Mayor of London,"

and may have his early associations roused, at seeing Whittington's College, for so I must call it, a magnificent structure in the immediate neighbourhood of Whittington's stone.

It has a central chapel, of the pointed style of architecture, the gable of which is surmounted by a lofty pinnacle. It has also two square and two angular buttresses, with pinnacles and finials in accordance. The two wings have also gables, buttresses, pinnacles, and finials in a corresponding style of architecture. The doors and windows are square-headed, and covered with moulded water tables; and the whole composition is at once useful and highly ornamental.

THE BREWER'S ALMS HOUSES, MILE END,

is a smaller, but very picturesque structure, in a very neat and effective style of domestic architecture. The front elevation is composed of a receding centre, between which and the wings are two slightly projecting transepts, if they may be so called, which are embellished at the corners with angular buttresses surmounted by pinnacles. The chimney shafts are capped in the old English style, with separate funnels connected at the top. The whole building is agreeably relieved by appropriate and at the same time useful breaks, which produce a gratifying diversity of light and shade over the entire elevation.

LONDON HORSE AND CARRIAGE REPOSITORY, GRAY'S INN LANE.

This may justly rank among the "Metropolitan Improvements." It is situated at the Junction of Gray's Inn Road with the New Road, and

Drawn by Tho. H. Shepherd. Engraved by W. Deeble.

NORTH WEST VIEW OF THE

LONDON HORSE & CARRIAGE REPOSITORY, GRAY'S INN ROAD.

Drawn by Tho. H. Shepherd. Engraved by W. Deeble.

SOUTH EAST VIEW OF THE

LONDON HORSE & CARRIAGE REPOSITORY, GRAY'S INN ROAD.

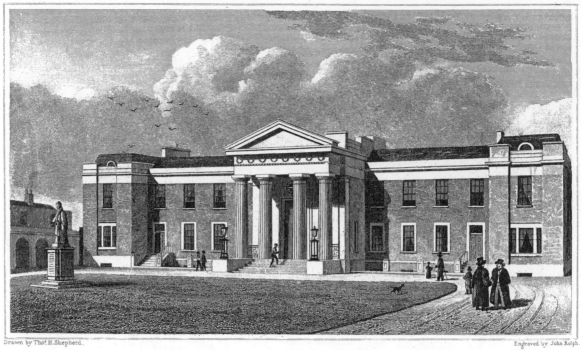

Drawn by Thoʰ H. Shepherd.   Engraved by John Rolph.

HABERDASHER'S ALMS HOUSES, HOXTON.

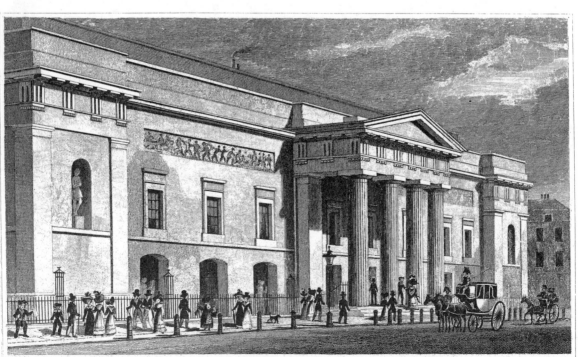

Drawn by Thoʰ H. Shepherd.   Engraved by John Rolph.

THEATRE ROYAL, COVENT GARDEN.

City Road, presenting a noble structure of a quadrangular form, with a spacious arena in the centre. The internal arrangements are on a grand scale, affording accommodation for about two hundred horses, and galleries for more than double that number of carriages. The lofty, light, airy stalls, and loose boxes, show that greater *regard* has been had to the *health* of that *invaluable animal* (as the *horse* may with great truth be styled), than will be found in any other public establishment in the British empire.

Besides the extensive horse and carriage departments, the south front comprises a spacious mansion, the principal story in which is wholly occupied by one entire grand room, in which, by the gratuitous permission of the spirited proprietor of this *unique* establishment, (William Bromley, Esq., of Euston Square,) some benevolent ladies lately held a bazaar, for the benefit of the Spanish Refugees, when this splendid room was proved to be capable of containing *upwards of one thousand persons!*

The large field (about ten acres), adjoining hereto, is about to be converted into a handsome square and gardens, *a la Tivoli*, with a superb theatre, to be called the *Panarmonion*, under the immediate patronage of His Majesty! The whole projected by Professor Lanza, and is without parallel in this country.

Lord Lowther's excellent Act— which comes into operation in January —by removing the turnpike gate *nuisances* from those delightful drives, the Edgeware Road, New Road, &c., will, together with the aforenamed novelties, combine to render this part of the metropolis a principal object of attraction with the fashionable world.

THE HABERDASHERS' ALMS HOUSES, HOXTON.

The original building, which has been recently pulled down to make room for the present neat structure, was a truly palladian design of that great philosopher and co-student of Sir Christopher Wren, the inventive Robert Hooke. It was erected in 1692 by the worshipful Company of Haberdashers, pursuant to the will of Robert Aske, Esq., a member of that company, who left an almost unexampled legacy of thirty thousand pounds for erecting a proper edifice for the accommodation of twenty decayed members of his company.

The former building was very spacious, being four hundred feet in length, with an ambulatory in front three hundred and forty feet long under a colonnade of the Tuscan order. The present building is much smaller in dimensions, and consists of a central Doric tetrastyle portico, with its frieze emasculated of its manly triglyphs, and a substitution of hybrid wreaths. The wings are decorated with brick piers instead of classical stone antæ. The apartments of the men are on each side of a spacious quadrangle (see plate of *the Haberdashers' Alms Houses, Hoxton)*, in the centre of which is a statue of its benevolent founder on a lofty pedestal, which bears inscriptions of his bounty.

COVENT GARDEN THEATRE.

One of the best views of the front of this theatre is from the opposite side of Bow Street, somewhat to the south of the south-east angle. See plate of the *Theatre Royal, Covent Garden.* This front, which is the principal, and in fact the only architectural front, if I may be allowed to use the expression, is two hundred and twenty feet in length, and divided into three principal parts, which project from the main body of the building and form its most attractive features. These are the portico and the wings. The former is tetrastyle of the Athenian Doric order, after that of the temple of Minerva Parthenon at Athens, and the latter are formed of antæ after the same example. The columns both in front and flank are equidistant, and have one triglyph and two metopes to each intercolumniation, and the antæ of the wings have the interval of two triglyphs and three metopes between them.

The entire entablature is carried over the portico and the wings; but the architrave, frieze, metopes, and mutules are omitted in the intervening portions of the front, to make room for the sculpture. The portico is crowned by a pediment surmounted by acroteria. The cornice of the wings and main building are surmounted by a blocking-course and parapet, crowned by a surbase moulding, like that which the same architect has used in the United Service Club House. Behind this, the lofty walls of the body of the theatre rear themselves in stern simplicity, and form an admirable architectural back ground to the ornamental façade below.

The lower part of the building on each side of the portico, and between the wings, is perforated by three arcades of segmental arches, which have been complained of, as not according in style with the Athenian purity of the other portion of the edifice. Above these, and over the plain square-headed doorways under the portico, are a row of nine sash windows, raised over a string-course that pervades the whole front, on lofty sills, decorated with architraves to the jambs and complete entablatures upon their upper surfaces.

Above these windows, on each side of the portico, are two long panels, extending their entire width, in which are sculptures in flat relief, and in niches between the antæ of the wings, of statues in the round, representing Tragedy and Comedy, from the chisel of Flaxman.

The bassi-rilievi in the panels are sculptured in freestone, from designs by Flaxman, one by Flaxman himself, and the other by Rossi, who also

Drawn by Thos H.Shepherd. Engraved by T.Dale.

COLLEGE OF THE CHURCH MISSIONARY SOCIETY,
ISLINGTON.

Published July 28. 1827 by Jones & Co 3. Acton Place. Kingsland Road London.

TO THE PATRONS & FRIENDS OF THE INSTITUTION, THIS PLATE IS RESPECTFULLY INSCRIBED.

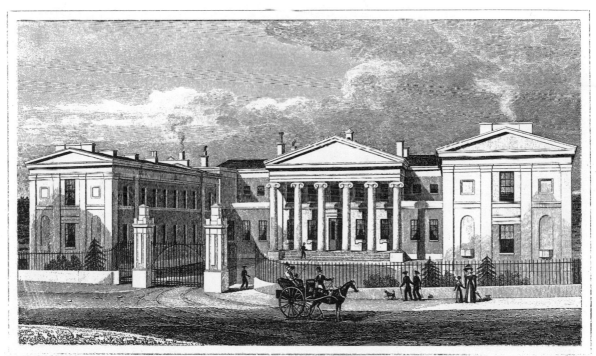

Drawn by Thos H.Shepherd. Engraved by T.Dale.

HIGHBURY COLLEGE, SOUTH WEST FRONT.
TO THOMAS WILSON, ESQ. THIS PLATE IS RESPECTFULLY INSCRIBED.

Drawn by Thos H. Shepherd.

Engraved by Wm Deeble

LORD GROSVENOR'S GALLERY, PARK LANE.

TO EARL GROSVENOR, THIS PLATE IS MOST RESPECTFULLY INSCRIBED.

Drawn by Thos H. Shepherd

Engraved by Wm Deeble.

THE ROYAL COLLEGE OF SURGEONS, LINCOLNS INN FIELDS.

TO SIR ASTLEY COOPER, BART. THIS PLATE IS RESPECTFULLY DEDICATED.

carved the figure of Shakspeare, in the anti-room of the principal box entrance; the northern compartments representing the *ancient,* and the southern the *modern* drama.

College of the Church Missionary Society,

a building more remarkable for strength and goodness of construction than for elegance of design. It looks more like the baldness of northern Calvinism, than the chaste beauties of the simply decorated church of England. Some one must have stripped this edifice of its laudable embellishments, as brother Jack did his garment in the Tale of the Tub. Its architect is Mr. William Brooks, whose works of the London Institution, Finsbury Chapel, and other ornaments of the metropolis, we have more than once had occasion to notice with approbation in these pages. It consists of a centre and two wings, without a single attempt at architectural decoration. See plate of the *College of the Church Missionary Society, Islington.* It is however a plain, substantial, useful building, adapted to a very laudable purpose.

Another similar establishment is,

Highbury College,

a building of more pretensions, and of more real architectural beauty. It consists of a centre and two very deeply projecting wings. In the middle of the centre building is an hexastyle Ionic portico, of the Ilyssus example, with a pediment above it. The ends of the projecting wings are tetrastyle in antis, and have also pediments and acroteria which conceal chimneys within them. See plate of *Highbury College.* The portico is raised a few steps above the court yard, which is enclosed from the high road by iron railings raised upon a lofty plinth, and a handsome carriage and two postern entrances. It reflects much credit on the architect for the selection of his materials from the choice storehouse of Ionian antiquities.

Lord Grosvenor's Gallery, Park Lane.

This building forms the western wing of a large and splendid town mansion, now in the course of erection from the designs of Mr. Cundy. It consists of a colonnade of the Corinthian order, raised upon a plain jointed stylobate.

Over each column of the principal building is an isolated statue with an attic behind them, after the manner of the ancient building called by Palladio the Forum of Trajan at Rome. On the acroteria of the building are vases and a balustrade (see plate of *Lord Grosvenor's Gallery, Park Lane)*, and between all the columns is a series of blank windows with balustraded balconies and triangular pediments, introduced in a manner that disfigures the other grand parts of the design. Over these are sunk panels with swags of fruit and flowers. But for these stopped-up windows, and the overpowering and needless balustrade over the heads of the statues, this building would rank among the very first in the metropolis; even with these trifling drawbacks, that can easily be remedied before the whole is completed, it is grand, architectural, and altogether worthy of its noble proprietor.

The Royal College of Surgeons, Lincoln's Inn Fields.

We have nothing that for chaste simplicity and harmony of proportion surpasses this fine portico, which, like a pension to a faithless patriot, is a good thing ill-applied, so little does it belong either in conjunction or relation to the awkward elevation behind it.

The portico consists of six lofty columns of the Ionic order, selected from the temple on the banks of the Ilyssus at Athens. See plate of the *Royal College of Surgeons, Lincoln's Inn Fields.* The entablature is in due accordance, and in the frieze is the following inscription:—Collegium · Regale · Chirurgorum ·

On the upper surface of the cornice is raised a solid stylobate, projecting, after the manner of pedestals, over each column. On these pedestals is placed a row of antique bronze tripods, which are attributes of the Apollo Medicus, and over the centre intercolumniation a second blocking is raised, which supports a shield on which is sculptured the armorial bearings of the college, supported by two very classical figures of Æsculapius with his club and mystic serpent.

The dwelling behind is so common-place that it can be compared, in relation to its fine portico, to nothing better than some of the additions by the modern Romans to the fine antique porticoes of their illustrious ancestors.

The New Corn Exchange, Mark Lane.

A new building recently erected by a joint stock company, as a market for the use of the corn factors, &c., of the metropolis. It is from the designs of George Smith, Esq., and is one of the most agreeable compositions in the city. See plate of *the New Corn Exchange, Mark Lane.*

It is composed of a centre, formed of a receding hexastyle portico of the genuine Doric order, but robbed of its triglyphs, *a la mode de* Mr. Nash, and for which laurel wreaths are substituted. The echinus is embellished with a lion's head over each column, which among the Greeks were used for the outpouring of the rain water from the roof, but which would be a libation, upon the heads of His Majesty's lieges frequenting the Corn Exchange, that the district surveyor would not allow.

The cornice is crowned by a magnificent blocking course of extraordinary height and boldness, which supports a stylobate bearing the imperial arms of the united kingdoms, with agricultural trophies, and the following inscription :—CORN EXCHANGE, ERECTED BY ACT OF PARLIAMENT, ANNO DOMINI M.DCCC.XXVII.

THE SUSPENSION BRIDGE, OVER THE THAMES, AT HAMMERSMITH.

A communication across the Thames by a bridge at Hammersmith had long been necessary to the neighbourhood, when a proposal for the erection of this bridge was made by Mr. J. Tierney Clarke, the Engineer to the Hammersmith Water Works Company, and a sum necessary for its execution was raised under the powers of an act of parliament.

The Bridge itself is composed of two square towers, with pilasters and cornices of the Doric order, just below low water mark, and with apertures in them for the road-way. In these towers the chains that carry the road-way are supported (see plate of *the Suspension Bridge, over the Thames, at Hammersmith)* in the same manner and on the same principle as that of the chain pier at Brighton. It forms a novel, picturesque, and highly agreeable feature among our recent Metropolitan Improvements.

NEW LONDON BRIDGE, WITH THE LORD MAROR'S PROCESSION PASSING UNDER THE UNFINISHED ARCHES, NOVEMBER 9, 1827.

The upper surfaces of the arches were decorated with flags of the principal nations of both hemispheres, and crowded with spectators, who cheered and loudly greeted the splendid and novel procession as it passed under and between the timbers of the centres which supported the huge masonry of the arches. See plate of *New London Bridge, with the Lord Mayor's Procession passing under the unfinished arches, November 9, 1827.* The workmen cheered, and the watermen and other persons connected with the river service added their voices and their hearts to the united shouts, as the stately barges glided nobly through the narrow aperture of the centre arch. This ceremony was repeated on the following Lord Mayor's Day, with equal splendour, and less difficulty, as more of the centres were removed from beneath the arches.

The New Treasury, Whitehall.

This work of legitimate art is by Professor Soane, and it comprises, besides the Treasury, the Privy Council Office, the Board of Trade, and other government offices. Several designs were made by Mr. Soane, but afterwards relinquished in favour of the present building, about which so much has been said both in and out of parliament. By way of apology or defence against those who have impugned his taste, Mr. Soane says, that " in every architectural composition, the style of the *exterior* determines the character of the *interior* decorations: and, whenever the application of this axiom is neglected, the want of sound judgment and good taste in the architect will always be manifested. Upon this principle, and with due regard to the character and destination of this building, the Privy Council Chamber assumes an appearance of magnificence; whilst the other rooms, as offices, are finished in the most simple and substantial manner, suitable to the character of public offices. The New Board Room of the Board of Trade owes the manner in which it has been finished to the same cause as determined the decorations of the Privy Council Chamber, and to the old Board Room, being the identical chamber in which the unfortunate Duke of Monmouth was born. To preserve the recollection of this room, the New Board Room is decorated, by Mr. Soane, in the same character; and such of the ornaments as could be taken down, and preserved, now form the enrichments of the new room of the Board of Trade. From these offices there is a direct communication with the Board of Treasury, the Treasury Chambers, and with the official residence of the First Lord of the Treasury.

The Italian Opera House, Haymarket, from Pall Mall, East.

This is a joint design of **Mr. Nash** and his tasteful pupil **Mr. Repton**. It is as fine a specimen of the Palladian style of architecture as any in London, and the difficulty of the inclined plane on which it is erected is overcome with the skill of a master. The design is eminently theatrical, and therefore characteristic. Its arcades and colonnades are necessary appendages to such a building. The sculptures in the panels over the colonnade, representing the origin and progress of music and dancing, are executed in terra cotta by **Mr. Bubb**.

Drawn by Tho. H. Shepherd.　Engraved by T. Higham.

SUSPENSION BRIDGE, OVER THE THAMES AT HAMMERSMITH.

Drawn by Tho. H. Shepherd.　Engraved by T. Higham.

NEW LONDON BRIDGE, WITH THE LORD MAYOR'S PROCESSION PASSING UNDER
THE UNFINISH'D ARCHES, NOV.R 9, 1827.

Drawn by Tho.ᵗ H.Shepherd.

Engraved by M. Fox.

THE NEW TREASURY, WHITEHALL.
TO JOHN SOANE ESQ.ʳ F.R.S. F.S.A. &c. THIS PLATE IS RESPECTFULLY DEDICATED.

Published Feb.ʸ 23. 1828. by Jones & C.ᵒ 3. Acton Place. Kingsland Road. London.

Drawn by Tho.ᵗ H.Shepherd.

Engraved by M. Fox.

ITALIAN OPERA HOUSE, HAYMARKET.
FROM PALL MALL EAST.

Drawn by Tho. H. Shepherd.

Engraved by J. Tingle.

ST. BRIDE'S AVENUE, FLEET STREET.

PITMAN & ASHFIELD   CHARLES TILT

MATHEWS MANUFACTURE

Drawn by Tho. H. Shepherd.

Engraved by J. Tingle.

ROYAL EXCHANGE, CORNHILL.

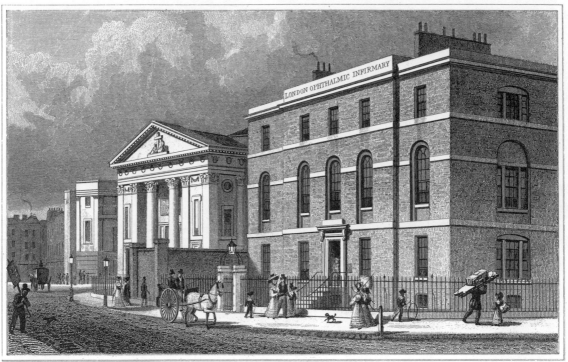

LONDON OPHTHALMIC INFIRMARY, &c. FINSBURY.

ASYLUM FOR THE INDIGENT BLIND, WESTMINSTER ROAD.

St. Bride's Avenue

(see plate)

opens to public view Sir Christopher Wren's majestic steeple of St. Bride, Fleet Street. This church is a fabric of great strength and beauty, and forms one of the most striking features of the metropolis. Its interior is at once spacious, commodious, and elegant, is one hundred and eleven feet in length, fifty-seven feet in breadth, and forty-one in height; composed of a lofty nave, covered with an arched ceiling and two aisles, separated below by solid piers, which form pedestals and support coupled columns of the Doric order above, from the capitals of which spring the arches of the nave aisles.

To a fire, which happened on the 14th of November, 1824, we are indebted for the present Avenue, designed by J. B. Papworth, Esq., thus opening to view a structure that is acknowledged to be the *chef d' œuvre* of one of the most eminent architects England, or perhaps Europe, ever produced.

London Ophthalmic Infirmary, &c., Finsbury,

has no architectural feature beyond that of plain utility in its entire composition. It is three stories in height, faced with brick, and divided by string courses of Portland stone, and crowned by a moulded cornice and blocking course, on which is inscribed, "London Ophthalmic Infirmary" (see plate.)

As this institution is for the cure of persons afflicted with incipient blindness, another laudable charity for those afflicted with total blindness presents itself in the

Asylum for the Indigent Blind, Westminster Road.

a building more commendable for utility than for its beauty, and apparently designed for its patients; any of whom would be supremely blessed, could they but see its glaring disproportions. The centre is composed of a ground story of three openings, covered with semi-elliptical arches, raised upon their narrow diameter, and on which is raised a principal story of three windows, with a façade of four ill-proportioned squat pilasters with Ionic columnar capitals. See plate of the *Asylum for the Indigent Blind, Westminster Road.*

On these capitals is raised an entablature and blocking course, with an inscription on the frieze and architrave, indicating the building to be a

" SCHOOL FOR THE INDIGENT BLIND, INSTITUTED M.DCCC.XIX.
SUPPORTED BY VOLUNTARY CONTRIBUTIONS,"

and also on the string courses of the principal and wing building, that articles manufactured on the premises by the indigent blind, such as hearth rugs, baskets, turnery, &c., may be purchased by the public.

In this praiseworthy and well conducted establishment, which it is quite a treat to visit, about sixty indigent persons, male and female, are supported and taught the arts of manufacturing baskets, mats, clothes' lines, sash cords, hearth rugs, &c., from which a produce of from eight hundred to a thousand pounds a year is generally produced. This institution was originally established in 1792, and the present erected in 1807, and enlarged in 1819, so as to accommodate two hundred children.

THE PENITENTIARY, MILLBANK, WESTMINSTER.

The plan of this building is principally on the *Panopticon*, or *all-seeing* principle of Jeremy Bentham, and was constructed for the purpose of trying the effect of a system of imprisonment, founded on the humane and rational principles of classification, employment, and reform. The prisoners, who are offenders of secondary turpitude, and who are confined here instead of being transported or sent to the hulks, are therefore separated into classes, are compelled to work, and their religious and moral habits, as well as those of industry and cleanliness, are properly attended to.

The external walls of this vast building, which resembles a fortification, or rather a continental fortified chateau, form an irregular octagon, enclosing no less than eighteen acres of ground. This large space comprehends several distinct though conjoined masses of building, the centre one being a regular hexagon, and the others branching out from its respective sides. By this means the governor, or overseer, can at all times have the power of overlooking every division of the prison, from windows in the central part. See plate of the *Penitentiary, at Millbank, Westminster.*

This institution is to accommodate four hundred male and four hundred female convicts. It is governed by a committee nominated by the privy council, which forms a body corporate, and has the appointment of all the officers, and the exclusive management of the prison. The prisoners are allowed a per centage on their labours, and the amount is given them when discharged. The expense of building this vast edifice amounted to nearly five hundred thousand pounds.

NEW BETHLEM HOSPITAL, ST. GEORGE'S FIELDS.

PENITENTIARY, MILLBANK, WESTMINSTER.

TRINITY CHURCH, CLOUDESLEY SQUARE.

NEW NATIONAL SCOTCH CHURCH, SIDMOUTH ST. GRAYS INN ROAD.
TO W. TITE. ESQ. THE ARCHITECT. THIS PLATE IS INSCRIBED FROM MOTIVES OF ESTEEM BY THO. H. SHEPHERD.

New Bethlem Hospital, St. George's Fields.

This building, which is for the cure of lunatics, presents a front of extraordinary grandeur and beauty, being scarcely inferior in harmony of proportion to George Dance's exquisitely proportioned hospital of St. Luke in Old Street, with more of architectural decoration. It is five hundred and eighty feet in length, and is composed of three principal and two subordinate parts, namely, a noble central building, embellished with an hexastyle portico of the Ionic order, which embraces only a part of its length, two side pavillions or wings, and two receding intermediate parts, which form the body of the building. See plate of the *New Bethlem Hospital, St. George's Fields.*

The central building, besides its before-mentioned Ionic portico, has a continuation of its main building to an extent of three windows on each side of its outer columns. It is surmounted by a pediment, above which is erected a handsome attic, which serves as a base to a cubicular building surmounted by a hemispherical cupola.

In the hall, which is entered under this beautiful Grecian portico, are the inimitable statues of *raving* and *melancholy* madness, by Cibber. These exquisite statues, which are quite *classics* in their way, formerly decorated the piers of the principal gateway to the former hospital in Moorfields.

The wings and body of the building are in happy accordance with the central composition. In these the patients are accommodated, and in the area behind, which comprises nearly twelve acres, are separate buildings for offices, &c., and enclosed grounds for the exercise of patients. This establishment contains accommodation for two hundred patients, exclusive of about sixty others, who are confined for acts of criminality, the charges of whom are defrayed by government. The building cost about one hundred thousand pounds, and the annual income of the institution is about eighteen thousand pounds.

The New National Scotch Church, Sidmouth Street, Gray's Inn Road,

where that spirit of the age, Rev. E. Irving, astonishes and delights his countrymen.

The elevation next Sidmouth Street is composed of three leading parts; namely, two towers, over the entrances into the aisles, and a central part surmounted by an embattled gable, that conceals the roof, over the nave. The doors are recessed into the thickness of the walls with clustered pillars and mouldings, and the central one is finished by a handsome crocketed gable and finial. Plain buttresses are introduced at the angles of the building and between the openings which run up the whole height of the lofty towers, and finish with pinnacles crocketed up the angles, and elaborately carved finials.

Over each door are windows that light the aisles, and over the centre a six light mullioned window, with rich tracery in the triangular part, with which it is finished. Over this is a triangular gable, intersecting a moulded string course, on which is inscribed in large capitals—ECCLESIA SCOTICA. The towers have on each of their faces handsome pointed windows, finished with crocketed labels and finials, and the parapets are embattled. The architect of this handsome specimen of the beautiful pointed style of our ancestors is William Tite, Esq.

SALTER'S HALL,

in Swithin's Lane, Cannon Street, is a handsome and very elaborate elevation, by George Smith, Esq., the architect of St. Paul's School, and many other excellent civic structures. It consists of a tetrastyle portico of the Ionic order, which supports an attic that forms a base or pedestal for the armorial bearings and supporters of the company it belongs to. See plate of *Salter's Hall*. The side portions of the elevation have semicircular headed windows, over which are tablets beautifully sculptured with the Grecian honey-suckle. The building is prettily situated in a planted garden, with dwelling houses and offices on each side.

THE GUILDHALL OF THE CITY OF LONDON,

the front of which is designed by the late George Dance, Esq., the city architect. The interior is ancient as high as the cornice, and the upper part, which was rebuilt after the fire of London, is about as ugly an upper story and roof as ever disguised a beautiful hall, and the corporation will be for ever deserving of censure, till they restore the ancient groined roof, the pillars of which are absolutely groaning for their airy partners in lieu of the mountains of masonry that now defile them. This fine—and, in spite of its roof, it is still a fine—hall is one hundred and fifty-three feet in length, forty-eight in breadth, and nearly sixty in height, and will contain, it is said, about seven thousand persons.

The windows of the principal front are all pointed, which has given occasion to some writers to call the style of its architecture Gothic. It is divided into three parts by four piers, pilasters, or buttresses, I know not which to call them, which are surmounted by octagonal pinnacles. The square parts of these pinnacles are ornamented with sculptural representations of the city sword and mace, and the central part with the shield, arms, and supporters of the corporation.

SALTERS-HALL.

TO ALDERMAN VENABLES, DURING WHOSE MAYORALTY THE EDIFICE WAS COMPLETED THIS PLATE IS RESPECTFULLY INSCRIBED BY THE PUBLISHERS

THE GUILD-HALL.

TO THE LORD MAYOR, ALDERMEN AND LIVERY OF LONDON, THIS PLATE IS RESPECTFULLY DEDICATED.

Drawn by Tho. H. Shepherd. Engraved by S. Lacy.

NORTH EAST SIDE OF BELGRAVE SQUARE, PIMLICO.
TO LORD BELGRAVE, THIS PLATE IS MOST RESPECTFULLY INSCRIBED.

Drawn by Tho. H. Shepherd. Engraved by S. Lacy.

BELGRAVE CHAPEL, AND WEST SIDE OF BELGRAVE SQUARE.

The King's Entrance to the House of Lords.

Early in 1822 Mr. Soane, the architect, was directed to prepare a design for the improvement of His Majesty's Entrance into the House of Lords, which being approved by His Majesty, the works were begun and carried on with such zeal and attention, that on the 30th of January, 1823, the carriage entrance and the royal staircase were finished as far as the door leading into the Prince's Chamber. During the progress of this work, Mr. Soane made other designs to complete the entrance from this staircase into the House of Lords, which having also been approved by His Majesty, the foundations of the building were laid on the 30th of October, 1823; and, by continuing the works night and day, the whole was completely finished on the 1st of February, 1824.

At the ceremony of the Sovereign's opening the Parliament of the United Kingdoms, His Majesty enters by this way. On arriving at the new carriage entrance (see plates of *the King's Entrance to the House of Lords, from Poet's Corner,* and *the Parliament House, from Old Palace Yard, Westminster*), the procession is formed, His Majesty alights, passes along the corridor which leads to the grand staircase, through the Ante Room, the Royal Gallery, and the Painted Chamber, into the Robing Room, and thence into the House of Lords, where His Majesty then takes his place upon the throne. For the better and more suitable accommodation of the King on these grand occasions, the floor of the noble apartment called *the Painted Chamber,* wherein the conferences between the two Houses of Parliament are held, has been raised to a perfect level, and the doorway from the Royal Gallery into the Painted Chamber suitably enlarged and decorated.

The exterior of these additions to the House of Lords are plain and simple specimens of the pointed style of architecture, embattled on the top, and composed in a corresponding style with the less recent portions of the building.

Belgrave Chapel and the West Side of Belgrave Square.

Belgrave Chapel is a chaste and elegant design of the Ionic order by Mr. Smirke, after the example of the temple on the banks of the Ilyssus at Athens. The cell or body of the chapel is parallelogramatic in plan, and Grecian in decoration, with antæ at the angles, the entablature carried over them, and a well proportioned stylobate by way of blocking course to the cornice and of parapet to the roof, crowning the elevation.

The principal front has a tetrastyle portico, flanked and supported behind with antæ, proper to the order, and raised on a handsome flight of steps above the street. See plate of *Belgrave Chapel, and West Side of Belgrave Square.* The columns are covered by a lofty epistylium, a plain frieze, and a cornice in flank, resolving itself into a beautifully proportioned pediment in front, which, by its becoming projection, adds a singularly effective play of light and shade over the whole composition.

Behind the central intercolumniation is a single doorway of large dimensions, embellished with architraves to the jambs, and an entablature *proper* to the lintel :—and windows, with diminishing jambs, like the little gem of a circular temple at Tivoli, ornament the wall between the antæ.

Beyond this is the west side of Belgrave Square, named after one of the titles of the Earl of Grosvenor, the ground landlord of this noble estate, which is of the great extent of nearly one hundred acres, lying between Knightsbridge and Pimlico from north to south, and between Chelsea and Buckingham gate from east to west.

This extensive area is now covering with mansions and handsome houses, laid out with beautiful plantations, into two spacious squares, a crescent, and several detached villas. This great undertaking, equal in extent and value to many cities, and destined (say the projectors) to be the future residences of the highest class of the fashionable world, is constructing over a district formerly known as *the Five Fields,* and as the resort, on Sunday mornings and Saint Mondays, of pugilists and blackguards.

North-east side of Belgrave Square,

is composed of five principal parts ; a lofty centre, with a row of dwelling houses on each side of it, forming the main body of the composition, and two extreme wings which terminate the façade. The centre is marked by a sub-portico or porch on the ground story, with an attached hexastyle portico above of three greater columns, which have always a poverty-struck would-be-fine sort of effect, particularly in the centre of a composition. The columns are of the Corinthian order of architecture, surmounted by an entablature bereaved of a third part of its fair proportions, and a consequent part of its height, and crowned by an attic, surmounted by vases.

The wings are *en suite,* but have tetrastyle porticoes, and a less aspiring attic, with a pyramidal form that is always graceful to the composition. The parapets of the wings and centre are unperforated, but those of the intervening houses have the common-place vulgarity, that Wren so vigorously but vainly tried to explode, of a useless balustrade.

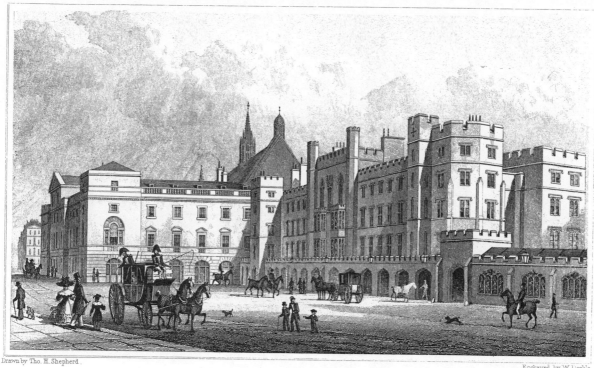

Drawn by Tho. H. Shepherd.

Engraved by W. Deeble.

THE PARLIAMENT HOUSE, FROM OLD PALACE YARD.
WESTMINSTER.

Drawn by Tho. H. Shepherd.

Engraved by W. Deeble.

THE KING'S ENTRANCE TO THE HOUSE OF LORDS.
FROM POETS CORNER.

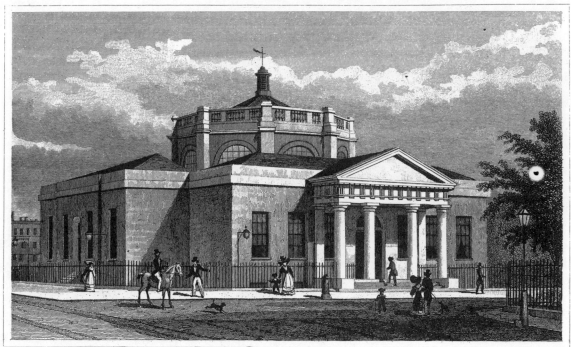

THE GUILDHALL, WESTMINSTER.

Published Aug. 9, 1828. by Jones & Cº 3. Acton Place, Kingsland. Road, London.

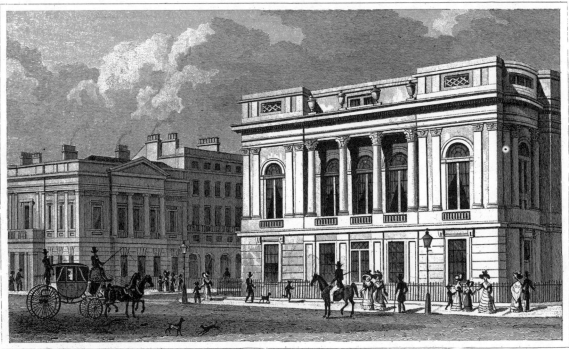

NEW BUILDINGS PALL-MALL EAST, AND UNIVERSITY CLUB HOUSE.

The Guildhall, Westminster,

is an insulated structure, designed for the use of the municipality of West-minster, standing on the south side of the ancient sanctuary, near to the Abbey.   In this building are held the sessions for the city, and the trials in the court of the High Bailiff, and it afforded accommodation for the various high courts of law and equity, during the repairs of Westminster Hall.   It is a quadrangular brick building, with recesses at the angles, that give it somewhat the form that continental architects call a Greek cross; and has a tetrastyle portico of the Doric order, with a pediment in the principal front.   The centre of the building is crowned by an octan-gular tower, with semicircular windows in every face, that give light to the principal court below.   At each angle is a pier that serves for a but-tress, which, with a connecting moulding that runs round the entire build-ing, crowns and connects the whole.   On this cornice is a blocking course, and a light and lofty balustrade, in three panels to each face.   The roof meets in a point over the centre of the building, on which is a lantern and vane.   It was designed and executed by the late Samuel Pepy Cockerell, Esq. a pupil of Sir Robert Taylor's, and father of the able and travelled architect, Mr. C. R. Cockerell, who designed the beautiful Ionic chapel of St. George in Regent Street, which is noticed at page 100 of this work.

New Buildings Pall Mall East, and the University Club House,

the former designed by Henry Rhodes, Esq. and the latter the united work of William Wilkins, Esq. R.A. and John Peter Dering, Esq. A.R.A.

The United University Club which meets at this house, is a society composed of members of the two universities of Oxford and Cambridge, elected by close ballot, which keeps them eminently select.

Being a corner house, it has the advantages of two fronts, one opening to Suffolk Street, and the other to Pall Mall East.   Both fronts are raised upon a rusticated surbasement, which is occupied by the ground story, and that next Pall Mall East, which may be considered as the principal, although not the entrance front, is distinguished from that next Suffolk Street by a tetrastyle portico of the Ionic order.   The entrance front, next Suffolk Street, has an enclosed portico or porch to the ground story, and a series of antæ in correspondence with those which appertain to the columns in the principal front.   Between all the columns and antæ are a series of spacious and lofty windows that give light to the grand apartments of the principal story.   Upon the upper surface of the entablature is a para-pet, designed in the proportions of a stylobate or continued pedestal, with piers over the antæ.

The other building before us, from the designs of Mr. Rhodes, is also elevated upon a rusticated surbasement, which is occupied by the ground story ware-rooms.   The windows are divided by rusticated and panelled piers, which are surmounted by a plain and efficient cornice, the lofty blocking course of which is used as a plinth for the Corinthian order of the principal story.   In front of each window is a perforated panel, which ingeniously converts the styles on interstices into sub-plinths for the columns above.   The front is divided into three parts, a centre of four Corinthian columns *in antis,* which forms a receding portico, and two slightly projecting wings, with coupled antæ at each angle.   In the inter-columniations of all the columns and antæ, are a row of semicircular-headed windows.

Upon the entablature of the Corinthian order is raised an attic story, with vases over the columns and dwarf pilasters over the antæ.   This handsome front is cleverly connected with that in Cockspur Street, to which it forms a very obtuse angle, by a circular recessed dyastyle portico in antis, and other ornaments above and beneath, in accordance with dif-ferent parts of the building.   See plate of *the New Buildings Pall Mall East, and the University Club House.*

The New Caledonian Asylum

is a chaste and classical design of the pure Doric order, consisting of a tetrastyle detached portico in the centre of the front, and four windows on each side.   The extreme angles are marked by antæ in accordance with those behind the columns.   The windows have architraves to their jambs, and lintels and trusses under their sills.   Those of the lower story have cornices above the lintels.   In the tympanum of the pediment is a shield containing the royal arms of Scotland, which for want of decorative and appropriate sculpture presents a very meagre appearance.   See plate of *the New Caledonian Asylum.*   Above the cornice of the pediment are plain acroteria, well adapted to the order of the building to which they are applied, and on the central one, is elevated a statue of St. Andrew with his cross.   This appropriate and useful building, which was instituted in 1815, for supporting and educating the children of soldiers, sailors, marines, &c. natives of Scotland, or born of indigent Scottish parents resident in London, is situated in front of a new cross road, leading from Holloway to Battle Bridge, by which a considerable distance is saved in the ap-proach to the west end of the metropolis from the leading North Road.

THE NEW CALEDONIAN ASYLUM.

TO THE FANCY-GIFTED SIR WALTER SCOT, BART. THIS PLATE IS RESPECTFULLY INSCRIBED.

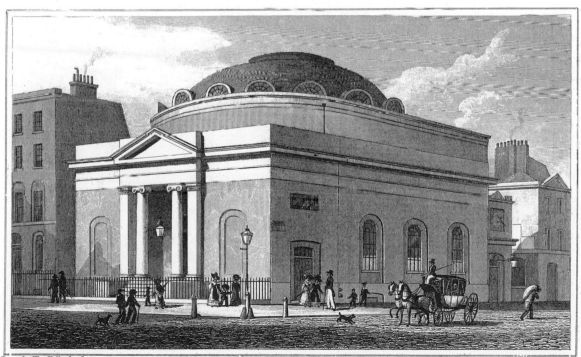

ALBION CHAPEL, MOORGATE.

Drawn by Thos. H. Shepherd. Engraved by R. Wm. Clatery.

ASYLUM FOR FEMALE ORPHANS, WESTMINSTER.

Drawn by Thos. H. Shepherd. Engraved by R. Wm. Clatery.

EGYPTIAN HALL, PICCADILLY.

The Egyptian Hall, Piccadilly,

was originally designed, in 1812, by P. F. Robinson, Esq. for W. Bullock, Esq. of Liverpool, as a receptacle for a Museum that went by his name, but was afterwards dispersed by auction. The elevation is completely Egyptian, that is, supposing the ancient Egyptians built their houses in stories. The details are correctly taken from Denons' celebrated work, and principally from the great temple at Tentyra. The two colossal figures that support the entablature of the centre window are novel in idea and application, picturesque in effect, and add variety to the composition; while the robust columns beneath them seem built exactly for pedestals to the sturdy Ethiopians above them. See plate of *the Egyptian Hall, Piccadilly*. The large projection of the superior cornice, rising from the colossal-sculptured torus that bounds the entire design, is grand and imposing.

Islington Tunnel, &c.

This Tunnel is a very successful and curious example of the modern method of canal work, and is worthy the inspection of the scientific. See plate of *the double lock, and east entrance to the Islington Tunnel, Regent's Canal*. Viewed from a short distance, such as from the intermediate space between the double lock, under the three-quarter elliptical arch of the Frog Lane Bridge, the western aperture in White Conduit Fields appears reduced to a point of great brilliancy, resembling a star surrounded by a halo of Rembrandtish darkness. It is perfectly straight and level through its whole course, and is upwards of nine hundred yards in length. Its form is an ellipsis, eighteen feet in height, and seventeen in width, having seven feet six inches depth of water, and being capacious enough for two canal boats, or one river barge to pass at the same time.

The Licensed Victuallers' School, Kennington,

is an establishment more to be regarded for the benevolent views of its patrons, than for the architectural beauty of the building. The Society was established, and is supported by the respectable body of Licensed Victuallers of the metropolis, as an asylum and school for the orphans and children of the destitute part of their brethren. The profits of the journal called "The Morning Advertiser" is also added to its funds, and every member is of course called on to contribute by taking in that newspaper. The building is a series of dwelling houses, added together at various times, as the funds and objects of the institution increased, and has been somewhat improved in architectural appearance, by a central tablet of stucco over the pedimented door as a sort of centre to the composition.   See plate of *the Licensed Victuallers' School, Kennington.*

THE NEW POST OFFICE, ST. MARTIN'S LE GRAND,

is a handsome structure by Mr. Smirke, begun in 1818, and for want of sufficient funds was for some time at a stand.   It is divided into three portions; namely, a central hexastyle portico of the Ionic order, the columns fluted, the entablature of good proportions, the frieze plain, and the cornice has the appropriate ornament of dentals in its bed mould. This central portico (see plate of *the New Post Office, St. Martin's Le Grand)* is finished with a pediment of just elevation, the tympanum of which contains the imperial arms of the united kingdoms.   This arrangement gives a pyramidal appearance to the group which forms the composition.   The side porticoes, which are tetrastyle of the same order, are finished with a low attic raised on the blocking course, instead of a pediment, which aids the composition and forms a pleasing contrast to the central or principal subject of the group.

The portions of the building between the centre and the wings have two stories of lofty windows, which are well arranged for harmony, and complete the composition, which is chaste, simple, and imposing.

The basement story is constructed of granite, and the superstructure of hard bricks, faced with Portland stone; the principal front, that which we have now been reviewing, is three hundred and eighty feet in length.

THE ROYAL EXCHANGE, CORNHILL.

The principal entrance is on the south side next Cornhill, and consists of a tetrastyle detached portico of the Corinthian order, with a lofty arch between the central columns.   The columns are surmounted by a lofty entablature, on the acroteria of which are sculptural armorial bearings of the United Kingdoms, the City of London, the Mercers' Company and Sir Thomas Gresham.   On each side of these is a balustrade surmounted by statues representing the four quarters of the globe.   These, as well as the bassi-rilievi below them, are by Mr. J. G. Bubb.   In niches below the architrave are statues of the unfortunate Charles the First, and his son Charles the Second, by Bushnell.   The new entablature, balustrade, bassi-rilievi, statues, and the new tower, are by Mr. George Smith, and in a purer taste than the original building.

Drawn by Thos H. Shepherd.   Engraved by F. J. Havell.

THE LIMEHOUSE DOCK, REGENT'S CANAL.
TO THE EARL OF MACCLESFIELD, THIS PLATE IS RESPECTFULLY INSCRIBED.

Published Augt 25. 1827. by Jones & Co 3 Acton Place. Kingsland Road. London.

Drawn by Thos H. Shepherd.   Engraved by F. J. Havell.

THE DOUBLE LOCK, & EAST ENTRANCE
TO THE ISLINGTON TUNNEL, REGENT'S CANAL.
TO COLONEL DRINKWATER THIS PLATE IS MOST RESPECTFULLY INSCRIBED.

LICENSED VICTUALLERS SCHOOL, KENNINGTON.

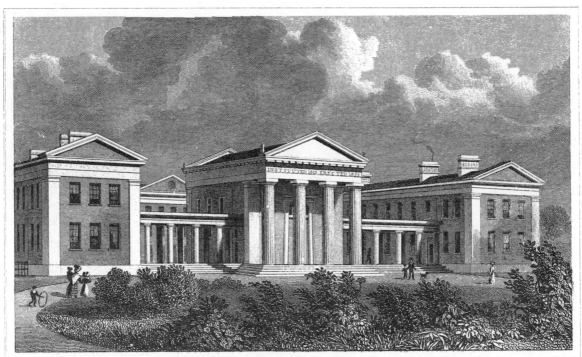

LONDON ORPHAN ASYLUM, CLAPTON.

CITY BASIN, REGENT'S CANAL,

TO SIR CULLING SMITH, BART. THIS PLATE IS RESPECTFULLY INSCRIBED.

ENTRANCE TO THE REGENT'S CANAL, LIMEHOUSE,

TO THE REGENTS CANAL COMPANY, THIS PLATE IS DEDICATED.

THE NEW CUSTOM HOUSE, FROM BILLINGSGATE.

THE NEW POST OFFICE, ST MARTINS LE-GRAND.

TO SIR FRANCIS FREELING, BART SECRETARY THIS PLATE IS RESPECTFULLY INSCRIBED.

VAUXHALL BRIDGE.

The first stone of this bridge was laid by the late Duke of Brunswick on the 21st of August, 1813, and on the 4th of June, 1816, being three years from the time of Mr. Walker's engagement with the company, the ceremonial of opening the bridge was performed.

The width of the river Thames at Vauxhall is about nine hundred feet, the depth at low water from eight to ten feet, and the rise of the tide about twelve feet. The bridge, as may be seen in the plate, consists of nine arches of seventy-eight feet span, and eight piers, each thirteen feet wide. The length of the bridge, clear of the abutments, is eight hundred and six feet; the rise of the centre arch above high water mark twenty-seven feet; the clear width of the bridge is thirty-six feet, divided into a carriageway of twenty-five feet, and two footways of five feet six inches each. The rise of the roadway upon the bridge is one foot in thirty-five to the middle of the fourth arch from each side; the line of the roadway over the centre arch, and half an arch on each side of it, being curved to meet the inclined planes formed by the roadway over the other arches, as shown in the view.

THE AUCTION MART, ST. BARTHOLOMEW LANE,

is a very useful commercial building, originally constructed by a joint stock company, principally composed of auctioneers. The front next Bartholomew Lane is rendered architectural by an attached portico of two stories, the lower of which is of the Doric order, and the upper of the Ionic surmounted by a pediment. The lower order is tetrastyle in antis, and occupies the height of the principal and mezzanine story. See plate of *the Auction Mart, St. Bartholomew Lane.* The side next Throgmorton Street is rusticated to the upper part of the mezzanine windows, and the cornice of the upper order is continued in both fronts.

The upper story is contained within the space of a curb-roof, and, being lighted by three large lantern lights, forms three spacious auction galleries. The area between the pavement and the building, which gives light to a basement story of offices, is protected by a plinth and balustrade instead of iron rails, and thus gives a very architectural appearance to this part of the structure.

THE NORTH-WEST FAÇADE OF THE NEW COVENT GARDEN MARKET

is erected in the centre of Inigo Jones's beautiful Piazza, which is now rendered by fire and alterations very incomplete. It is composed of four great principal parts, each of which have similar characteristics. The centre consists of an arch raised upon the entablature of two Tuscan columns, with a single-faced archivolt supported by two piers, which carry a lofty triangular pediment, the tympanum of which is embellished by the armorial bearings of the noble owner of the soil, the Duke of Bedford. On each side of this appropriate centre, which is high enough to admit a lofty loaded waggon into the central area, is a colonnade of the Tuscan order, projecting before the shops. The columns are of granite, and of the Palladian or rather Chambersian Tuscan, disfigured by an ornamental balustrade, which has no use but to contain market business, totally out of keeping with the massiveness of the order. See plate of *the North-west Façade of the New Covent Garden Market.*

At each of the extreme angles of the four portions of this new market is a raised quadrangular pavilion, which breaks the monotony of the composition in a very satisfactory and artist-like manner.

APSLEY HOUSE, HYDE PARK CORNER,

is now the town mansion of his Grace the Duke of Wellington, as it was formerly that of his brother the Marquess of Wellesley. This splendid mansion, has been recently enlarged, renovated, and made architectural; the situation being one of the finest in the metropolis, standing at the very beginning of the town, entering westward, and commanding fine views of the parks, with the Surry and Kent hills in the distance.

The principal front consists of a centre and two wings. See plate of *Apsley House, Hyde Park Corner.* The portico is tetrastyle and of the Corinthian order, raised upon a rusticated arcade of three apertures, which lead to the entrance hall; the wings have each two windows in width, and the whole of the ground story, which forms the basement of the building, is also rusticated. The west front has two wings, and the centre slightly receding has four windows, to which are appended a handsome balcony, and the portico here is surmounted by a pediment of graceful proportions.

THE NEW SHOT MILL, NEAR WATERLOO BRIDGE.

VAUXHALL BRIDGE, FROM MILL BANK.

THE N.W. FAÇADE OF THE NEW COVENT GARDEN MARKET.

AUCTION MART, ST. BARTHOLOMEW'S LANE.

The Gas Works, near the Regent's Canal,

are an immense pile of buildings, in the parish of St. Pancras, in the road leading to Kentish Town, and have a degree of architectural beauty arising from their intrinsic magnitude, the simplicity of their component parts, and the imposing grandeur of the two large columnar chimneys that surmount the roofs. See plate of *the Gas Works, near the Regent's Canal*. The composition of the principal front is pleasing, although deviating from the generally received notions of composition, by having its centre lower than its sides, which is improved by a slightly projecting centre and a pediment. The flanks have each a series of circular-headed windows in each story, which, like the arcades of an ancient aquæduct, are pleasing from the reduplication of a number of simple parts, which when alone produce scarcely any effect.

Buildings, Highfield, Camden Road.

Among the various recent improvements of the Metropolis and its Environs, there are few more likely to be permanently useful than the new line of road now made from the Gloucester Gate, Regent's Park, to Holloway, and intended to be continued through Stamford Hill to Essex and Hertfordshire; thereby shortening the distance between and approximating all the adjacent villages and the western parts of the metropolis, the parks and places of public resort.

It is upon the highest point of this road where it crosses the road leading from Battle Bridge to Highgate that these buildings (see plate of *Buildings, Highfield, Camden Road)*, have been erected, being the first of any importance in that part of the environs of the town, and which from its elevated site and magnitude forms a most distinguishing object. The view from the top is without exception unequalled within the same distance from town, being completely panoramic, and taking in the surrounding country to a vast extent, far into Essex, the hills near Rochester, the Thames, Shooter's Hill, the Surry hills, Richmond, and to Windsor, with all the intermediate objects.

The principal building we have shown is ninety feet long, forty-five wide, and sixty-six high, besides others of nearly equal dimensions, which, we are informed by the proprietors Messrs. Mann and Sargon, are required to contain their stock of cloth, the quality of which depends in a great degree upon its age and long exposure to the air, and to accomplish which the stock on hand is always from 30 to 40,000 yards.

The New Library, &c. in the Temple.

The pile of buildings called the Temple is divided between two societies, named the *Inner* and the *Middle* Temple, both possessing a hall, a library, a garden, chambers, &c. but using the ancient church described in our former pages in common.

The new library now in progress of execution, belongs to the society of the Inner Temple, whose improvements of their ancient structure deserve high praise. See plate of *the New Library, &c. in the Temple*. The design is in the pointed style of ancient English architecture, by Mr. Smirke, and is in complete accordance with the ancient parts of the Temple, which I learn will be persevered in till complete. The style of architecture is simple, useful, appropriate, and the works are most substantially and scientifically built.

Church of St. Barnabas, King Square,

between Goswell Street Road and the Regent's Basin in the City Road, an edifice built more for use and duration than particular ornament. The portico is tetrastyle of the Ionic order, without a pediment, having a blocking course and balustrade in its stead. On either side of the portico is a circular-headed window of true tabernacle cut, and sunk panels above them, like attic windows bricked up to avoid the window duty. Above the balustrade that crowns the portico is a square tower with belfry windows, and a dial in the upper part of the one that faces the west; and upon this is raised an octagonal obeliscal spire of good proportions, which however does not harmonize with the Ionic building beneath it.

The New Church, Camden Town.

The western front of this church is light, airy, and Grecian in an eminent degree. The portico, which forms the centre of the composition, is semicircular in plan, the entablature of which, projecting over the centre door, is supported by four columns of the Ionic order, and connected to the building by antæ. The cornice is surmounted by a series of sepulchral stêle, which, being introduced instead of the bold blocking course or plain scamilli, detract from the simplicity of the design. The side buildings or aisles have doors in correspondence with those of the nave, and the windows in the flanks are raised on a species of stylobate, which contribute

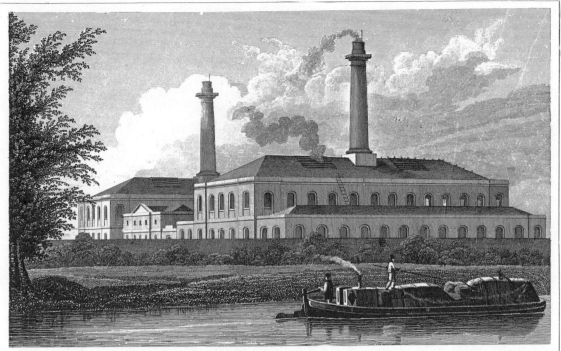

Drawn by Tho. H. Shepherd. Engraved by A. Mc Clatchie.

GAS WORKS, NEAR THE REGENT'S CANAL.

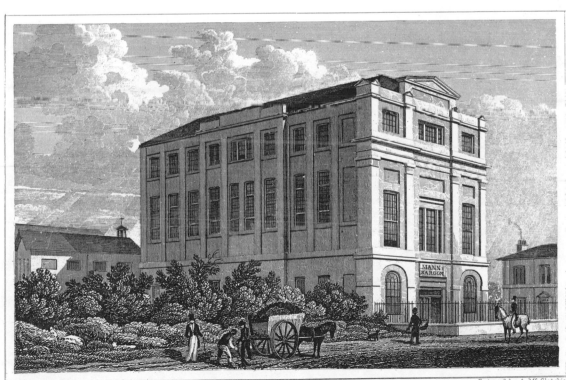

Drawn by Tho. H. Shepherd. Engraved by A. Mc Clatchie.

BUILDINGS, HIGHFIELD, CAMDEN ROAD.

ST. JOHN'S CHURCH, HOLLOWAY.

Drawn by Tho. H. Shepherd.

Engraved by J. Hinchliff.

THE NEW LIBRARY, AND PARLIAMENT CHAMBERS,

TEMPLE.

Drawn by Tho. H. Shepherd   Engraved by J. Cleghorn

ST. BARNABAS, KING SQUARE.

Drawn by Tho. H. Shepherd   Engraved by J. Cleghorn

NEW CHURCH, WATERLOO ROAD.

Drawn by Thos H. Shepherd.   Engraved by T. Dale.

THE NEW CHURCH, CAMDEN TOWN.

Drawn by Thos H. Shepherd.   Engraved by C. Westwood.

THE NEW CHURCH, REGENT SQUARE SIDMOUTH STR.

Drawn by Thos. H. Shepherd.

Engraved by Thos. Barber.

THE CATHOLIC CHAPEL, FINSBURY.

TO HIS GRACE THE DUKE OF NORFOLK &c. &c. THIS PLATE IS RESPECTFULLY DEDICATED

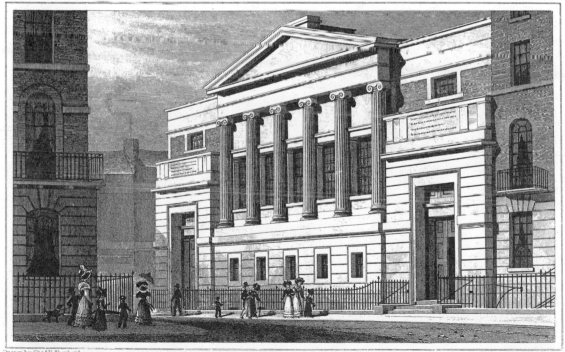

Drawn by Thos. H. Shepherd.

Engraved by Thos. Barber.

FINSBURY CHAPEL.

TO Wm. BROOKS ESQ: ARCHITECT. THIS PLATE IS RESPECTFULLY INSCRIBED.

Drawn by Thoˢ. H. Shepherd.   Engraved by Wᵐ Deeble.

NEW CHURCH, HAGGERSTONE.

Drawn by Thoˢ. H. Shepherd.   Engraved by Wᵐ Deeble.

NEW CHURCH, SOMERS TOWN.

Published December 1. 1827 by Jones & Cᵒ 3 Acton Place, Kingsland Road, London.

by their plain simplicity to the general good effect of the whole. The tower, or steeple, in accordance with the circular portico, is also circular in plan; which form pervades every story, as the octangular does that of St. Pancras.

FINSBURY CHAPEL,

is from a design of William Brooks, Esq. the architect of the London Institution. The principal feature in its front is an elevated hexastyle portico of three-quarter columns of the Ionic order, standing on a rusticated basement, and crowned by a lofty entablature and a well-proportioned pediment. Two wings, which occupy the whole of the rusticated basement, and about two-thirds of the Ionic columns in height, form the entrances; and, as they project beyond the main line of the building, they break the formality, and give a pleasing relief of light and shade. The entablature of the order is carried over the main wings, with the omission of the cymatium or sima. The intercolumniations of the Ionic order have apertures, formed by dwarf antæ on a string course supporting an architrave cornice, which serve as the windows. The lower story is lighted by dwarf windows, with dressings, which occupy four courses of the rusticated masonry. The entrance doors in the wings are ornamented on the jambs and lintel, with an architrave in accordance with the order of the building. They are covered by a cornice, surmounted by a blocking course and an attic order of two pair of coupled antæ; between which are inscriptions of texts from Scripture. The composition is pleasing and full of variety. It was erected by a congregation of Protestant Dissenters for the Rev. Alexander Fletcher, formerly of Albion Chapel at Moorgate.

CHAPEL OF EASE, WEST HACKNEY,

which, without the bell tower, and aisles, would be a respectable version, or rather abridgment, of the portico of Covent Garden Theatre, and almost as characteristic. As a portico, it is a good copy from that of a Grecian temple, but its effect is destroyed by the wings and conventicle-headed windows, and the incubus of a bell tower that is riding upon its back.

THE NEW CHURCH, HAGGERSTONE,

a design of the style termed Gothic, and by Mr. Nash. The west front is divided into five principal parts, which have variety and picturesque beauty. The central portion of the design is the lofty tower, which rises from the ground. Each angle of the tower is protected by an octagonal buttress, between two of which is the entrance door leading to the nave. Above this door are two plain stories separated by moulded bands or string courses, and a small pointed window to each. The parapet is terminated by a battlement on every face, and at each angle the buttresses run up to a lofty elevation, and are terminated by crocketed pinnacles and finials. Between these pinnacles, and behind the battlements, is a lofty quadrangular lantern, supported by flying buttresses. The doors leading to the aisles are covered by pointed arches and square water tables. Above each door is a narrow loop-hole window, surmounted by a gable, with a pinnacle on its apex, and at each side of these entrances is a spacious flanking octangular tower, two stories in height, which contains the gallery stairs.

St. John's, Hoxton.

The front is composed of three parts, a centre, which defines the width of the nave, and two wings, which belong to the aisles and galleries. The centre has a portico of three-quarter fluted columns of the Ionic order, between two antæ, which are repeated, slightly receding, at the angles of the aisles. An entablature and blocking course crowns the order and connects the entire building.

Above the entablature is a square panelled tower with a Grecian-shaped window, filled in with louvres. The tower then sets off to a circle in plan with projecting piers on four of its faces, and a lofty cylindrical tower is erected on this base. It is divided into eight parts, by slightly projecting Grecian antæ, which have windows with semicircular heads between them.

New Church of St. Luke, Chelsea.

The western or principal front of this church, by Mr. Savage, is a lofty commanding elevation of three parts; namely, a central tower of great originality and beauty, and two equally good side porticoes in front of the aisles.

The portico, for it is too decided in its character to be called a porch, consists of five principal parts, a grand central arch under the middle of the tower, and two side arches of smaller dimensions on either side. These arches are separated from each other by piers and buttresses, and are surmounted by a perforated parapet of tracery work and pinnacles with crockets and finials.

Behind this arcade, or portico, which is terminated at either end by an arch in correspondence with those in front, and a perforated parapet following the rake of the roof, is seen the western windows and raking pa-

Drawn by Thos H Shepherd.

Engraved by W.Bond.

CHAPEL OF EASE, WEST HACKNEY.

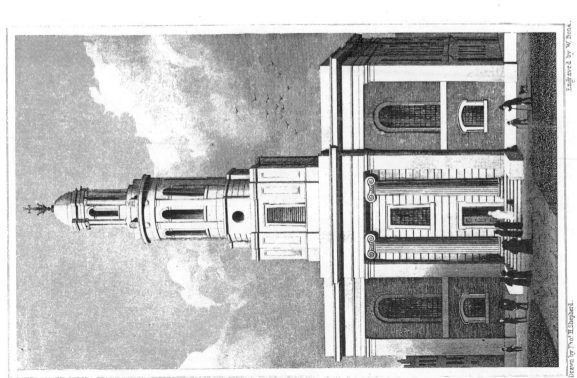

Drawn by Thos H Shepherd.

Engraved by W.Bond.

ST JOHN'S. HOXTON.

Drawn by Thos H Shepherd.

Engraved by S.Lacey.

ST. MARK THE EVANGELIST, PENTONVILLE.

Drawn by Thos H Shepherd.

Engraved by S.Lacey.

ST. LUKES CHURCH, CHELSEA.

rapet of the two aisles, and the flying buttresses which spring from the lower wall-buttresses of the aisles to the upper buttresses of the lofty nave. These upper buttresses rise beautifully above the panelled tracery of the upper parapet, and are richly decorated as they rise with delicate foliated crockets and finials; illustrating the practice of our ancient English architects of adding richness as they rise.

The Chapel of Ease to Mary-le-bone, Stafford Street, New Road,

is a composition of the Ionic order of architecture, consisting of a tetrastyle portico in front, which faces or represents the nave, and an Italian window on each side of this Athenian colonnade to bear witness to the aisles, and on the flanks are repetitions of the columns. The parapet is balustraded, and above and behind the pediment rises a plain square tower. Above this square tower, whose monotony is broken only by the clock, is a square portico of four columns on each face, somewhat resembling one of the tiers of that strange building called the Septizonium of Severus, and the steeple is finished by a campanile and cupola which support a ball and cross. It is substantial, but inelegant and inappropriate.

St. Mary-le-bone Chapel, St. John's Wood Road,

is a substantial unpretending chapel of the Ionic order, designed by the late Thomas Hardwick, Esq. It is divided into two stories, with square windows to give light to the pews under the galleries, and with lofty semicircular-headed windows to light the galleries and body of the edifice. The portico is tetrastyle, and has a dial or clock-face in the tympanum of the pediment. Above this is a cubical tower, with steps, which forms a pedestal to a handsome lantern of the Roman Doric order. Apertures between the columns give light to the belfry, which is covered by a hemispherical cupola, ball, and vane.

The Church of St. Mark the Evangelist, Pentonville,

a design by W. C. Milne, Esq. is a small but pleasing composition of three parts, in the western or front principal elevation; namely, a tower of four stories, which contains the entrance to the church generally, and two lancet-headed windows, which light the aisles.

The door is deeply recessed, within a series of pointed arches, supported by circular pillars, between two square projecting panelled buttresses. The upper surface of the outer arch is decorated with crocketing, which terminates in a finial beneath the great western window, and the spandrells are filled up with panelling. The parapet is ornamented externally by triangular panels, and the angles of the towers are strengthened by square projecting buttresses, carried up above the parapet and finished with crocketed pinnacles and finials. The flanks have angular buttresses, finished in a similar manner at each corner, and dwarf buttresses, which finish below the parapet, between each window.

St. Mary's Church, Wyndham Place, and District Rectory to St. Mary-le-bone,

is, like the before-mentioned church at Camden Town, composed of a semicircular portico, and a circular tower. It is a substantial structure of brick and stone of the Ionic order, and from the designs of Mr. Smirke. The novelty of the porforated parapet, as a substitute for the orthodox balustrade, is no improvement, and the steeple is deficient in lightness for want of that pyramidal gradation which distinguishes the steeples of Wren above those of every other architect. The interior is in the same plain unornamented style as the exterior, except that over the altar is a large window of stained glass, representing the resurrection of Christ.

The New Church of St. Pancras

is an edifice of a very commanding character, and designed by Messrs. W. and H. W. Inwood, after the purest Athenian examples. The portico to the west front is hexastyle, of a very elaborate and highly enriched specimen of the Ionic order, copied from the celebrated temple of Minerva Polias at Athens. On the columns is raised a lofty entablature, which is covered with a tympanum, and its cymatium sculptured with the foliage of the Grecian honeysuckle. The tower is octagonal, with eight isolated columns on a stylobate and an entablature of the order of the temple of the winds at Athens. On the cell of this story is raised another octangular stylobate, which also supports a similar octangular temple of smaller dimensions; the summit of which is crowned by an octagonal attic, with sculptural figures on each face. The eastern end is in imitation of the half of a circular temple of the Ionic order, with attached or three-quarter columns. The side elevations are decorated with continuations of the entablature, and of the heads or capitals of the antæ. On each side are two sub-porticoes, supported by four canephoræ, after those of the Erectheïum at Athens, and behind them are entire sarcophagi, to indicate that they lead to the mansions of the dead. The vaults or catacombs beneath the church, and to which these side porticoes lead, are constructed to hold two thousand coffins.

St. Philip's Chapel, Regent Street.

The portico is tetrastyle and of the Doric order. The central inter-columniation is wider than the rest, having a metope in the centre, and the entablature is surmounted by a triangular pediment. The metopes are ornamented by bulls' sculls and pateræ, the emblems of pagan sacrifice, and so far inappropriate to a Christian temple. In the wings, the cornice and mutules only are continued, the triglyphs being judiciously omitted, which gives room for a loftier window than could otherwise have been introduced. Above the cornice of the wings is an attic decorated by sculptures of bulls' sculls and sacrificial wreaths, surmounted by a blocking course with an acroterium in the centre. The campanile is erected on a lofty cubical pedestal, which is embellished by a square panel including a circular one. The tower itself is a copy from the beautiful little circular temple at Athens, called the choragic monument of Lysicrates, but better known to travellers as the lantern of Demosthenes.

St. Peter's Church, Eaton Square, Pimlico.

This classical edifice is composed of an hexastyle portico of the Ionic order, which extends the whole width of the church. The columns are fluted and detached the entire width of an intercolumniation from the cell or body of the building. They support a lofty entablature, which is crowned by a pediment. Between the columns, in the main west wall of the church, are three doorways, panelled with square lacunariæ and equi-distant styles, bounded by bold architraves, and crowned by handsome cornices supported by cantalivers. Above the pediment, and in the perpendicular line of the back wall of the portico, is a raised building the whole width of the church, terminated at each end by pediments, much resembling the excrescences on the Mansion House in the city, and similar erections on the church of St. George, Hanover Square. Upon this species of stylobate is raised another parallelogrammatic pedestal, occupying the width of the four central columns, and decorated with panelled piers at each extremity; and upon the upper surface of this, as upon a platform, the square bell tower is abruptly placed. This portion of the steeple is a handsome moulded cube, with a dial in each face, upon which is erected a classical tower and circular finial, the former being of the Ionic order.

St. Paul's Church, Ball's Pond,

is a church very recently built from the designs of Mr. Barry, whose new church at Brighton has given such general satisfaction. It is one of the most rural looking of all our suburban churches, and wants but a little discolorisation, and better planting around it, to pass for a veritable country church. It is composed of a lofty nave lighted from above the roofs of the aisles, a square substantial brick tower with angular buttresses surmounted by crocketed pinnacles, and two aisles lighted by lancet-headed windows, which are separated by dwarf buttresses. The design is pure in taste, and drawn from the best sources of our ancient English architecture.

The New Church, Regent Square, Sidmouth Street,

a composition similar, but inferior to that of St. Pancras, which may be considered at present as the masterpiece of the Messrs. Inwood. The western front consists of a hexastyle portico of the Ionic order, but which has the incorrect architrave of three faciæ. The doors are in a similar style of majestic boldness with those of St. Pancras, and the steeple is a variation of the other, converting the octagon into circles. The windows in the flanks harmonize well with the front, and the whole edifice is a chaste and pleasing composition.

The New Church, Somers Town,

is a district church in the parish of St. Pancras, in the pointed or English style of Gothic architecture, built of brick with stone dressings. The western front is simple and unpretending, and divided into five principal portions, the central of which forms the tower and entrance to the nave. The next two portions are plain, and the two extreme divisions are perforated by doorways which open into the aisles. These are separated by plain buttresses and surmounted with pinnacles. The tower is divided into three stories, the lowermost of which contains the principal entrance; the next, which is mezzanine, holds the clock, its apparatus and dial, in a square sunk and moulded panel, and the upper story is appropriated to a belfry. The parapet is perforated and panelled, and at each angle is a buttress finished with an octagonal pinnacle and foliated finial.

ST PAUL'S CHURCH, BALLS POND.

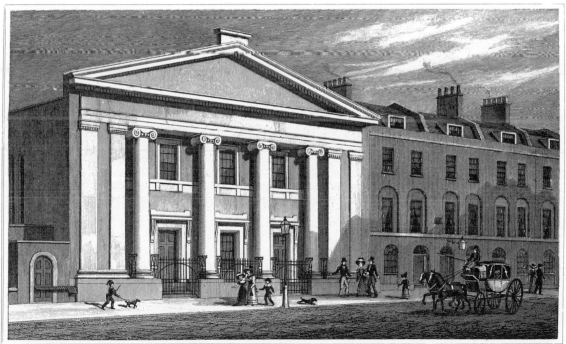

THE UNITARIAN CHAPEL, FINSBURY.

The Church of the Holy Trinity, Cloudesley Square, Islington,

a Gothic edifice of similar good taste to that recently mentioned at Ball's Pond, and by the same architect, Mr. Barry, and it deserves the same praise, for characteristic design and solidity of construction, as that very ·ural looking church.

The Unitarian Chapel, Finsbury,

s unorthodox in every respect, and dissents from the true faith of legitinate architecture. Its principal front consists of four three-quarter Ionic columns, guarded by two pairs of antæ, and a remarkably ill-proportioned entablature and pediment, which is surmounted by something like a miniature stack of chimneys. It is also disfigured by the introduction of dwelling house sash windows.

The New Church, Waterloo Road,

dedicated to St. John the evangelist, was built from the designs of Mr. Bedford in 1824. It has some faults and many beauties; the columns of the portico are of the lightest style of the Doric order, and, though rather effeminate for that masculine order, are beautifully proportioned and systematically arranged. The portico is hexastyle and joined to the body of the church, with antique propriety, as a continuation of the lateral cornice and roof. But all this propriety of annexation, and real beauty of proportion, is absolutely destroyed by the atrocity of a steeple, the ugliest perhaps in London, which is straddled a cock-horse across the pediment.

The entablature is weak and fragile, when the order to which it is adapted is taken into consideration. The frieze is denuded of its characteristic triglyphs and metopes, and trivial wreaths of laurel inefficiently substituted; the steeple is a series of quadrangular buildings, placed one upon the other and diminishing *seriatim* as they arise. At the angles are affixed quadrants of spheres and Grecian honey-suckles sculptured in their sectional faces.

The New Church of St. John, Holloway,

is another of Mr. Barry's examples of pure ancient English architecture, and is equally creditable to his good taste in that beautiful department of our art as his new church in Cloudesley Square, his restoration of St. Mary (Stoke Newington), his new churches in the Ball's Pond Road and at Brighton. It is composed, like that of St. Paul's, Ball's Pond, of a nave and two aisles, with pointed windows and dwarf buttresses between them, and a substantial square tower, with angular buttresses surmounted by crocketed pinnacles. This durable and handsome church is built with brick and stone, after the ancient English method, which is as pleasing in appearance as it is strong in principle.

ALBION CHAPEL, MOORFIELDS,

is a neat and unaffected building, with a pretty little diastyle portico in antis of the Ionic order, designed by a young architect of the name of Jay. The roof gives it somewhat the air of a theatre, but it possesses a character of original thinking in its design that is highly pleasing. It was formerly occupied by the Rev. Alexander Fletcher, a clergyman of the Scots Secession Church, who has removed to the more spacious and handsome chapel in the neighbourhood, before noticed under the name of Finsbury Chapel.

THE LONDON ORPHAN ASYLUM, CLAPTON.

This laudable charity provides for and accommodates three hundred destitute orphans, and is situate at Clapton, near Hackney, and is from a classical design of the Grecian Doric order. It consists of four parts, a centre and two wings, and a chapel connected with the latter by a dwarf colonnade. The most striking feature of this pleasing edifice is the central building in front, which is used for the chapel. It is a pure Greek prostyle temple, with a tetrastyle portico of the Doric order, bearing an inscription on the frieze, instead of triglyphs, importing that it was instituted in 1813, and erected in 1823. The pediment is plain, but in just altitude to the order, and has mutules under the corona. The wing buildings have antæ at their angles, and the roofs form pediments to the order. The centre behind the temple accords in elevation with the wings, and has a wide and lofty pediment to give it its proper consequence. The central temple is joined to the wings by a low Doric colonnade, the roof of which affords shelter to an ambulatory below, that leads from the wings to the chapel.

ASYLUM FOR FEMALE ORPHANS, WESTMINSTER,

a charitable institution, originally established by Sir John Fielding, in 1758, for the laudable purpose of preserving poor friendless and deserted girls under twelve years of age from the miseries and dangers of prostitution; whilst its neighbour, the Magdalen, endeavours to reform those who have fallen into such ways.

The centre of this architectural composition is a portico, or rather porch, of the Ionic order, selected from a choice example of the purest Grecian elegance, and the whole building, notwithstanding some defects of detail, is one of the prettiest productions of the present day.

TEMPLE OF THE MUSES, FINSBURY SQUARE,

a building so named by its eccentric founder, the late James Lackington, who realized a competency, by the sale of second-hand books, on the sure principle of small profits and quick returns; and was succeeded in business by his nephew, of the firm of Lackington, Allen, & Co. On their removal westward, this large concern was for a long time empty, till it was taken by Messrs. Jones & Co. the proprietors of the present work, and opened by them for the publication and sale of their works only. It may be thought unseemly here to descant on the merits of these particular editions, nor can it be necessary, since the immense circulation, not only at home, but throughout the Continent of Europe, America, and India, is a sufficient test of superiority and of the successful issue of a bold and original plan. Suffice it to say, that the object was to combine a vast saving of expense, portability, and facility of reference, with correctness, typographical beauty, and good taste. This has been effectually applied to the most popular and valuable works in English literature, comprising an HISTORICAL SERIES—THE BRITISH CLASSICS, or ESSAYISTS— a DRAMATIC and a POETICAL SERIES, all in an OCTAVO library size— a CABINET EDITION of Select BRITISH POETS, in Four Volumes Duo-decimo, (comprising nearly as much as the Sixty Volumes of "Johnson's Poet's," and including recent authors, in lieu of those of inferior merit,)— A DIAMOND EDITION of the POETS—CLASSIC TALES, &c. (the smallest ever printed—and each author detached, as a sort of waistcoat pocket companion), besides many other works of miscellaneous character. Last, though not least in success and popularity, has been the present work, forming part of a general series, under the title of "JONES' GREAT BRITAIN ILLUSTRATED;" and of which *London—Edinburgh—Bath, Bristol, and Wales—and Gentlemen's Seats,* (North and Western Series,) are now in progress. In addition to the above-mentioned series of British authors, and intended as a companion, they have also announced

a SERIES of the most approved TRANSLATIONS from the GREEK and
ROMAN CLASSICS, which is in a forward state of preparation—to commence with BAKER'S LIVY, complete in One Elegant Octavo Volume,
at one-fourth the price of former editions.

ALPHABETICAL LIST

OF THE

ENGRAVINGS,

WITH A

REFERENCE TO THE DESCRIPTION OF THE SUBJECTS.

Achilles (Statue of), p. 133.
Asylum, Orphan, p. 170.
————— for Indigent Blind, p. 149.
Andrew's (St.), Place, p. 80.
Auction Mart, p. 159.
Albany Cottage, p. 49.
Apsley House, p. 160.

Bank of England, from Bartholomew Lane, p. 128.
————————, North and West Front, ib.
————————, East Front, ib.
Brewer's Alms Houses, p. 142.
Burlington Arcade, p 141.
Belgrave Square, Pimlico, p. 154.
Bride's (St.) Avenue, p. 149.
Bethlehem Hospital, p. 151.
Buildings, Highfield, Camden Road, p. 161.
Bridge over the Serpentine, Hyde Park, p. 136.

Coliseum, Regent's Park, p. 68.
—————, and Part of the Lake, p. 19.
Clarence Terrace, p. 46.
Cornwall Terrace, ib.
Cumberland Terrace, p. 23.
————————, Centre of, ib.
Chester Terrace, p. 67.
Cambridge Terrace, p. 68.
College, Church Missionary, p. 145.
————— of Surgeons, p. 146.
————— of Physicians, p. 124.
City Basin, Regent's Canal, p. 157.
Charing Cross, Improvements, p. 124.
Custom House, New, p. 132.
————————— from Thames Street, ib.
Crockford's Club House, p. 140.
Corn Exchange, New, p. 146.
Caledonian Asylum, p. 156.
Covent Garden Market, p. 160.

East, or Gloucester Gate, Regent's Park, p. 23.
Egyptian Hall, Piccadilly, p. 157.
Entrance, Grand, to Hyde Park, p. 138.
————————— to the King's Palace, p. 133.

Furnival's Inn, p. 138.

Guildhall, London, p. 152.
—————; Westminster, p. 155.
Greenhough's, Mr., Villa, Regent's Park, p. 30.
Grosvenor's, Lord, Gallery, p. 145.
Government Mews, p. 139.
Gass Works, Regent's Canal, p. 161.

Hanover Terrace, Regent's Park, p. 48.
————— Lodge, Ditto, p. 50.
Highbury College, p. 145.
Holme, The, Regent's Park, p. 27.
Hertford's, Marquess of, Villa, p. 51.
Haberdasher's Alms Houses, p. 143.
Harmonic Institution, p. 102.
Hammersmith Suspension Bridge, p. 147.
Hall, New, Christ's Hospital, p. 140.

Islington Tunnel, p. 157.
Island on the Lake, Regent's Park, p. 19.

King's Entrance to the House of Lords, p. 153.
Katherine's (St.) Hospital, p. 59.

London, General View of, p. 1.
————— Bridge, New, p. 147.
————— University, p. 125.
————— Institution, p. 126.
————— Orphan Asylum, Clapton, p. 170.
————— Ophthalmic Infirmary, p. 149.
————— Horse and Carriage Repository, p. 142.
—————, Another View, ib.
Lodge, New, Hyde Park, p. 137.
Limehouse Dock, p. 157.
Langham Place, p. 94.
Licenced Victuallers' School, p. 157.
Library, New, Temple, p. 162.

Macclesfield Bridge, p. 58.
Maberly's, Mr., Villa, p. 24.
Milbank Penitentiary, p. 150.

Opera House, Haymarket, p. 148.

Opening, New, to St. Martin's Church, p. 123.

Paul's, St., School, p. 126.
Post Office, New, p. 158.
Park Village East, p. 20.
————————, Second View, ib.
Park Crescent, p. 92.
———————— and Diorama, p. 80.
——— Square, p. 88.
Parliament House, p. 153.
Pall Mall East, New Buildings, p. 155.

Royal Exchange, p. 158.
Regent's Park, Plan of, p. 19.
————————, View in, p. 20.
————————, Canal, Entrance, p. 157.
————————, Junction, p. ib.
————————, Villa in, p. 24.
————————, Doric Villa, ib.
Regent's Quadrant, p. 114.
————————, and part of Regent Street,
    ib.
Regent Street, part of East side of, p. 98.
——————— Another View of, p. 110.
———————, Ditto, p. 114.
———————, Buildings in, ib.
———————, Ditto, p. 115.
———————, from Circus, Piccadilly, p. 99.
———————, from Quadrant, ib.
———————, part of West side, p. 97.
———————, Ditto continued, ib.
Richmond Terrace, p. 137.
Russel Institution, p. 132.

Sussex Place, p. 48.
South Villa, p. 24.
Southwark Bridge, p. 127.
Surry Theatre, p. 134.
Salter's Hall, p. 152.
Suffolk Street, Pall Mall East, p. 123.
Shot Tower, p. 127.

Treasury, Whitehall, p. 148.
Taylor's, Sir Herbert, Residence, p. 65.
Temple of the Muses, Finsbury, p. 170.
Theatre Royal, Drury Lane, p. 135.
———————, Covent Garden, p. 144.

Ulster Terrace, p. 79.
United Service Club House, p. 125.

Vauxhall Bridge, p. 159.

Waterloo Bridge, p. 127.
——————— Place, p. 121.

Wittington's Alms Houses, p. 141.
West Gate, Regent's Park, p. 19.

York House, p. 122.
——— Terrace, p. 44.
——— Baths, ib.
——— Gate, p. 35.

NEW CHURCHES AND CHAPELS.

All-souls Church, Langham Place, p. 97.
Albion Chapel, Moorgate, p. 170.

Barnabas, St., Church, King Square, p. 162.
Belgrave Chapel, Pimlico, p. 153.
Catholic Chapel, Moorfields, p. 170.
Camden Town New Church, p. 162.

Finsbury Chapel, p. 163.

George's, St., Chapel, Regent Street, p. 100.

Hackney, West, Chapel of Ease, p. 163.
Haggerstone New Church, ib.

John's, St., Hoxton, Church, p. 164.
———————, Holloway, p. 169.

Luke's, St., Church, Chelsea, p. 164.

Mary-le-bone Chapel of Ease, Stafford Street,
    p. 165.
———————, John's Wood Road, p. 165.
Mark's, St., Pentonville, p. 165.
Mary's, St., Church, Wyndham Place, p. 166.

Pancras, St., Church, New Road, ib.
Philip's, St., Chapel, Regent Street, p. 167.
Peter's, St., Church, Pimlico, ib.
Paul's, St., Church, Ball's Pond Road, p. 168.

Regent Square Church, Sidmouth Street, p. 168.

Somers Town New Church, p. 168.
Stepney New Church, p. 139.
Scotch Church, Gray's Inn Road, p. 151.

Trinity Church, New Road, p. 81.
———————, Cloudesley Square, p. 169.
Temple Church, as restored, p. 131.

Unitarian Chapel, Finsbury, p. 169.

Waterloo Road, New Church, p. 169